JIMMY KAVANAGH

Roses In December

I hope you enjoy the book
Jimmy

© Copyright 2005 Jimmy Kavanagh.
All rights reserved. No part of this publication may be reproduced, stored in a retrieval system, or transmitted, in any form or by any means, electronic, mechanical, photocopying, recording, or otherwise, without the written prior permission of the author.

Note for Librarians: A cataloguing record for this book is available from Library and Archives Canada at www.collectionscanada.ca/amicus/index-e.html
ISBN 1-4120-6892-4

Printed in Victoria, BC, Canada. Printed on paper with minimum 30% recycled fibre. Trafford's print shop runs on "green energy" from solar, wind and other environmentally-friendly power sources.

TRAFFORD PUBLISHING™

Offices in Canada, USA, Ireland and UK
This book was published *on-demand* in cooperation with Trafford Publishing. On-demand publishing is a unique process and service of making a book available for retail sale to the public taking advantage of on-demand manufacturing and Internet marketing. On-demand publishing includes promotions, retail sales, manufacturing, order fulfilment, accounting and collecting royalties on behalf of the author.

Book sales for North America and international:
Trafford Publishing, 6E–2333 Government St.,
Victoria, BC V8T 4P4 CANADA
phone 250 383 6864 (toll-free 1 888 232 4444)
fax 250 383 6804; email to orders@trafford.com
Book sales in Europe:
Trafford Publishing (UK) Limited, 9 Park End Street, 2nd Floor
Oxford, UK OX1 1HH UNITED KINGDOM
phone 44 (0)1865 722 113 (local rate 0845 230 9601)
facsimile 44 (0)1865 722 868; info.uk@trafford.com
Order online at:
trafford.com/05-1803

10 9 8 7 6 5 4 3 2

*For May
And the next generation*

Someone said

> *God gave us memory so that we might have*
> *Roses in December*

THE ROAD NOT TAKEN

Two roads diverged in a yellow wood,
And sorry I could not travel both
And be one traveller, long I stood
And looked down one as far as I could
To where it bent in the undergrowth;

Then took the other, as just as fair,
And having perhaps the better claim,
Because it was grassy and wanted wear;
Though as for that, the passing there
Had worn them really about the same,

And both that morning equally lay
In leaves no step had trodden black.
Oh, I kept the first for another day!
Yet knowing how way leads on to way,
I doubted if I should ever come back.

I shall be telling this with a sigh
Somewhere ages and ages hence:
Two roads diverged in a wood, and I –
I took the one less travelled by,
And that has made all the difference

Robert Frost

CONTENTS

FOREWORD	**9**
PROLOGUE	**11**
The Beginning – Momentous Years	13
1 EARLY YEARS	**25**
A Quiet and Easy-going Man	27
Sunday Amongst the Cypress Trees	31
Remembered with Great Affection	34
Germany Calling – Germany Calling	37
No longer Babies	41
Necessity - The Mother of Invention	43
Singing for your Supper	49
A Riot of Colour and Activity	54
2 A CHRISTMAS MEMORY	**61**
A Dickensian Christmas Scene	63
Home for the Holidays	66
Holidaying in Brittas Bay	75
3 THE ADOLESCENT YEARS AND BEYOND!	**79**
All there for the Taking!	81
A Summer Occupation	85
A Welcome distraction	90
An accusing Finger	94
How Green was My Valley	99
4 HAYFORKS, WEDDINGS, AND TROPICAL ISLANDS	**103**
Not the most Courageous Individual!	105
A Beautiful Autumn Day	110
A Most Stark and Visible Manner	113
Ghosts in the Garden	133
The Cottage on the Rocks	136
Pass Me Your Head Line	140
Does this Lifeboat really go to Sea?	145
Camelot - a Magnificent Show	153
An Unforgettable Experience	162
5 POLITICS - A LIFELONG INVOLVEMENT	**167**
The Widowed, the Orphaned and the Aged	169
The Uncertainties of Public Life	175

6 A WHOLE NEW LIFE — 181
- "Cut Your Teeth on That" — 183
- Gladys White – Remembered. — 191
- Two Remarkable Ladies — 194
- The Weekly Prayer Meeting — 198

7 LIFEBOAT YEARS — 203
- They came like Swallows — 205
- Ability for Getting Things Done — 213
- A Cosy Domestic Scene — 217
- The Wettest Day — 219
- A Thrilling Experience — 230
- Now you're flying the Aeroplane — 236
- A Room with a View — 239
- "White of Morn" — 242
- Home from the Sea — 247
- A Noble Visitor — 252
- The Great Maureen Potter — 256
- A Royal Visit — 259
- A Rather Special Party — 263
- My Turn to say Goodbye — 268

8 RETIREMENT — 273
- A new beginning — 275
- A visit to the Aras — 280
- The Lake of Kings — 284
- " The Decent Church " — 293
- Old Kylemore — 298
- The Dog simply disappeared — 302
- A Home for the Arts — 307
- The fuller View of Retrospection — 310
- Amongst the Memories — 313
- The End of the Journey — 316

EPILOGUE — 319
- February 2004 — 321
- Acknowledgments — 325

FOREWORD

It is a very personal thing to decide to write down your lifetime memories from early childhood and onwards. It is all the more remarkable if you are a person as self effacing as Jimmy Kavanagh. In his own words his story is "a simple and unpretentious tale of reflections and remembrances of times past and the many friends and acquaintances I have made over the years."

Jimmy was encouraged by those who had the pleasure of reading his manuscript to go ahead and publish it. His story is a pleasure to read for he has only good to say about the people who influenced and interested him throughout his life. There is no rancour or bitterness recorded. In its place are humorous anecdotes that make you smile and a forthright insightfulness that you only learn about when someone shares with you their innermost thoughts.

Roses in December is a fascinating story of his life in Wicklow town throughout the twentieth century. The story is embellished by Jimmy's unimpaired memory and an ability to seamlessly link his reminiscences to major political developments in Ireland and more momentous World events and personalities of his era.

It is essentially a story about growing up in a large and loving family and how the Kavanaghs managed to cope in the hard times with fortitude and the help of an inspirational Irish mother, good neighbours and great friends. It records the Kavanagh's contribution to an ever-changing Wicklow, successes in business life and politics and in Jimmy's case, his work with the RNLI.

I must confess that I turned the pages at the first opportunity to read about the Lifeboat Years where Jim and I shared the experience of working together during a time of extraordinary expansion of the RNLI around the Irish coastline. I was not disappointed but fascinated by Jimmy's ability to liaise personally with so many generous Lifeboat volunteers throughout the length and breadth of Ireland. In the process he made memorable friendships that last to the present day. I should mention that he was supported generously by his beloved wife May in his untiring work for the Institution.

The main thrust of the story is told with simplicity and integrity against the fascinating background of the evolving new Ireland of today. The writing style of the narrative is distinctive which no doubt Jimmy would credit to the Dominican Sisters in Wicklow while not failing to mention the De La Salle Brothers too. This is the measure of the man – thoughtful, considerate and generous at all times.

It was my privilege to write his foreword and my pleasure to read Roses in December- an experience I am sure you will enjoy sharing with me.

Ronnie Delany

Prologue

The Beginning – Momentous Years

In many ways, life was not easy in those years of the early forties. Although Ireland was mercifully saved the awful horror of the Second World War, (we in Ireland referred to this period of Irish history as "The Emergency"), times were far from easy. As a small emerging nation with little or no industrial base, Ireland depended almost entirely on agriculture. Fortunately the Irish people were in a position to be able to keep themselves fed and nourished to a reasonable degree in those unhappy years while war was raging across Europe and the Pacific; and indeed to feed those many visitors who could afford to cross the water for a short visit, to escape from war torn Britain, and to relax in a city which was gloriously free from nightly air raids. Many years later, through my work as National Organiser for the RNLI in Ireland, I was to meet and talk with people who took that opportunity to visit Dublin in those years, and recount pleasantmemories of their visits to such places as "Jamais" in Nassau Street, or the Russell Hotel at Harcourt Street, and partake of good and wholesome food not available to them back home.

Although Ireland officially took a neutral stance, it was clear where her sympathies lay. As in the "Great War" of 1914/18, many Irishmen served with the British Forces in the "Second World War", even up to the very highest ranks. Field-Marshals Montgomery and Alexander were both Irishmen to name but two. A great many Irishmen who served in the British Army, Navy and Air Force distinguished themselves by being awarded Britain's highest honour, that of The Victoria Cross. The RAF airman accredited with shooting down the greatest number of enemy aircraft, thirty-eight in all, over the whole period of the war was Group Captain James Edgar Johnson "Johnnie", also Irish.

There were of course German sympathisers, those who believed in the adage, 'England's difficulty is Ireland's opportunity'; these were to be found mainly in the membership of the Irish Republican Army (IRA) and were very much in the minority. Lines of communication were, however, maintained between Germany and the IRA during the war years, with arrangements made for the supply of arms to the IRA by the German Government. Just before Christmas 1939 the IRA successfully raided the Magazine Fort in the Phoenix Park; as a result, on 4th January 1940 in emergency session Dail Eireann passed the establishment of an internment camp at the Curragh, Co. Kildare. During the period of the emergency several hundred IRA prisoners were held at the camp. The Curragh also comprised of two other separate blocks, which accommodated German and British internees. In the case of British subjects, in most cases Airmen, these were usually and quietly returned across the border to Northern Ireland.

To appreciate the economic situation in Ireland during the 40's and on through the 50's it is necessary to look back to the previous decade, the 30's, which of course will always be remembered internationally as the decade which was to see the emergence of

Pickering Public Library
Central Library
One The Esplanade

Automated Phone Renewal
905-831-8209

Today's date 2/9/2008 3:20:00 PM

33081007689897
Dirty work /
Due back on 3/1/2008

33081004052933
Package holiday   part one of the Th
Due back on 3/1/2008

33081006290200
The haunted abbot /
Due back on 3/1/2008

33081005132528
Valley of the shadow /
Due back on 3/1/2008

33081003919744
Katharine, the virgin widow /
Due back on 3/1/2008

Phone: 905-831-6265
www.picnet.org
Note: For security, client barcode
information has been removed

the most horrific power the world has ever known, the Nazi Party under the leadership of Adolf Hitler.

The early 30's were momentous years for the Irish Free State for a different reason. The February 1932 General Election saw the defeat of the Cumann na nGaedheal Government led by William T. Cosgrave, who many would say had steered the country out of the chaos that was the Civil War and laid the foundations for a well organised democratic state. On the 9th March 1932, Eamonn De Valera, with a Fianna Fail minority, entered Government for the first time since the foundation of the State. The new government within twenty-four hours of taking office released the IRA prisoners from gaol; the Cosgrave government had only declared the IRA an illegal organisation some five months earlier.

And so started for good and otherwise, "the De Valera years", a towering and austere figure who was to dominate constitutional politics in Ireland for years to come.

The 30th January 1933 would be remembered in retrospect all over the world as possibly one of its darkest days. Adolf Hitler became Chancellor of the Weimar Republic of Germany. Over a period of twelve years Europe and the World would suffer calamity on an unimaginable scale at the hands of this evil and depraved dictator. However, that's another story.

The days immediately following De Valera's rise to power were tense days in Ireland. The Civil War of only several years earlier was still very much in the minds of the people. The deep divisions, even within families, would take many many years to heal. While the Regular Army was still largely under the command of the officers who had defeated the Irregulars led by De Valera, in a most bitter and bloody civil war. Now De Valera would be their de facto Commander-in-Chief. It should also be remembered that De Valera had not won an overall majority but led a minority government. It was to William T. Cosgrave's great credit and statesmanship that the smooth and peaceful transition of power from the Cumann na nGaedhail Government to Eamon

De Valera's Fianna Fail Government took place in March 1932

On 16th March 1932, De Valera announced his plan for government, some of the main points being, the merging of the office of the President of the Executive Council with that of the Governor-General, and the abolition of the oath of allegiance. The plan also included the withholding of the land annuities paid to Britain and the introduction of protective tariffs. Many regarded as a serious mistake the withholding of land annuities and particularly the introduction of protective tariffs against Britain at this time. This decision would involve Ireland in a different kind of war, and would have very serious implications for a fragile Irish economy, for many years to come. The "Economic War", as it became known, was a dispute this country could not possibly win against the might of a strongly based British economy on which Ireland was still almost totally dependent. The counter tariffs that Britain imposed succeeded in almost totally halting economic growth in Ireland. The "Economic War" was to last until 1938 when it was agreed that Ireland would pay Ten Million Pounds to Britain in a final financial settlement. In return, Britain would lose control of the military installations in Lough Swilly, Co. Donegal and also in Cobh and Bearhaven in Co.Cork. The effects of this period, followed by the Second World War, were to drastically impede economic growth in Ireland until well into the late 1950's

Ireland in the 1930's and 40's was a poor and somewhat stagnant country, inward looking and with little employment opportunity for her largely poorly educated population. For many thousands of young men and women emigration was not an option, it was a necessity. The Irish Government was in no position to provide more than a basic education to age fourteen. With little or no education, many of these unfortunate emigrants were faced with accepting the menial jobs that nobody else wanted, be it in New York or London, Liverpool or Birmingham; some of them sadly never to return, but live out their old age in lonely bed-sits left with only sad memories of their native home. Could they but return today what massive changes they would see in Irish life, Social, Political and Religious?

The education of the masses was in the main left to the religious teaching orders. We hear much these days of the appalling failings of a number of religious; and it is correct that these cruel and vile people be removed from any contact with innocent children, and brought before the full rigors of the law. The abiding sympathy of all must be with those people who in childhood suffered such appalling and unspeakable debasement, leaving their lives, in many cases, almost in total ruin. But the sadness does not end there, the deep sense of betrayal and hurt felt by parents, who totally trusted, indeed were proud of, and even encouraged the association of their innocent children with men they revered as men of God, a trust they would have believed to be totally beyond question. Then there is the harrowing sadness of the vast majority of Priests, Christian Brothers and Sisters whose lives were, and are, dedicated to the spiritual and educational welfare of those in their care. They cannot comprehend how fellow Religious could abuse defenseless children in this awful manner; and of course who see what is to them, their sacred ministry, demeaned and ridiculed. Sadly of course, we can all witness the awful damage done to that institution, so beloved of and fought for by generations of Irish people down through the centuries, The Catholic Church. We can only speculate with particular sadness the effect that such example will have on the Church in Ireland in the years to come.

Having said all that, I am sure the gratitude of the Irish people does go out to the great many excellent members of those teaching orders who down through the years dedicated their lives to the education of Ireland's young boys and girls. Their dedication was given in generosity, with the minimum support and resources at that time from central government. A great many successful people across the professions, in politics, in business and in many other fields will readily give credit for their achievement in life to the selfless dedication of the men and women of Religious Orders, all over Ireland.

In this regard Wicklow Town was no exception. We had our success stories from Wicklow's learning establishments over the years. We no longer have a community of De La Salle Brothers in Wicklow and the Principals of the two Dominican Convent Schools are both laypersons. While I have no doubt there are those who may view the departure of the Religious Orders from the teaching profession with some enthusiasm, I feel sure that the vast majority will view this departure with a deep sense of loss, for what in most cases was a very special force for good not only in education but also in the wider community life of many towns throughout Ireland.

The town of Wicklow, of those days, was a world apart from the town we know today. The population stood at around 2500. From the centre of town at say the old Post Office (then in Main Street opposite the junction of "Morton's Lane") you could walk to the edge of town, in any direction you chose to take, in a matter of a few minutes. Proceeding south, when you passed the terrace known as "The Coastguard Station" you were leaving the town. The only house beyond this point was "Ard-Keen" where the Vize family lived, now demolished to make way for a number of modern town houses. Some 100 yards beyond was Wicklow Golf Club, you were then well and truly in the country.

To the North, the town, more or less ended at the Tennis Club. There were some houses on Rocky Road but the people living there were generally regarded by townie's as being country folk. Going west, Bayview Road to the Dominican Convent and the terrace on Convent Road ending at the home of Mrs O'Reilly, "Mount Carmel" now the home of my brother Liam, marked the western boundary. In those days and for many years to come, in fact well into the 70's, Wicklow seemed to languish in a state of enervation, being in a sort of no-mans-land. It was too far from Dublin for many who worked in the city to commute on a daily basis, and yet was close enough to the city for most people to shop there for the more expensive items of clothing and household goods, etc. The effect of this situation on the town over many years, when money was scarce, was for business to almost stand still. While Bray in north county Wicklow, being closer to the city and well within the commuter belt, tended to develop, and conversely Arklow in the south of the county for the opposite reason, being that much further removed than Wicklow Town, tended to develop through a necessity for a higher degree of self-sufficiency. Also, Bray and Arklow unlike the county town of Wicklow, were widely acknowledged as tourist destinations, which greatly influenced their development and economies.

Wicklow had one other serious disadvantage on the other major towns in the county; there was no through flow of traffic to the south. What is now the southern exit, through Dunbur, on past Blainroe Golf Club and joining the Brittas Bay road near Three-Mile-Water; did not exist then. The road terminated at Silver Strand. In order to leave Wicklow town wishing to travel south you had to back track from the centre of the town and turn left by the Grand Hotel onto Marlton Road to pick up the main Dublin / Wexford route. If proceeding south from Dublin, by turning right in the village of Rathnew you could by-pass the town altogether. This in effect meant that Wicklow was to some extent in a backwater, cut off from the natural flow of through traffic.

This situation may be considered an advantage in these times of serious traffic congestion, but back then being off the beaten track was certainly a drawback and contributed to Wicklow's comparatively slower rate of development.

All that has changed drastically in the last fifteen or so years - Wicklow and its environs have grown almost beyond recognition; the town is now a very busy centre of trade and commerce. Ironically the Council is at the advanced planning stage for the building of an inner by-pass route around Wicklow to alleviate the serious traffic congestion in the town centre. The population of the greater Wicklow area now stands at close to ten thousand, while the projected growth over the next ten years is expected to reach twenty five thousand. Housing estates have sprung up in every part of town, some of questionable quality. It is no longer necessary to shop in Dublin; the shops in Wicklow can cater for all one's needs and for everything and anything you care to purchase.

Main Street has changed little in appearance over the years, apart from the greater variety of shops and places to eat, what has changed is the now extremely difficult task of driving through it without encountering a traffic jam somewhere between Abbey Street at one end and the new Market Square at the other, while expecting to park at any convenient spot is understandably out of the question. One particular area in which Wicklow has greatly advanced is that of sports facilities. All three ball games - The GAA, Rugby Football, and Association Football have developed quality-playing pitches and modern club houses, these facilities were badly needed and long overdue. We are also delighted that Wicklow can now boast its own fine new indoor heated Swimming Pool, which is enjoyed by people of all age groups. Golf is another sport that has seen tremendous growth in popularity over the years, the massive coverage of the professional golf circuit on television and the great successes of our young Irish professionals in recent times being major contributing factors. Wicklow town is certainly to the forefront in the development of the game of golf, now boasting two fine 18-hole courses close to the town, with another "The European Club", listed in the top one hundred golf courses of the world and sited just a mile or so south at Brittas Bay.

Wicklow, for all the advances made in sport, has in the area of entertainment stood still or even gone backwards; maybe it's the social attitude of Irish society as a whole that has changed. Fifty odd years ago the greater Wicklow area boasted four dance halls and two cinemas, both cinemas were capable of multi-functional use, which facilitated different activities. With the exception of the Assembly Hall, all are now gone. The old "Catholic Club" which as I remember it, was not confined to Catholics but which did have a friendly social atmosphere, is no more. Entertainment for young people these days is centered on the Public House. The "Pub Culture" is alive and well in Wicklow, as it is all over Ireland. We certainly have our share of glitzy pubs in town. We also have many more licensed clubs than in the old days, and of course most people, especially young people have more disposable income to indulge in this particular form of entertainment. Another serious problem in these times of affluence and wealth is the "couldn't care less" attitude to environmental matters, in particular to the condition of our public areas.

The South Quay, which was always a pleasant place to stroll and watch the shipping and boating activity in the harbour, is now one long car park, with heavy commercial and private traffic, making it almost impossible and in fact dangerous for walkers. The "Smoothing Iron" at Fitzwilliam Square with what used to be its well maintained rose beds and manicured grass, is now neglected and left in it's present sorry state. The Fairground opposite the "Leitrim Lounge" was up to very recently used as an unofficial travelers halt, as is part of the upper Murrough and Station Road, although thankfully efforts are being made to improve and secure the Fairground area. The Shelters on the seafront where many a romance blossomed, gone! The Promenade, as its name implies, a popular walking and meeting place on summer evenings; most of the time littered with rubbish and broken glass, and daily showing the remains of last night's teenage drinking parties. The Town Council and the Gardai certainly have a part to play, but can do little without the support and cooperation of the general public, in their efforts to solve this serious problem - a sad catalogue of carelessness and neglect of the "Garden of Ireland's" county town.

I appreciate that growth is vital to the future development of any community. It is understandable that in order for a community to develop, change and compromise is a very necessary part of that growth, and a price must be paid to facilitate the change. Have we had to pay too high a price? I think in order to answer that question we need to ask ourselves another question. Is living in this "Modern" Wicklow of today a better way of life for its citizens? You must answer that question for yourself, maybe it's an 'age thing', but for me, I believe the answer is 'no'.

However, one has to watch not to fall into the old trap - that hackneyed phrase 'back in the good old days'. There is no doubt in my mind that as one of Ireland's loveliest located towns, Wicklow, with the enthusiasm and passion of its citizenry could score at the very highest level in the National Tidy Towns Competition.

Having looked back over those last several paragraphs, much of the criticisms made could easily be put right. Then Wicklow really could be a better place in which to live for all of us. After all who would dispute but that we are all at present living in better times than "the good old days".

Looking back to a less hectic age, the mid.30's; although conditions were harsh, life was less complicated; the pace was less pressurized, less stressful than life is today. As one grows older and relaxes more into the calmness of senior citizenship it can be fascinating to just sit and drift back in time, and try to recall one's earliest memories. In these pressurized times, those whose lives are still crammed with the concerns of just getting through each working day, have little time or inclination to indulge in such "day dreaming". No! such matters as those that mark one's earliest recollections of bygone days are not the stuff of youth. This is the prerogative of age, one of the pleasures of advancing years, when one has the time to relax and luxuriate in thoughts of times long past. It is amazing how, with a little effort, long forgotten memories of all kinds come flooding back with absolute clarity, while events that happened in the recent past are often difficult to recall with the same, if you like, chronological clarity. I suppose if one is approaching the other end of life's journey, and the frenzy of daily life begins to lessen these early recollections assume a somewhat greater significance. While maybe at times such harmless indulgence may often have its melancholy moments.

Looking in retrospect on my own early years, although it didn't concern me then, rearing a family was undoubtedly a real struggle, wages were small and making ends meet was always a problem for most families. With none of the modern facilities that one takes so much for granted today, mothers, especially those of large families and there were many, quietly accepted a huge burden of hardship. No one would disagree that that particular generation of mothers were wonderful women who single-mindedly and without any thought for themselves devoted their every waking moment to the protection and wellbeing of their families. While it should be said that the fathers worked extremely hard, in many cases from dawn until dusk for meagre wages, many would have found some little release in meeting with a friend or two for a drink at least once a week. As the breadwinner of the family, once the housekeeping money was handed over on Friday night, it was generally accepted that the father's obligation, so to speak, was done. The rearing of the children and the efforts to make ends meet was seen as the responsibility of the mothers of Ireland, which they carried out not only without complaint, but in almost every case with selfless dedication.

It was into this background and social order that those of us who were born in the "thirties" started our journey through life, and what changes we were to witness over that short span of several decades!

1

✻

Early Years

A QUIET AND EASY-GOING MAN

I can trace my earliest childhood memory back to when I was four years of age. How I know this to be true is quite simple, I can recall vivid, if only very selected memories of my father. I had just turned five years of age when he died on 5th of April 1941. I was the eighth of a family of ten children; Frank my younger brother was just over three years of age. While the youngest member of the family Therese was only one year and nine months old. It is difficult to comprehend the desolation my mother must have experienced at that time, being left as the sole parent of ten young children. The future years must have looked bleak and frightening to her, having to take on the role of mother and father of ten, the eldest still of school going age, her only regular source of income being a small widows pension. Our parents had bought the house on Dunbur Road with a loan from the bank and of course regular repayments were still due and would be for some years to come. Being a woman of strong religious belief, one can only assume that her faith in God gave her the strength to carry on at this awful time. She simply got on with the job of rearing her family the best way she knew how.

My father as I remember him was a quiet and easy-going, but hard-working man with little spare time or money for anything but to attend to the needs of the family. He came to Wicklow from his native Galway and managed a grocery and bar business in Main Street owned by the firm of S.V. Delahunt & Co. Ltd. The story as my mother told it.

"He being one of the Liam Mellows brigade and on the run, he had to leave his native Galway during the Black and Tan era, which brought him to Wicklow." While working in Delahunts he met my mother and they were married in 1926. The family lived at Two Dunbur Road, a small terraced house, while my aunt, my mother's sister and her husband - Jim and Ellen (Nellie) Everett, lived at the larger number seven, known as "St Patrick's." Jim and Ellen Everett were to play a major part in the life of our family after the death of our father. The Coastguard Service had originally built the terrace that both houses occupied, and were stationed there until the withdrawal of British Forces from Ireland in 1922. On the departure of the coastguards the houses were individually sold off.

Part of the property with each house was a very large garden extending to more than half an acre. My earliest memory is of my father working in the garden, where he cultivated every square inch. Each evening when he wasn't working late, during spring and summer, after his evening meal, he would change to his gardening clothes and boots and while daylight lasted his time was spent in the garden. I can still see him clearly, grey hair, although only in his early forties, falling across his forehead as he bent over the drills placing the seed potatoes on the manure between the freshly dug drills. He grew all the vegetables needed for the household for most of the year. We were never short of potatoes, cabbage, onions, carrots, beet, turnip, peas, and many more. We also had lots of gooseberry, blackcurrant and redcurrant bushes, raspberry canes and the lovely wine rhubarb.

My mother made enough jam to keep the family going for

the whole year. Our job was to pick whatever fruit was in season. Having enough sugar for the operation was no great problem. Even during the war years our family ration was more than enough for daily needs, my mother saved what was left from week to week. I can still remember the butter box, which in our case was the "sugar box", getting fuller and fuller as the jam-making season approached.

As time went on and our father was no longer with us the garden still continued to be tilled and the jam continued to be made, but now my older brother Liam was given the responsibility of the garden, without much complaint or indeed without much help from me or any other member of the family. I hated gardening and got into trouble many a time for not pulling my weight. Liam, of course, went on in later years to achieve very high office, but more about that later.

As I mentioned earlier I was the eighth of ten children, the first three were girls Carmel, Marjorie, and Monica, then came the first boy Michael, then Breda and then four more boys, Paddy, Liam, myself and Frank, and finally the baby Therese. All ten grew up and did what adults do, nine got married, one remained single, five had families of their own, three adopted wonderful children, four moved and made their lives away from Wicklow. Two having moved away returned to settle back in Wicklow, and happily all ten remained extremely close throughout our lives.

Some years after my father and mother married, in order to add to the family income, my father built or had built, a small single story bungalow at the back of the house. During the summer months the family would move out to the bungalow and our parents would let the house by the month to people wishing to spend their holidays by the sea at Wicklow. Most summers for years to come we were to spend the months of June, July and August and some times the month of May as well in our little bungalow, that extra month being a bonus in terms of earnings for my mother. During the summer period, because the bungalow was small, the two oldest girls Carmel and Marjorie stayed at no 7 with my aunt Nellie and uncle Jim. This was the start of the exodus of part of the family to live permanently at no 7. Paddy later joined the two girls and was followed by Michael.

These were very happy times and looking back, life in the bungalow was always associated with long hot, and carefree summer days, which I am sure if one were to check the weather statistics for those years, such perfect conditions were not always the reality. However, "memories through rose coloured spectacles" or whatever. Nevertheless, even in bad weather, life back in those far off summers remains in my memory as cosy and happy in our little bungalow. There was one glorious fact; summertime also meant holidays from school and freedom to go and do whatever one wished. For me that was heaven, all the time in the world to indulge all sorts of "flights of fancy", I was always more the dreamer while my other male siblings were of a much more focused and pragmatic disposition.

SUNDAY AMONGST THE CYPRESS TREES

My father wore a heavy grey herringbone tweed overcoat in Winter and, of course, a trilby hat, head-dress for men even in summer, was very much part of the dress code back in those days. Occasionally, when he was going to work in the mornings, I would skip along by his side holding his hand as we proceeded out from the back of our house and around by 'Brennan's wall' and the Coast Guard Apparatus house, as far as what we called "the red-gate". I can still see his form in the long gray coat and soft hat, hands deep in his coat pockets or waving back as he proceeded on down Summer Hill before I turned and retraced my steps to our back door. My mother, of course dealt in Delahunt's of Main Street for her weekly shopping and I remember her telling me, later in life, that our father would weigh everything to the last ounce and make sure that she did not get even a fraction of an ounce over what she was entitled to in anything she purchased.

In wintertime most young boys wore boots to school. My father did the re-soling of the boots and shoes for all of us. I remember vividly, and looking back for some reason with a contented and secure feeling, him sitting on a cushion on the floor by the warm glow of the old range in the kitchen, the last between his knees, working away with leather, tacks and sharp knife, his pipe in his mouth; while we the younger kids happily climbed all over him - My mother seated at the other side of the fire darning a mountain of socks.

My last memory of my father was when he was very ill with pneumonia, and the ambulance came to take him to the local hospital. The men carried him on the stretcher down the twisty stairs and I clearly remember putting my hand on his warm forehead as he was carried through the hallway to the waiting ambulance. My father died some days later. I have no memory of the funeral or if we were even brought to the cemetery but I do remember Liam and myself, being taken out of class by Miss Wall and Mother Angela of the Dominican Community and being put kneeling to pray at a big statue on a stand outside in the hallway of the old school. I also seem to remember a lot of activity as my father's family arrived from Galway.

It is strange how the mind of a child works; I have no memory of sadness at my father's death. Although I have these vivid memories of him in life, I have no memory of missing his presence in the life of the household after his departure. It seems to me, trying to recall this terrible event in the life of our family, when my father was carried out of the house on that day in April 1941, his existence was simply eradicated from my memory. As I write these lines, trying to think myself back into what must have been such a painful time for my older sisters and brothers, I am unable to recall any memory of sadness or loss. I can only assume that the exclusion from the memory of a child of such events is a form of safety mechanism, to protect the young mind from the worst extremes of trauma, while allowing that young mind to grow and develop unaffected by such harrowing memories.

I have often heard it said that the strongest of ones senses is our sense of smell, and although these days I possess little or no sense of smell; all through my life the smell of the evergreen Leyland

Cypress trees brought me back instantly to Rathnew Cemetery. Most Sunday afternoons back in those times, we walked with my mother to spend some time at my father's graveside amongst the cypress trees in Rathnew Cemetery. Of course as time went on we, the younger end of the family, became more aware of the absence of a father figure within the home, although Jim Everett was as close to a father figure to all of us as any man could possibly be. After my father's death Uncle Jim, as he was known to us, although no blood relation, and his wife Aunt Nellie, my mother's sister, with no family of their own, devoted their lives almost totally to the welfare of the Kavanagh family. Jim Everett was an uncle by marriage only; he had no obligation to take responsibility for any member of our family, yet from this time on until his death in 1967 he regarded all of us as his own family. He extended to each one of us no less love and support, as he would have shown his own children. In return we all afforded both he and Aunt Nellie the same love and respect for as long as they lived, but more than that, a total acknowledgement by all of us of their absolute membership of the Kavanagh family. When Jim Everett died in Sir Patrick Dunne's Hospital, my mother was recovering from surgery not far away in St. Vincent's hospital. When we broke the news to her of his death later that evening I remember her saying "God Bless Jim Everett, he is surely in Heaven tonight".

REMEMBERED WITH GREAT AFFECTION

Back in my young days and I believe up to comparatively recent years, all the children both boys and girls started school with the Dominican Community in the convent school. The large imposing red brick building that you see today, known to all as Holy Rosary School, was built after my time. The old school stood beyond the grassy mound to the left, as you approach the main convent building. After the age of seven or eight when the children had made their First Communion the boys transferred to the De La Salle Brothers School and remained there until they achieved their Primary Leaving Certificate.

On the first day of school at the Convent the mothers and children were met at the door by Miss Wall who sympathetically and with great understanding took over the child in each case from its mother, and in some cases I might add kicking and screaming and upsetting the quieter children. Like the Pied Piper, Miss Wall, followed by all those little kids now almost too terrified to make a sound proceeded to her classroom. Of course in some cases it was the mother that needed to be consoled and re-assured rather than the child. Cecilia Wall was a wonderful teacher and brought many talents to her very special calling. She possessed one particular advantage above that of many teachers, most especially with the very young children; because of her diminutive size, the children never found her in any way intimidating.

She was a great lady, possessed of a wonderful sense of humour, who for years and years had taken responsibility for the younger children as they started school. She had a special gift of being able to settle the children very quickly into the routine of school life. Miss Wall was always the essence of kindness and understanding while at the same time in full control of her class. On First Communion day I remember she would bring all the First Communicants to the Altar, and move along behind each child as they received First Communion from the Priest. In some cases placing a reassuring hand on the head of the more nervous child. In our case, Liam and myself, together with many other children, made our First Communion with the celebrant of the Mass being Fr. Michael Ryan. We were accompanied of course by the ever-attentive Miss Wall. Afterwards all the children were taken back to the convent for a special breakfast.

Miss Wall lived on well into her nineties, and looked exactly the same to the end, as when we were all in school with her. In later years it was always a great pleasure to meet and chat with her. She had a story to tell about almost every child she put through her hands, and could relate funny incidents and events for hours that happened with the children in her classroom down through the years. She had the remarkable ability of recall in her later life of specific events in great detail, of ones schooldays, with almost anyone she taught. For many years before she died, on the Sunday prior to Christmas Day, Miss Wall joined May and her mother Mrs. Lambert and myself in our home with a number of Mrs. Lambert's elderly friends for Christmas Lunch. On those occasions Miss Wall was always the life and soul of the party. We used to call it the Granny's Lunch. Had we been blessed with children of our own to carry on the tradition, and had Miss Wall lived on, we would by now have graduated to join her together with the others as recipients of the "Granny's Lunch" as Christmas approaches.

Miss Wall was a most remarkable lady, who will be remembered with great affection by thousands of Wicklow people, all of whom have childhood memories of a special time when they passed through her care. To borrow an analogy from the old Gregory Peck film "To Kill a Mocking Bird"-

"Stand Wicklow Miss Wall has passed on."

GERMANY CALLING – GERMANY CALLING

I suppose much of the early memories of those of my age, and of those somewhat older, was the impact on their lives of the Second World War. I was three years of age when war was declared in 1939. Of course I was too young to be aware of the detail of the day-to-day events as they unfolded. As time went on what seems to have made an impression on me was the occasions when our parents would appear to take particular interest in the daily news bulletins, on these occasions I remember we were urged to be quiet while they listened intently on the old valve radio to the latest reports from the front. I imagine such occasions were battles of particular moment or importance. They say that the first casualty of war is truth, I suppose much of what was broadcast was propaganda and I am sure it was difficult to know where the real truth lay.

Saturday night was a special night, amongst all the fuss of baths in the tin tub in front of the kitchen fire, and preparations for Sunday Mass, suddenly complete silence was called for; even in the bath one couldn't move a muscle or make a splash. We all waited in anticipation, not knowing why, and suddenly through the crackle of the old radio came, GERMANY CALLING, GERMANY CALLING, and the voice of William Joyce known as Lord Haw-Haw, delivering his particular weekly slant of German propaganda to the British people from Berlin, and I am told, on at least a few occasions reference was made to Ireland saying on one particular broadcast –

"Greystones that little British Colony on the Irish coast we are watching you." Even at that tender age one was aware of a strange uneasy feeling listening to that voice. I suppose adults would have used the word sinister. William Joyce was born in America of Irish parents and spent much of his life in Britain. In the late 1920's he became involved with the British Union of Fascists and in 1939 at the age of 33 moved with his second wife to Berlin. At the end of the war he was captured tried and executed as a war criminal. He possibly believed that being an American citizen he would be spared the death penalty, however, he had for a short period in earlier life served in the British Armed Services. For many years people continued to question whether justice prevailed when William Joyce (Lord Haw-Haw) was hanged in January 1946.

One of the memories I have of that time was watching the shipping proceed north or south off the coast of Wicklow, which we could clearly see from my mother's bedroom window; it was so strange to see a huge Balloon floating high above each ship. The purpose of these balloons was to act as an anti-aircraft barrier to prevent enemy aircraft from attacking shipping from a low level. When ever I see on television these days the large blimp delivering aerial photography from a high level over one of the major golf tournaments it brings to mind the Barrage Balloons of the war years.

Another memory of those years, a necessary measure by the government, which added to the hardship of the times, was the rationing of all essential foodstuffs and many other items. For larger families such as ours, the quantities were generous enough.

I remember when serving my time to the Bar and Grocery trade in S.V. Delahunt & Co Ltd., having to weigh the regulated quantities of particular foodstuffs, rationing was still in place into the fifties. Each person was allowed on a weekly basis under the regulations, two ounces of Tea, six ounces of Butter and three-quarters of a pound of Sugar. We used to weigh multiples of these weights in huge quantities each week. When the customers came to buy their groceries the Ration Book had to be presented and marked by the assistant. Other items were also rationed such as Flour and Cigarettes. Although the rationing of cigarettes ceased soon after the end of the war as I remember it. While it was in place it seemed to create far greater hardship than food rationing for those addicted to the habit. Smokers it appeared would go anywhere or do almost anything to enhance their meagre ration of 'fags.' I would have thought it much easier to break the habit once and for all, rather than put up with a short supply and with continuous craving all through the war years. A song that was popular at that time which went like this - Bless 'em all, bless 'em all, the long and the short and the tall, Bless all the Sergeants and W. O. ones, Bless all the Corporals and their blinking sons,

The Irish version went like this:
Bless 'em all bless 'em all
Bless all the TD's in the Dail
Bless de Valera and Sean McEntee
They gave us brown bread and a half-ounce of tea
But the smokes they're the scarcest of all
And they say that supplies must still fall
They're bringing starvation to this little nation
So welcome St. Vincent de Paul

Just a couple of years ago, at the fiftieth anniversary celebrations of Holy Rosary School, I spoke to Sr. Mary Theophane now happily enjoying her well-earned retirement. When I was in the convent school over sixty years earlier Sr. Theophane was teaching there, but has long since left Wicklow, and had just returned for the celebrations. I introduced myself and asked her did she remember me?

"I remember you very well, you were always drawing airplanes, dropping bombs,"

She replied.

NO LONGER BABIES

The beginning of September following the making of ones First Communion the boys transferred from the Convent School to the De La Salle Brothers National School. It was with mixed feelings I believe that most young boys approached this move. As I remember it, the younger classes in the convent were to some extent cosseted and taken care of, almost like babies. The names of the then classes even lend credence to this, Senior Infants, Babies, and so on. However, in the brothers we were all moving into First Class, we were no longer "infants", we were young boys. We were beginning to feel a little more independent and it was a good feeling. But in the back of our minds we were also being thrust into a scene where we were the youngest and also the most vulnerable in the pecking order of this new and strange environment; we no longer had Miss Wall or the good nuns or in my case older sisters to look out for us, older brothers just weren't the same. We were entering the rough and tumble of the boys' school.

Well we settled in and it was rough by comparison but we got on with it. The De La Salle brothers of the primary school were all conscientious men dedicated to their profession of teaching, if at times maybe a little over earnest, if you take my meaning, but as they say "it never did us any harm" and maybe it didn't. We had Brother Fridlin for the first two years who I remember spent hour after hour making us sing out our tables until we were able to multiply or divide figures almost without thinking. We progressed to Brother Leo who stayed with us through third, fourth and fifth class. Bro. Leo was a County Cork man and as I remember never missed an opportunity of singing the praises of Christy Ring the great Cork hurler. My favourite lesson during this period was singing I still remember some of the songs he taught us which were mostly in the Irish language. I, like the youngsters of all generations was more interested in the popular music of the day. At that time due to over-crowding in the school, sixth class was conducted in a room in the Parocial Hall just down the road a piece from the school. Brother Patrick who was the Superior of the De La Salle Community in Wicklow at that time, was our teacher for the sixth and final year in the National School, a stern disciplinarian, always fair, but well liked and respected by the pupils.

NECESSITY - THE MOTHER OF INVENTION

Back in those years in most households Monday was washday and before going to school each Monday morning it was our job to get the fire going in the back yard and fill the big wash-pot with water in preparation for the days wash. "Necessity is the mother of invention", and with coal not being available during the war years, it was necessary to find some other alternative, for such purposes as boiling water for washing clothes etc, sawdust which was in plentiful supply was the answer for many household purposes. The fire was built outdoors with the sawdust, which we collected weekly from the local sawmill on the quay. The method was simple but very effective. The container used for the fire was an open topped five-gallon drum; a hole about the size of an old penny was cut in the centre of the bottom. The drum was placed on two red bricks to create ventilation under the fire. We would then stand a sweeping brush handle upright in the drum with its end out through the hole in the bottom. Holding the handle perpendicular we would fill the drum with sawdust, while at the same time compacting it all the time with a milk bottle as we filled. When the drum was full we would carefully ease the brush handle out of the drum leaving a neat hole up through the centre of the sawdust. We would light the fire from the vent underneath the drum.

When we were sure the fire was lighting we would lift the large wash-pot up on the drum. If the sawdust was damp it would be more difficult to start the fire, we might have to resort to using a little paraffin poured down the centre hole to help it along. Our job was finished when the fire was lighting, it was then time to go to school. We would as a rule leave the house at 9.10am. each morning as the signature tune for "Housewives Choice" a BBC daily radio programme, introduced more often than not by a presenter named George Elrick, allowing us twenty minutes for our journey on foot to school for start of lessons at 9.30am. As I write I can still hum the tune! An hour or so later the water would be boiling for my mother to start boiling the clothes prior to washing them. She would still be washing clothes in the old zinc bath when we returned home from school in the late afternoon, the fire would stay lighting all day supplying plenty of hot water. Washday must have been a really hard days work for my mother back in those days. I never heard her complain, it was just another chore that had to be taken care of in the course of her weekly routine. How times have changed; I still have that old cast-iron oval wash-pot, these days it is home to a display of geraniums at the front of our house.

Another weekly event that took place each winter of our youth, my mother being a widow was entitled to some free fuel during winter months this was supplied weekly by Wicklow County Council, however, delivery was not included. Michael and Paddy had constructed a trolley for the purpose, which consisted of a plank about eight feet long. At the front end a heavy wooden cross piece was attached by one single bolt allowing the cross bar to swivel for steerage purposes. To this cross bar an axle was fitted which received the wheels – probably from some discarded pram. A heavy rope each end attached to the cross bar - rein like, for steering was fitted. Towards the back end or the load-bearing end of the plank a box like structure about two feet six inches wide and about five feet long was fitted, with another wider axle and two more wheels fitted at the rear end. In those days one could find many old wheel less prams lying about. During the war years the only fuel available from the Council was turf, (peat) and more often than not it was too wet to burn. Each Friday when we came home from school Michael, Paddy, Liam and myself, and later Fran when he was old enough, complete with fuel dockets would head for Hamilton's yard on the quay.

Anyone familiar with the topography of Wicklow town will know that the journey from Dunbur road to the quay is all very much downhill. We would all pile onto the trolley and with Michael at the controls take off down Summerhill, turning sharply at Flynn's Corner, and thankfully remaining upright with the help of a makeshift brake; down Monkton Road and left at breakneck speed into the tee junction with Castle Street, down the "Hollow" past Turner's little shop and sharply turning right at Kane's Yard onto Quay Lane and into Hamilton's Coal Yard, to join the many other trolleys, old prams and the many other modes of make-shift conveyance used to transport the turf to keep the home fires burning for another week.

Thinking about those down hill journeys, I feel five unfortunate and hard working Guardian Angles must have had some anxious moments in their efforts to keep us safe. I often wondered how we were not all killed. On one occasion a certain guardian angel I'm afraid did stumble a little in his efforts on Fran's behalf. On one of our downhill trips Fran came off the trolley and landed rather heavily, after a sleepless night he was brought to the local hospital where it was discovered he had broken his arm. Needless to say, Fran being the youngest of the boys, life for the rest of us was somewhat tense, to say the least for a while at home. For some six weeks or so Fran became the celebrity and in some respect the envy of the gang with his arm from wrist to shoulder in plaster.

There were two old sisters who lived together on our terrace, Miss Byrne and Mrs Redmond who because of their status were also entitled to the free fuel, so it became our responsibility to bring home the fuel for the two ladies. The journey back with a heavy double load was another matter altogether; with Michael out front pulling on the rope and the rest of us pushing, occasionally maybe loosing a wheel along the way, all hard work indeed. Miss Byrne was a small and austere lady with the whitest white hair I have ever seen, she always wore one of those wraparound aprons popular back then with ladies of advancing years. She made regular visits to our house especially when she had some news to relate to my mother. It was clear to me that she didn't like children very much; she would insist that which ever, or as many of us who were in the kitchen when she called would be promptly removed before she would start to impart her news.

Each evening after we finished our tea and all the crockery, etc. was washed and put away on the big dresser in the kitchen by my mother or Monica or Breeda, my mother would call us all together. It was then time to recite the Rosary. We would all kneel down facing the large picture of "The Sacred Heart" with below it, the perpetual lamp burning. With elbows resting on individual kitchen chairs as we knelt, the little ones kneeling two to a chair, our Rosary Beads dangling out through the spindles of the chair backs, the Rosary would begin. My mother would give out the first decade and then the older members of the family would take it in turn through the mysteries. On occasions, the person leading the prayers would forget to move the beads through their fingers, until my mother would finally announce – we are now on the thirteenth Hail Mary!

We had a little smoky grey cat called "Topsy" at that time. One was never sure when Topsy would come to life during the Rosary and discover the Rosary Beads, dangling between the legs of the chairs, which he assumed were there for his amusement.

With one pounce – paws flailing – beads flying around the legs of the chairs, which in the middle of the prayers would put us into chinks of laughter. The more we would try to suppress it of course the more we would laugh. I'm afraid on these irreverent occasions the mysteries were more joyful than sorrowful. Eventually my mother would give instructions for the cat to be put outside, the sanctity of the Rosary would then be restored. The closing prayers at the end would start with the "Litany of the Saints" and would go on interminably through many other prayers, and lasted almost as long as the Rosary itself.

Just down the road from where we lived about fifty yards or so, a new family had moved in, which was unusual in those days. Really the only people back then whose work necessitated moving from place to place, apart from the clergy, were bank officials and the occasional new member of the Garda Siochana. Everybody living on Summer Hill or the Dunbur Road district was local to Wicklow as I remember it, so when the Tumulty family moved into "Ard-na-Graine" Terrace they were, just for a little while, somewhat of a curiosity to us locals. Mr. Tumulty was a member of the Garda Siochana and took up duty in Wicklow Town. The Tumulty and Kavanagh families became close friends as the years passed. My brother Michael and the oldest member of the Tumulty family, Ray were of an age and went through school together, Roy the second member was roughly Paddy's age, while the third and youngest member Brendan was just a month or so younger than myself. We spent all our time together as we grew up, we must have looked like the newspaper cartoon characters Mutt and Jeff, Brendan even as a young boy stood head and shoulders over me.

Like his dad, on leaving school Brendan joined the police. Unlike his dad he emigrated from Ireland and became a member of the New York Police Department. Brendan like myself is now retired and still living in New York. He returns to Wicklow each year for the Regatta Festival. My mother and Mrs Tumulty were close friends for the rest of their lives. Their salutations towards each other through the years, remained formal, never using first names, they always referred to each other as Mrs. Tumulty or Mrs Kavanagh, I suppose in those more formal days, not having grown up together, such familiarity did not come easy to them.

Some few years after the arrival of the Tumulty family in Wicklow another family came to live on our road, the family's name was Rodgers. My uncle had built a bungalow beside their own house; the Rodgers family, as did their predecessor in the bank, rented the bungalow and became the latest new people on the block. Mr Rodgers was a bank official on the staff of the Hibernian Bank in Abbey Street. The family at that time consisted of two girls and a boy, Maeve being the oldest, Fiona was next and then came Adrian, two further children were born while the family lived in Wicklow namely Kieran and Ian. Adrian was a couple of years younger than me but very quickly fitted in and became one of our group. Mrs Rodgers was a very friendly lady and made us welcome anytime we called to the house, in fact their garden became the play ground for all of us during those years. As the years passed Mr Rodgers was transferred, which was normal practice for Bank people back in those times, and we lost touch with the family for some years. I was delighted to meet up again with Maeve and Fiona several years ago and reminisce about old times. Maeve and Fiona both married, Adrian I believe remained single, qualified as a dentist, and practiced for most of his working life in Wexford. During the formative years of my childhood my closest friends were the members of these two families.

SINGING FOR YOUR SUPPER

As a young fellow, it was recognized by some people in our immediate circle that I had a reasonably good ear for music and could carry a tune pretty well. This, I discovered was not altogether a bad thing, I found I was being brought places on the understanding that I would 'sing a song', well I didn't mind inflicting my singing on unsuspecting hosts if it meant being taken on special trips. Again, somebody, I can't remember who, apparently persuaded my mother to do something about my voice. Now I'm sure my mother had many more pressing matters on her mind, rather than spend her time considering if she had another Bing Crosby or John McCormack on her hands, which, again I'm sure she understood was highly unlikely. However, she was the kind of woman who, if someone she respected outlined to her, a serious opportunity concerning one of the family, she felt duty bound, and would not spare herself to give that family member their chance or opportunity.

So, I was duly entered to audition for a children's radio program on Radio Eireann, the national radio station. In the weeks prior to the audition I was dispatched several times to the home of Maeve Finlay a close friend of my sister Breda. Maeve was a fine pianist from a very musical family in the town. Well, Maeve and in fact her mother also an excellent pianist, very kindly gave me all the help they could, finally the day of the audition arrived which, strangely enough was on a Sunday morning.

At that time Radio Eireann was housed on the upper floors of the GPO building in O'Connell Street. My mother and one or two friends and myself complete with music arrived at the appointed time, and were shown into a very large room with some chairs around the sides, and a full grand piano stood in the centre of the room. There was no evidence of anybody else presenting themselves for audition. A very friendly lady put me standing at a large microphone placed on a stand, which stood about a foot above my head, and instructed me on what she wanted me to do. The lady started to play; the song I had chosen was "The loveliest Night of the Year". All seemed to go OK, and when I finished singing the lady thanked me and said they would be in touch with me. A letter duly arrived from RE, confirming yes that I had a pleasant voice but the song I had chosen was wrong for my voice, and recommending that I should concentrate on songs like "The Road to the Isles" or such, and then I should re-apply again for another audition. Well, "The Road to the Isles" was not really my kind of music, so I never re-applied and really never thought anymore about it.

However, music and singing has always played an important part in my life; in fact to me a life without music would be a barren and lacklustre affair indeed. I remember all those years ago we had an old gramophone at home, not the "Henry Higgins" type with the large horn but the type that opened like a suitcase. We also had a large number of records most of which I've forgotten, but I do remember several recordings of short sketches by Jimmy O'Dea and Harry O Donovan, one of the sketches was entitled "Sixpence each way on Water Spray;" as I remember, the scene was Jimmy O'Dea trying to place a bet on a horse. One particular record we used to play all the time, the song was "Tip toe through the Tulips," and on the flipside a tune called "Painting the clouds with Sunshine;" although I can't remember the singers name. We got great value from that scratchy old gramophone; you had to change the needle for a new one after every ten or twelve tunes, we eventually wore out all the needles. My sister Monica studied shorthand in school, I used to get her to take down the words of all the popular songs of the day from the radio and type them up for me. The top singer back then was Bing Crosby with the younger Frank Sinatra and Perry Como also making big names for themselves. Another name I remember from those times was Dick Haymes, my sister Breda's favourite crooner.

My particular favourite from as early as I can remember has always been Bing Crosby. Over the years I must have collected nearly everything Bing has ever done from 78s to LPs to CDs, and videoed over thirty of his feature films. Many a evening or night when I was driving home from far flung parts of the country the strains of Bing have kept me company on the car radio and helped to shorten the often long journeys. I remember back in the early 70's reading in the paper that Bing Crosby was coming to Ireland and would be playing a charity exhibition round of golf with the late great Harry Bradshaw, Christy Green, another Irish professional golfer and the American Ambassador. The event would take place at Woodbrook Golf Club, Bray Co. Wicklow. I prevailed on Michael Butler to go along with me, it was a lovely warm day we followed the golf together with a great many other people, at one stage in the afternoon we had the opportunity to meet and shake hands with Bing, which really made my day.

Sometime later he did a show in the Gaiety Theatre accompanied by Rosemary Clooney, Dermot Desmond kindly offered to queue for tickets. Dermot, Mary, May and myself went along to what for all of us but especially for me was indeed another very special and really memorable occasion.

I think looking back over the years the first purchase I made shortly after I started work was what was called in those days a Pick-up, which was essentially a modern gramophone that could play 78's as they were known, which had one single song on each side of the record. It could also play LP's, long play or multiple tune records. The pick-up was the forerunner of the radiogram. You simply plugged two leads into the speaker of your existing radio and the radio picked up the sound. The sound reproduction was infinitely better than the old gramophone of our childhood.

The first two records I bought were the LP soundtrack recordings of "South Pacific" and "Oklahoma" which cost in those days thirty-nine shillings and six pence each and which I still have today. While over the years as I became interested in the musicals shows I collected many original stage recordings of the great Stage Musicals and Operetta. Of the many hobbies and pastimes that have held my interest at various times over the years, music and song has always been and remains the abiding passion of my life, so in the words of the great ABBA –

"Thank you for the music, for giving it to me"

However, I digress, getting back to the point, the years in the brothers National School were I suppose uneventful. We did our lessons and most of us got into the routine of having to do home exercise, which was new to us on transferring to the Brothers School. Our lunch period was between 12.30pm and 1.15pm, leaving us with little time to get home to the other end of town, have our lunch, and get back to school. We would always race down the 'Chapel Hill' and around "Lalors Corner" and up Main Street. On one occasion having rounded the corner at full tilt and on by Long's Drapery shop, now FBD Insurance, I tripped and apparently hit my head on the shaft of a Horse and Cart parked, if that is the word, outside the shop and fell under the horses hooves. I knew nothing more about this situation until I eventually came around in Wicklow Hospital with a large bandage over one eye and the mother and father of a headache. I remember the Matron whose name was Nurse Corless, as a large lady with a commanding presence who wore glasses and ruled the roost in the hospital at that time. Dr.Roche a local doctor in Wicklow apparently stitched me up and I spent a couple of days as a patient being cared for by Nurse McDaniel and Nurse Nevin. The great thing about this event was that I got a week off school and was treated preferentially for some time at home, especially if I complained of a 'headache'.

A RIOT OF COLOUR AND ACTIVITY

One of the great event memories of my younger days, and of all the young lads who made up our group, was The Wicklow Regatta Festival. As the carefree summer days of July went by, we as youngsters all looked forward eagerly to the August Weekend. Wicklow Regatta Festival in those times was one of the major festivals of the east coast, and I believe one of the oldest in the calendar of festival events in Ireland. First established in 1876, down through the years the festival had become a special day out for many thousands of people from all the villages in the wider Wicklow area. Emigrants working in Britain looked forward all through the year to returning home and renewing friendships at the Wicklow Regatta. The festival for us got under way with the arrival of the "Amusements" during the week prior to the August Weekend, and was set up on the green close to the Leitrim Bar, as we all watched with eager expectation of the weekend to come.

Friday evening of the August Weekend and the influx of people really got into full swing. Saturday afternoon and the yachts started to arrive from Dunlaoghaire. Although I'm sure it was not always the case, but looking back; the sun was always shining and the yachts always had a fair wind and fetched up sailing magnificently between the piers. We never left the Old Pier on Saturday and Sunday except when we got hungry, and then only to run home and back to the pier as soon as we could, as the yachts continued to arrive in great numbers. Cruising yachts and racing yachts of all sizes and colours. The Dublin Bay Twenty Fours, and The D.B. Twenty Ones, and the other various racing classes all arrived regularly as clockwork. We all had our favourite yacht, which we claimed as our own. One particular yacht, our special favourite, for which we eagerly awaited each year, and always arrived on Sunday afternoon, was the J.B. Kearney owned yawl "Mavis." In its immaculate black livery with gold strip along its length, and beautifully maintained bright work, she would tie up proudly as if she knew that she was being admired, stern on to the East Pier.

We could then head for home for our tea in the knowledge that once again all our favourite yachts that we knew so well had arrived - all present and correct. There was one other boat that usually arrived late Sunday evening and tied up in the "turn hole", close to what are now Herbst's sheds. She was a large old sailing smack, I think from Ringsend, the name of which escapes me, with a carefree crew of a dozen or so happy-go-lucky people on board. Not for them the immaculate doeskin reefers and special deck shoes, which was the regular dress of the well-healed 'yachties' of those times. This high-spirited almost rag tag looking crew by comparison, arrived fully equipped with a range of musical instruments and I feel a well stocked "locker," they had come to Wicklow to have a good time, and they were most welcome. We would be back down to the quay after tea, with many others to enjoy the fun as the crew sat on the deck while their music making floated over the whole quayside and went on late into the night, and indeed a great time was had by all. Finally tired but happy we made our way home through the darkness, having had a wonderful day and full of anticipation of all the events of tomorrow the actual Regatta Day in Wicklow. "Sure why would anyone want to be anywhere else."

The great day dawned and we couldn't get our breakfast over quickly enough, meet up with our pals and get back down to the quayside. As we approached from the "bank wall" overlooking the harbour, the whole scene was really a sight to behold. From the old "Sarah rocks" at the upper end of "Batney's strand" to well past where Hopkins Hardware is now, was chock solid with yachts. In places you could almost cross the harbour, climbing from boat to boat to the other side. Some of the yachts would have their sails up airing in the sun or gently flapping in the light breeze, while many of the crew were frantically preparing for the racing later in the day. While still other crewmembers prepared breakfast, as the smell of bacon, eggs and sausages cooking in the open air, wafted across the boats to the quayside. The whole scene and atmosphere was spellbinding. On the Murrough side of the harbour the lorries would soon start to arrive with the Racing Skiffs from Greystones, Dalkey, Dunlaoghaire and Ringsend while of course Wicklow's own "Guiding Star," which always featured in the major Skiff Racing events all along the East Coast stood ready and in top condition for the great skiff racing events of the day.

The special "Sea Breeze" trains would start arriving during the morning with the supporters of the various Rowing Clubs and the many families and individuals for whom the annual pilgrimage to the Wicklow Regatta was a must. By noon-time and for the rest of the day the seafront would be black with people. The Dodgems, the Chair-o-Planes, the Swinging-Boats and the Hobby-Horses as well as all the other sideshows were all operating at full capacity. This special day would always draw many hawkers selling fruit, sweets and minerals. There would be caravans with fortune-tellers and goodness knows what else, while the cacophony of sound from the amusements and the crowds of people was at all times in competition with the pop music of the day blasting out at full volume from the Amusements headquarters.

The Lifeboat also played its part in the Regatta Festival. During the morning she would be lowered from the house to stand proudly on show in its always immaculate condition on the slipway until early afternoon, when she would be launched and do trips for all who wished, along the course during the Skiff races. A long tradition of support for the RNLI existed even in those days and the Lifeboat Flag Days were a well-established part of the Regatta even back then. I remember the Lifeboat Day emblems in those times were round stiff paper badges depicting a lifeboat steaming through the centre of a lifebuoy and were attached to ones coat or whatever with a straight pin. As small kids it was our job to fix the pins to hundreds of flags in preparation for the older members of the family who with a great many others helped with the collection. Little did I know that I would in later life find myself endeavoring to organize Lifeboat Flag Days all over The Republic of Ireland.

The action in the afternoon took place largely on the Murrough side of town, all the yachts having sailed out on the bay in preparation for the racing in the afternoon. The Swimming Races and the Diving Competitions could be viewed to the harbour side of the West or New Pier as it is called, which was bedecked with flags and bunting. The "Greasy Pole" event was great fun to watch. The pole, which was greased, was fixed to the pier with its length extended straight out over the water and a small flag attached to the outer end. The idea was to walk the pole and remove the flag and return without falling into the water below. With many of the competitors slipping and falling straddle-legged in their efforts to walk the pole I feel sure it was more fun for the spectator than for the competitor.

Meanwhile on the seaside of the New Pier and along the Promenade you could watch the start and finish of each of the skiff races. On the water many small boats and yawls followed the course of the races while cheering on their own particular favourite boat. Further out in the bay all the different classes of yachts with their multicolored spinnakers were in evidence as their racing went on a pace, all creating a riot of colour and activity in the bay. Many of the yachts did not return to the harbour on the completion of the racing, but took advantage of a favourable tide or wind if that was the case to carry them back to Dunlaoghaire. The cut and thrust of the All Ireland Senior Open Skiff Race, which generally took place at approximately 6pm. with tremendous vocal enthusiasm all along the seafront from the great many supporters of each boat taking part, while a full commentary very capably delivered by an old friend of our family the late Jim Murphy and broadcast from the course. There was always great disappointment if the local boat didn't win, but whatever happened it was always and still is an exciting and enjoyable spectator event.

By now the train whistles were beginning to blow and the people were making their way back to the train station. Some of them who had spent more time in the pub than they should have were a little under the weather, we often followed on part of the way to the train in the hope that we would see the occasional argument between supporters develop into something a bit more boisterous. And usually we were not disappointed!!

For the younger adults of course the best was yet to come with the big Regatta Dance, with one of the well known Show Bands of the era engaged for the dancing event of the festival. For us, the younger people the final event of the day and probably the most spectacular took place at about 10.30pm at the end of the East Pier, as many hundreds of people including ourselves watched from the grassy banks at the Black Castle. The Fireworks display which for us kids was the enthralling climax, marking the end of August Weekend. What wonderful memories!

A story told I believe by the late Miss Gertie Carroll but worth repeating. During a Confirmation Ceremony in "St. Patrick's" Church Wicklow many years ago, The Bishop asked a child,

"What is the greatest Feast Day of the year?" The child re-

plied without hesitation,
    "The Wicklow Regatta"

2

❋

A Christmas Memory

A DICKENSIAN CHRISTMAS SCENE

One of the magical times each year in our young lives was the Christmas season; right back to my earliest memories of that great Feast Day of all the Christian Churches. Any Churchman will tell you that The Easter season is the most important celebration in the Church's year and liturgically I am sure they are correct, however, for me together with children of all ages, and throughout the ages, the Christmas season has always been a time of particular magic. Today it is the major holiday of mid-winter and usually lasts for almost two weeks, when spending goes through the roof and commercialism seems to reach even dizzier heights as each new Christmas approaches. Nevertheless, if I said it still manages to awaken the child in all of us and lift our spirits during the long dark and dreary days of winter; I believe I would be making an understatement.

Since we married forty plus years ago May and I have never spent Christmas in our own home. When my mother passed on, and indeed for several years before, we have spent Christmas with my brother Liam and his wife Margaret and their children Conal and Rosemary at their home "Mount Carmel" overlooking

Wicklow and the Bay.

My brother Frank and his wife Maura made up the rest of the party for Christmas dinner. Margaret is a marvellous homemaker and cook and Christmas in that lovely old house "Mount Carmel" has always been very special. The house is decorated in a very traditional festive fashion with lots of holly and ivy and coloured bells and decorations everywhere, and with the largest Christmas tree possible in the grand old Sitting Room, and of course The Crib; in fact every room rivals a Dickensian Christmas scene. Liam is usually busy tending to the massive log fires, which burn in two or three different rooms or making sure everybody has a drink; all giving an atmosphere of warmth and genuine welcome. Meanwhile the kitchen where eventually everybody seems to gravitate towards is full of happy and good-humoured activity. Margaret spares no effort in the preparation of Christmas Dinner, which is always a veritable banquet.

Having attended Midnight Mass on Christmas Eve, with its always-wonderful sense of the real meaning of Christmas; our routine on Christmas morning usually goes like this! We visit each of the family homes and exchange gifts. First to May's sisters Peggy, Noeleen and Eileen and their families then on to my sister Breeda and husband James and their daughter Maritta and the other members of their family, by the time we visit all the houses, ending up calling to Mary's home, my sister in law on Dunbur Road, by then it is usually into the early afternoon. As we drive through the gates, full of anticipation of what has always been a very special occasion; I am grateful that we have been spared to enjoy another wonderful Christmas in "Mount Carmel." We all sit down for a leisurely Christmas dinner around 5pm, which with the good wine, the many excellent courses, the happy and lively conversation a couple or three hours seem to pass very quickly. It has always been my job to flame the Christmas pudding which gives a spectacular climax to Christmas Dinner, after gaelic coffee for those who wish to indulge, it is then time for Rosemary to pass around the gifts.

HOME FOR THE HOLIDAYS

Christmas was very different in our young days to what it is today, much of the almost daily pleasures that we enjoy and take for granted as the everyday norm, was for most people very much the luxury to be experienced only at Christmas or on very special occasions. The present generation of young people who are used to almost instant access to all their desires and wishes, comparatively speaking, would be horrified to have to endure the frugal lifestyle of our youth.

Paradoxically, that prudent lifestyle of those days had to my mind its upside for our generation, particularly at Christmas, which I believe the children of today are possibly missing. All the little luxuries our parents struggled to provide for us at this one very special time, that weren't part of our lives on a daily basis, became for us part of the magic that was Christmas. They helped to intensify the special pleasure of those times and the memories that will always remain with us; the one toy we received from Santa that we so much appreciated and cherished and were so grateful to receive. The anticipation of the wonderful food of that special time, the visitors to our home, and so many other simple experiences by today's standards, that heightened that spirit of Christmas in our young lives so many years ago.

As you will have gathered, school was not my favourite pastime, I was always too free-spirited to be fenced in and having to focus on matters educational for several hours every day. Even school as we approached Christmas became more than tolerable, at times even verging on the "pleasant experience", - but lets not get carried away! One of those happy school times was when we started to rehearse the Nativity Play, with Sister Mary Cyprian, one of the great teachers of music and singing in the young lives of all who attended the Dominican Convent primary school. We had by now progressed from Miss Wall's groupings of babies. The Nativity School Play for me marked the beginning of the Christmas season; and seemed to create in school life an atmosphere of good will and benevolence to all; that was of course, as long as you acted or sung your part to Sister Mary Cyprian's high standards. If not, you invoked the wrath of this formidable woman, a wrath that to a small child could seem considerable. That was the beginning of Christmas and our spirits and expectations began to rise. In retrospect, I believe the Nativity Play bestirred in me at that early age a lifelong interest in theatre and the magic of stagecraft.

About this time things started to happen at home beyond the usual round of regular household chores that took up almost all of my mothers waking hours. Extra shopping was done, space had to be found in cupboards for all sorts of stuff that was not part of the normal weekly shopping list, such as raisins and sultanas, candied peel, cherries and exotic spices and all the other ingredients that go into the special fare of Christmas cooking. The old gas cooker was thoroughly checked over to make sure that it was in tip-top condition for these very special cooking events. You had to remember to avoid peak cooking times when baking the Christmas cake in order to avoid a catastrophe as gas pressure tended to drop at these times.

The first big cooking event was the making of the Christmas pudding. The large kitchen table with its scrubbed white boards was cleared in preparation, and all the vital ingredients including the essential bottle of Guinness, were placed strategically on three sides around the perimeter of the table, leaving the centre free for the star of the performance, the massive mixing bowl; while several of us sat around the table intrigued with my mother's preparations and proceedings. Another step towards the magic that was Christmas was taking place. The special pudding cloth, which had been washed and put safely away last year had been retrieved earlier and greased in readiness to accept the mixture when prepared. We watched with great intent as my mother added each element of the ingredients in its correct order into the mixing bowl - the flour the suet the bread crumbs the eggs the sultanas and raisins the muscatels etc. which she thoroughly mixed; finally the stout was added. At this point we all took our turn at stirring the mixture and my mother told us all to make a silent wish as we stirred - an old Irish custom. The greased cloth was spread and the contents of the mixing bowl was turned out on the cloth, when the bowl was finally scraped almost clean the cloth was gathered and firmly tied at the neck. Having been boiled for four or five hours the pudding was removed from the water and suspended to dry, over a basin from a broom handle resting across two kitchen chairs. In our kitchen there was a large meat hook firmly fixed in the ceiling, on the day following the cooking, the pudding was hung from the hook by twine fastened around the neck of the cloth, where it would remain until Christmas Day.

Some days later the main event would take place, while the pudding was mixed and cooked in the traditional way, the making of the Christmas Cake was a much more scientific event altogether. All the ingredients would be measured to the last detail; fruit again would be washed and dried days before the baking was to take place, flour would be very finely sieved and the cake tin painstakingly lined. All the preparation would have to be completed and entry to the oven timed to avoid the peak gas pressure period in the town. The following day when the finished cake had cooled a good measure of the best Irish whiskey was poured over it; the cake was then wrapped in greaseproof paper. Nearer to Christmas the icing of the cake would take place, first the almond icing followed by the white icing. After a few days the cake would be decorated, my mother approached this task with the precision of an artist approaching a blank canvas, with layers of different coloured trellising and rosettes all around the edge, while finishing off with Happy Xmas piped across the centre, she took great pride in this particular operation.

As the days slowly passed the shop windows in the street took on a more festive air, decorated with simulated snow and Christmas decorations and all sorts of exciting and wonderful Christmas fare appearing as each day went by. It took us longer to walk home after school as we did our dream window-shopping along the way. I clearly remember one particular Christmas; on my way home stopping at Edmond O'Reilly's little shop in Market Street, there in the window was a beautiful little red bicycle, which I fell in love with. Each day from then on, on my journey home I made my way quickly to Market Street and each day there was the little red bicycle. On some occasions even after I went home I would go back down to the shop. I implored Santa to bring me that little red bicycle that Christmas, but even at that early age the situation was clear to me; and I had figured that it wasn't to be.

Some time around mid-December on a particular day each year as we made our way to school, the Market Square would be transformed and almost impassable, with vans, cars, traps, and donkey carts of every description; even at that early hour another great Christmas occasion would be in full swing, the annual Turkey Market. There would be turkeys of all sizes, Bronze and White although stripped of their plumage, they all looked white to me, with their red heads hanging lifeless from the rear end of every type of conveyance. Looking through the centre door of the

Town Hall, now the main entrance but back then it opened into a store- room, and inside hung a huge weighing scales which was suspended from a large wooden beam in the ceiling, on market day it was used for weighing the turkeys. The Town Sergeant Mr. Bartel O'Toole and his staff would be working away weighing birds by the score.

For days before the talk was of nothing else but what price the turkeys would make at the market, would they be dear or cheap, or would we be able to afford one at all. I think I am correct, as I remember it, the local butchers bought their turkeys early in the morning at the market, and whichever butcher struck the first price with the farmers, that deal set the price of the turkeys for the day. If the price set was considered high, the butcher was ridiculed for pushing up the price. In retrospect, I'm sure the normal market forces of supply and demand played a greater part in the price setting of the turkeys.

We would hurry back to the Market Square after school to see what was happening, but usually by then most buying and selling would be well finished, leaving only the last few holding out to sell, which by that time left only birds of poor quality. However, this was the time when a bargain could be struck.

My happiest day in school was invariably the day we broke up for holidays, on those occasions I left the house in the morning with a spring in my step, all bright eyed and bushy tailed, and of course the day we got our Christmas holidays was even that bit more special. Little schoolwork was done that day and little was expected. I think the teachers were almost as excited as we were, and who could blame them, getting away for a well-earned break from the horrors of so many noisy children. The lay teachers possibly to spend Christmas with their families in maybe Kerry or Donegal, while the nuns had time to relax and re-charge their batteries in the peace and quiet of a student-free convent.

By noon we were all set and free to go, giving the teachers from these far-flung parts of the country a chance to make their way home for the holidays. We were now approaching the final days and the excitement was palpable. The older members of the family busied themselves putting up the Christmas decorations and cleaning the house from top to bottom, while we were free to meet with our friends and amuse ourselves playing the games of the day. Although I had several close friends I was equally happy mixing within the closeness of the family or on my own, drawing, or even at that age having a go at making things with my hands.

Christmas Eve arrived with most of the hustle and bustle of preparation taken care of. The turkey, which had been hanging in the back pantry since the market day, was retrieved by my mother, cleaned out, and the stuffing prepared. Unlike much of the other Christmas preparations we all gave the kitchen a wide berth during this operation. Nevertheless it was all part of the activity in the kitchen on Christmas Eve.

I remember our first Christmas tree, which reached from floor to ceiling, Michael, my oldest brother brought it home, and we were all very excited, trimming the tree, preparing the stand and placing it in the corner of the Parlour. Nobody dared to ask where or from whom he got the tree. When it was decorated with crepe paper and anything we could make or find and covered in snow which we made from my mother's lux flakes washing powder, Michael fixed a dozen or more clip on miniature candle holders to the branches. When all was ready we gathered round, in the fading light of the afternoon on that Christmas Eve, and lit the candles, our first Christmas tree was a truly wonderful sight, which exemplified for all of us the magic that is Christmas for that short period of ones childhood.

After tea my mother set up the big red Christmas candle in the front window, she was very conscious of safety in this operation because the candle would remain lighting overnight, so it had to be well secured and anything inflammable had to be removed from the general area of the lighted candle. With little or no traffic in those days it was so peaceful to walk around the town in the calmness of the late afternoon and see all the windows with the candles lighting; the moment I suppose for that generation which came closest to the manifestation of what Christmas was all about, as my mother told us – welcoming the new born Baby Jesus into our homes. What a pity the lighted Christmas tree has all but replaced this lovely old Irish tradition. For us younger kids, our minds were filled with the anticipated arrival of Santa Claus later that night. Bedtime came early on Christmas Eve although with excitement running high, sleep did not come easily. Before going to bed Liam, Frank, and myself would have hung up our stockings by the fireplace in the kitchen while Therese's would hang on her cot at the foot of my mothers bed.

Time passed very slowly as we lay silent and wide-awake. When we figured that the older members of the family had finally long gone to sleep, Liam, Frank, and myself complete with torch would creep as quietly as possible down stairs; conscious of every creak on each step we took of the old twisted staircase; our young hearts racing, barely able to contain our excitement. As we entered the kitchen, the rich aroma of the turkey, which my mother had put in the oven to slowly cook through the night before she went to bed, together with the warmth from the gas cooker in those pre-central heating days, added a heightened sense of Christmas spirit to this very special moment in our lives. We very quietly closed the kitchen door behind us, before switching on the light to discover the fulfilment of all the hopes and dreams of the many weeks preparation that built up to this special moment. As well as receiving the toys, which I suppose looking back, we were subtly steered towards over the previous several weeks; we also received all kinds of sweets, chocolate and fruit, which filled our stockings from the toe to the rim. As tiredness eventually took its toll, we eventually and very quietly crept back upstairs and sleep finally came.

Christmas day started early, there was no Midnight Mass then, the first Mass of the day took place at 7am. and was generally attended by most families. With no cars, we all left the house in darkness at about 6-30am, to walk to the church. Like Midnight Mass of today we had the Church Choir singing all the beautiful well-known Carols, which created a special and rarefied atmosphere in the crisp winter chill in those days of mass at dawn. Wherever we sat in the crowded church for Mass we would crane our necks to try to see the priest as he placed the infant in the crib while the choir sang Silent Night. Walking home, as dawn was breaking everybody seemed to be filled with the spirit of the season, the greeting of "Happy Christmas" could be heard all through the street as friends and strangers alike exchanged greetings while making their way back from Mass on this happiest of mornings.

All the meals were special on Christmas day but the ceremony of the Pudding was a really special event. Having removed it from the hook in the ceiling earlier in the morning and again boiled it for an hour or two, the problem was to divest it of its boiling hot cloth and place it on the biggest plate that could be found, always a tricky operation. The Pudding made in this very traditional way had a distinctive aroma and flavour which was different from that which is more usual today, my mother was always very proud of her traditional Christmas Pudding and took particular pleasure in this moment.

In the afternoon while some of the older members of the family went to meet their friends we would again walk to the church, this time specifically to visit the Crib. For tea the formal moment was the cutting of the Christmas cake as we all gathered round the big oval table in the parlour with all the best china liberated from the china cabinet for the occasion. Later in the evening Auntie and Uncle and those members of the family who now resided with them at "St. Patrick's" together with some friends, gathered around the fire, we would sing songs to our hearts content not wanting the day to end. Inevitably Christmas passed, but with the closeness of our family, these happy days left us with wondrous and lifelong memories.

HOLIDAYING IN BRITTAS BAY

Annual holidays were not a feature of everyday life for most people back in the 1940's, or rather should I say, going away on holidays was as a rule not an option for those moving in our circle. Although some of the family as I remember made it to Galway to stay with the relatives there. However, back in those years we did manage to have a holiday in Brittas Bay, which I suggest hardly counts as going away. My uncle who was a member of Dail Eireann at that time rented a cottage in Cornagower from a friend of his named Andy Doyle, the year I believe would have been probably '43 or '44. Some of the family packed up and moved out to Brittas Bay. We had a big white tent and when the weather was fine some of us would sleep in the tent in the garden. Needless to say we spent a lot of our time on the beach. A little way up the road from the cottage was a farm place owned by people called Newman. It came to our notice that the property had a fairly good orchard; well we did make one or two sorties to the orchard during the holiday, but one of the members of the household named Alec, was a good-natured chap with the products of the orchard, which was much appreciated.

My sister Monica was recognised as being the strong willed member of the family, I remember during our stay in Brittas Bay some dispute arose between herself and another family member, I don't remember who, but whatever the problem was that Monica took exception to, she cycled all the way home to Wicklow, which to us at that time seemed a colossal journey to undertake.

Our next break away from Wicklow was in August 1948 when again my uncle and auntie took a house, on this occasion in Dun Laoghaire. We enjoyed the change from the then sleepy town of Wicklow, to the city like hustle and bustle of Dun Laoghaire. Georges Street the main thoroughfare was full of life and activity with many fine shops. Although we had little money in our pockets Woolworths was always an exciting store to walk around. A particularly thrilling occasion was our first trip on the Tram from Dun Laoghaire to Dalkey, with all its banging and clanging over the tracks along the way. Each end, front and back of the upper level of the tram was open to the elements and it was exciting up there so high above the street with the wind in our faces as we trundled our way to Dalkey.

We spent much of our time, my younger brother Frank and myself around the seafront, St. Michael's Wharf and the Coal Harbour, watching all the boating activity. The two great mail boats "Cambria" and "Hibernia" plied their way back and forth morning and evening, between Dun Laoghaire and the Port of Holyhead in Anglesey, North Wales. Such places for us may well have been on the other side of the world, which later we had to seek its whereabouts on our school maps. We often watched the arrivals of the happy homecoming holiday makers, in many cases men in their fawn belted gabardine coats and flat caps, carrying their well used brown suit cases and glad to be back on Irish soil for a short break from their work in London, Liverpool, Birmingham or Manchester. Of course watching the departures was a very different story and a much sadder affair indeed. Each Saturday we would go down to the Pier to watch the yacht racing.

Occasionally we would recognise some yachts familiar to us from their visits to Wicklow.

To us the whole Dun Laoghaire scene was prosperous and exciting, as we wondered at this boating spectacle, which only happened once a year at home; it seemed to me, in my childish way, what a wonderful place! The Regatta Day happened in Dun Laoghaire every week.

3

✷

The Adolescent Years And Beyond!

ALL THERE FOR THE TAKING!

Time of course, to use a hackneyed phrase, does not stand still and so our years in the Boys' National School inevitably came to a close. It was time to move on to Secondary school. It was also a time when although still far from adulthood the thoughts and trappings of our childhood years were being subtly replaced by new concerns. We were starting to embark upon what they say are the more difficult and mixed-up time of ones young life "the adolescent years."

One hears a lot these days on radio and on television about the problems of teenagers and the crass behaviour of many in this age group both in the home and on the street. It is universally acknowledged that this period in the development of many young people can be a difficult and fractious time. However, today a more sinister behavioural condition appears to exist with a sizable number of young people during this transitional period to adulthood. Many of today's teenagers are much more aggressive than I remember in my youth. Violence resulting in serious injury, tragically in many cases ending in death, often without reason or rationale is a regular occurrence particularly on the streets of our major cities. Today's youth have been raised in a time of plenty where almost immediate access to all their demands is almost expected.

There appears to be a belief or a perception amongst more than a small minority, that "it's all there for the taking," without obligation or responsibility on their part. Yet the social conscience of a great many young people today I feel has never been higher; unfortunately little seems to be heard about this facet of teenage behaviour. It seems to me that there is a deeper intensity in the character of today's youth towards life; they are better educated than any previous generation, by constant exposure to television their knowledge of world events and the many injustices they see on their screens is much more immediate. As a result many are more questioning, less accepting, more confident and more vocal in their attitudes and opinions. This I believe is to be encouraged, and if directed in a positive manner, that they can accept, could be a great force for good; if it is not, well 'God help us all'.

When I started these scribblings, harking back to times long past I tended to think in terms of "the happier experiences of those early years." I think it is natural that we all tend to recall those happier times and experiences of our past. However, life for most of us does not progress sublimely from one happy experience to another, and if the years that followed were not wholly unhappy, they were not a period I recall with much pleasure. It is undoubtedly a sad admission, but the time I spent at "St. Joseph's" College was as I look back, neither a happy nor I believe a fruitful period of my life.

The 'school going' experience should be a carefree and happy time in ones young life, a time I believe that one can look back on with a sense of gratitude and appreciation; not a time of intimidation and coercion. It is true that the teacher should entreat the student to be serious and hard working in his or her approach to their studies, while encouraging an atmosphere of assiduousness in class. School life and home life for the young should be an all-embracing time in the development of the whole person. It should be very much more, from the aspect of school life, than just the "cramming in", by whatever means necessary of the very minimum of subjects for examination success, as I remember the system at "St. Joseph's". Success in the examination system is very important for advancing to further education. I believe however, of greater importance is the influence that a properly organised school life will play in the forging of a well-rounded character; capable of dealing with the problems and difficulties that life will inevitably throw at them.

Knowledge should not be misconstrued as intelligence. Knowledge is dispensed through the teacher and assimilated by the pupil; intelligence is not in the gift of any teacher, it is God given. It is my firm belief that no child comes to this life "gift less" so to speak; it may on occasions require the skills of that rare gifted teacher, together with a much wider curriculum than we were exposed to, to seek out that gift and encourage it to blossom.

All this is not to say that the school didn't achieve results, a great many of the pupils went on to acquit themselves very well in third level education and to successfully achieve positions of very considerable responsibility across the professions, in the church, in public life and whatever. This it has to be said is to the school's credit. My own two brothers Michael and Liam are two past pupils of "St. Joseph's" who could be considered amongst this group and their memories of secondary school life may well be different to mine. I may be wrong, but 'hand on heart', I believe that many of the average pupils like myself, would not look back with a great deal of pleasure on their "St. Joseph's years." My brother Frank boarded in Terenure College and was, all through his life extremely proud of his school, attending with great enthusiasm the sporting events of the college and supporting the functions of its Past Pupil Union. That lasting pride in one's school can only be reflected through happy memories of ones school days, contrast that to just one of my memories of our "St. Joseph" days!

I recall one incident when we were in first year; a new teacher a tall athletic figure of a man whose name was Brother Augustine had joined the teaching staff, and was taking our Latin class for the first time. It was usual for the class to recite "The Angelus" at noon each day, which occurred about midway through the period of the class. On this occasion when the prayer was finished the brother without question, struck one of the boys hard on the head and berated him loudly for his disrespectful behaviour during the prayer. Knowing the situation the whole class stood there stunned and amazed. It appeared that the boy had stood with his hands by his sides and had not recited the prayer with the rest of the class. The boy quickly explained that he was a member of the Church of Ireland faith, to a rather sorry looking De La Salle Brother. I have no memory of an apology being made! The boy's name was Joe Murray. Over the next year or two Joe and myself became very close friends and remain so to this day. Something good - lifelong friendship came out of that school for both of us.

Whatever ability, if any, I may have brought to future positions I held in life, little I believe came as a result of my time spent at "St. Joseph's" De La Salle College Wicklow.

Recently I had occasion to do some video photography during classes in "The Holy Rosary School" in Wicklow in connection with that school's Fiftieth Anniversary celebrations, I was delighted to see so many happy children being taught in an interactive way with their teachers.

Thank goodness in this more enlightened age 'teacher training' appears to be directed towards a more encouraging and inspiring approach to teaching, rather than in the confrontational manner of the old ways.

A SUMMER OCCUPATION

I had for many years been interested in photography; even as a young boy I had an old Kodak Box Brownie camera. I would buy a film when I could get the money together and take shots of the older members of the family and sell the photos to them; this I quickly add was not the early signs of an entrepreneurial propensity but simply gave me the where-with–all to buy the next film, and on it went. While I was still at school I made friends with a chap who had started a photographic business in Wicklow, his name was Paud Noonan, a son of the well-respected local reporter Mr. Paddy Noonan of the "Wicklow People" newspaper. I spent a lot of time after school hours in Paud's shop and when the summer holidays came he offered me a summer job. I enjoyed the opportunity of working with him, developing films, printing and enlarging photographs; the money also came in handy.

The following year Paud needed to take on another hand to cope with the extra summer work. I asked my friend Joe Murray if he wanted a job for the summer. Joe worked with us for the summer period and went on to build a very successful career in photography, in the neighbouring town of Arklow. He and h wife Lily carried on their photographic business in Arklow up to recently when they retired, Joe by then being the most sought after wedding photographer in the South Wicklow/ North Wexford district. Paud Noonan gave up the photographic work and settled in London where he still lives with his family.

I left "St. Joseph's before my Intermediate Certificate Examination, and joined the staff of S.V. Delahunt & Co. as an apprentice to the bar and grocery trade. Although I enjoyed working in Delahunts, I did not really see shop-work as a lifetime ambition. It did, however, get me out of that school and I suppose in a way I was following in my father's footsteps.

The firm of S.V. Delahunt & Co. was an old Wicklow firm, established I believe at the end of the nineteenth century and still in business today, having passed through four generations. The then owner was Tom Delahunt an affable man who was well liked and respected by the staff. The business essentially consisted of two shops, one which was known within the organisation as "Main Street", for obvious reasons, and consisted of Bar and Grocery; which was where my father came to from Galway. Then there was the much larger store, which was known as "Abbey Hill" at the north end of town. As well as comprising of Bar and Grocery there was also a very busy Hardware and Builders Providers Department. The firm also operated a successful wholesale Wine, Spirits and general Bottling department.

I made lifelong friends while working in Delahunts Michael Butler and his wife Rose who also worked in the office in Delahunt's and was a classmate of my wife's in their school days in Dominican Convent Wicklow. It was Rose who first encouraged me to write down some of my memories. Noel Furlong whom I knew in school started in Delahunts a year before me, Noel spent his whole working life in Delahunts and was eventually appointed General Manager. Jerry Phelan now also retired, Jerry had a wonderful infectious sense of humour. It would have been difficult to be in bad form while in Jerry's company. The late

John Conway was a popular member of the hardware staff whose sense of humour was always quietly understated. Then there was the General Manager Pat Dunne with whom I had a friendly if sometimes stormy relationship.

Many of the larger stores in those times tended to provide indoor accommodation for their staff, as it was then in the case of Delahunts, the staff was boarded in rooms over the shop at Abbey Hill. It was normal practice in Delahunt's back then to recruit all shop staff from out of town. The first local to be taken on, I believe, was John Conway. Later Noel Furlong and Dick Kavanagh (no relation) and the following year I joined the staff. The housekeeper, Mrs. O'Neill and her assistant, Mrs. Malone looked after the indoor staff members and both were always kind and helpful to all. As the junior in the grocery department it was my responsibility to see that the kitchen was kept supplied with all the necessary provisions to run the house. At approximately 11 am each morning I would take my passbook to the kitchen where Mrs. O'Neill would give me her list of requirements for the day, and the ladies would have a cup of tea ready for me as I wrote out the order. Many a time I would have to duck into the pantry adjoining the kitchen when we would hear Mr. Dunne's foot on the stairs possibly looking for me, if he thought I was taking too long in the kitchen.

Shop work in those days was much more labour intensive by comparison with say today's supermarkets. There was no such thing as "self service", all orders were assembled by the staff. Much of the goods supplied for the shop were delivered in bulk and then were weighed into suitable packs for sales purposes. In the early '50's rationing of essential foodstuffs was still part of everyday life. Each person in the household, under the regulations, was allowed on a weekly basis – 12 ounces of sugar, 2ounces of tea and 6 ounces of butter. We would spend Monday of each week weighing in multiples of these amounts in preparation for the business of the week ahead. Of course at Christmas time all the dried fruit, sultanas, raisins, currants, valencia and muscatel raisins, cherries and peel had to be weighed in appropriate weights. On Wednesday and Thursday each week all the country grocery orders had to be prepared and dispatched by van to places as far away as Brittas Bay, Barndarrig, Glenealy and generally around the outlying town lands of the greater Wicklow area.

The bar end of the business was no different, and all deliveries came in bulk. At that time the only draught beer sold was what was known as Plain Porter, which cost the customer in the bar 1s-8d per pint, less than 10p in pre euro money. Porter was delivered in small wooden barrels called firkins, which held, as I remember, about one hundred pints. The firkins were mounted on a stand in the cellar and connected by lead pipe from tap to pumps on the bar counter. The method used for tapping the firkin, which had a small round wooden bung in one end, was this. You held the large brass tap to the indent on the bung in the firkin and with a heavy wooden mallet hit the tap one mighty blow. This usually worked well; however, if you didn't connect straight on the tap, or didn't hit it hard enough you could possibly split the bung and with the porter under pressure in the firkin you can imagine what would happen. You could end up being sprayed with porter from head to toe, more than once I have to admit to ending up in this condition.

Jack Ryan was the manager of the wholesale Wine and Spirits Department, which supplied many of the Public Houses in East Wicklow. Stout was delivered from Guinness's to the bottling store at Abbey Hill in very large barrels called Hogsheads. A hogshead contained seventy-two dozen bottles of stout, we regularly bottled, labelled and stacked six hogsheads each week and up to eight or more during busier periods such as Christmas time or "Bank Holiday" weekends. The bottled stout was then left to mature for about two weeks before distribution could take place. Under Jack's supervision we also bottled Ales, Ports, Sherries, and Whiskey. I remember on occasions being almost overcome from the fumes as we racked and bottled whiskey. As deliveries were made to the different pubs, the empties would be collected by the delivery men and brought back, we would then have to wash the bottles, and the whole cycle would start all over again.

While I was working in Delahunt's, Noel Furlong and myself decided to join the woodwork class in the local Vocational School. One reason, more than any other, was to find a pastime for winter evenings, which on the meagre wages of an apprentice would involve little or no expenditure. Well I really enjoyed working with wood so much that I continued with the class for many years and even up to today carpentry and woodwork is one of my favourite hobbies.

A WELCOME DISTRACTION

Some of my happiest memories of those teenage times were of attending the weekly dances in the "The Mall Ballroom." Our family and the O'Toole family had been friendly for years and Mrs O'Toole always invited me for supper during the weekly dances. Sadly The Mall Ballroom was demolished recently. Nothing remains of the building today except an ugly gap in the streetscape. We all learned to dance at the weekly hops at the Mall, to the music of Chris O'Toole and his band. At one of these dances I made a new friend, a girl, her name was May Lambert. May was a fifth year pupil of St. Anne's College, Dominican Convent, what I suppose these days would be called transition year. She was most diligent and serious about her studies. The eldest of four girls, her mother and father tended to worry about her being almost too serious about her studies and not getting out and about more, the all work and no play syndrome.

The other members of the family were Peggy, Noeleen, and Eileen. I arranged to meet May the following weekend and go to a particular film showing locally. The film was a new musical called "Kiss Me Kate" with Howard Keel and Kathryn Grayson, which marked our first date. Jim and Winnie, May's parents were very friendly towards me; I think they saw me in those early days as a welcome distraction from their daughter's somewhat overzealous attitude to her studies. During school terms we continued to date at weekends and snatch the occasional mid-week meeting, while May spent most her time poring over her books. As time went on our relationship became more serious, I was a constant visitor to the Lambert household, included in all the family events and excursions. Jim was the Works Manager in the local garage of Coleburn & Hopkins Ltd. (present site of the Allied Irish Bank) and as such he quite often had access to a car, this at a time when only the well off owned a car in Wicklow; the whole family and myself included would take off regularly to all sorts of places at weekends.

The summer holidays finally came and we spent every available moment together. We went with the family to Brittas Bay, or a group of us would go to Silver Strand, in the evenings we would meet up with friends, or maybe just go for a walk together on the Murrough, or just talk. It was a wonderful summer with vivid and lasting memories for both of us. Although several summers were to pass before our relationship became permanent, by the end of that summer I think we both knew that there was no one else for us but each other. In September May started her final year in St. Anne's and continued her study regime as in previous years. Needless to say she passed her Leaving Certificate with flying colours and went on to take a job in Dun Laoghaire Public Libraries. Over the next few years I was to become very familiar with Dun Laoghaire and its environs.

I of course was still working in Delahunt's and by then had been transferred to the Main Street shop. Our half-day off was Thursday and I would generally make my way to Dublin and later in the afternoon to Dun Laoghaire and meet up with May after she finished work at the library. Usually on Thursday morning Mr. Dunne, our aforementioned General Manager, would ask me if I wanted a lift to Dublin and I was always very grateful and glad to accept his kind offer.

I suppose it is reasonably normal for a person of my years to ponder on ones mortality, although one is loath to overly dwell on such matters. However, it is not usual for one in his late teens to bring that subject to mind on a regular basis, that is unless you were travelling regularly with Mr. Pat Dunne. Pat was arguably the worst driver I have ever known, particularly his night driving. I remember on one Thursday night we were coming home late and Pat was driving, I was in the front seat beside him and Michael Butler for some reason or other was in the back. We were approaching a corner near Kilpedder, but instead of rounding the corner it seemed to me that our near side front wheel was heading straight for a high sloping bank, I was certain if we hit the bank the car would turn over, I caught the wheel and pulled the car away from the bank, to Mr. Dunne's consternation. I think Michael was asleep in the back but came to life very quickly as the car veered from side to side for some distance along the road, while I in the front was being admonished severely by Mr Dunne for touching the steering wheel. Nevertheless we both continued to travel and take our chances with Pat on Thursday afternoon. I suppose the young will do anything for love.

Through a contact of May's father, May went to stay in Dun Laoghaire with a couple named Quigley. Cecil Quigley was a very fine handsome man with a friendly and outgoing personality; his wife Lena was an elegant lady if small in stature but always warm and welcoming. Cecil worked for the cigarette people W.D. & H.O.Wills as a commercial representative, which suited his personality perfectly; in fact in any group Cecil was always the centre of attention. His job took him away down the country most weeks, returning home on Friday afternoon for the weekend. May stayed in lodgings with Lena during the week returning home to Wicklow at weekends. The arrangement worked well and was a win/win situation all round.

At that time The Gas Company Theatre in Dun Laoghaire was at the height of its success staging many fine professional productions by such celebrated writers as Tennessee Williams - "Cat on a hot tin Roof "or Noel Coward's "Blithe Spirit" and many other fine plays such as "Picnic" which as I remember we particularly enjoyed. These were wonderful evenings, which we looked forward to with great enthusiasm. Unfortunately this excellent little theatre had to close, owing I believe to some difficulties with fire regulations.

On summer evenings we often walked the length of the East Pier or sat and watched the summertime activity in the harbour. Over the years while May continued to work in Dun Laoghaire the Quigley home became a home from home for both of us. Cecil had a small boat, which he kept on a mooring in Bullock Harbour, and on the occasional Thursday afternoon when he happened to be home early he and I would take off on the bus for the harbour carrying his little Seagull engine. We spent many enjoyable summer afternoons fishing off Dalkey Island or the " Muglins." while waiting for May to finish work. Later when we were living in Wicklow, and Cecil and Lena came to visit, I would borrow one of the yawls from the harbour and we would spend the afternoon out in Wicklow Bay.

Cecil was a very keen rugby enthusiast; we never missed any of the Five Nations Rugby matches at Lansdowne Road; watching some of the greats of Irish and international rugby of the time. Just this year Michael Butler and I went to Lansdowne Road to see Ireland play Fiji, which brought back memories of those far off days with Cecil.

Cecil and Lena Quigley are two of a small group of people who stand out in a very special way as May and I look back over the course of our lives together.

AN ACCUSING FINGER

One aspect of bar work that I did not like was the unsocial hours; it seemed to me that when all my friends were off duty and enjoying themselves especially at all the major holiday periods throughout the year, I appeared to be always on duty in the bar.

Our family had a small Green Grocery and Fruiterers shop in Fitzwilliam Sq., which was run by my brother Paddy. He had found a new job and wanted out from the shop so I was asked to take over from him. I left Delahunt's and took over the running of the shop at a time when business generally in Ireland was very slow, and Wicklow town was no exception. I had to have some means of transporting supplies of vegetables and fruit etc. from the markets in Dublin so I bought my first car. It was a Fiat Multipla, which had six seats in a two/two/two formation. The four back seats were collapsible leaving a huge free space for carrying the supplies for the shop. It was very suitable for our needs if somewhat underpowered when loaded with goods or occasionally with possibly six people. Needless to say it was exciting to have my own wheels as they say these days, for the first time. When the shop was closed we were free to take off where ever we wished to go.

Each Thursday I would go to Dublin to the Fruit and Vegetable Market to pick up the supplies for the shop for the weekend, on these occasions I would come back to Dun Laoghaire to meet up with May. One particular Thursday Michael Butler came with me to the markets; I had no arrangements to meet May later that day so Michael and I decided to have an evening out in the city. We went to the theatre to a play, "The Rose Tattoo", by Tennessee Williams with Anna Managhan playing the lead part; the play was controversial at the time. Although it was not banned, the imaginary or whatever reference on stage to a contraceptive brought the wrath of the Garda Siochanna down on the play's director Alan Simpson who ended up in gaol. With today's more broadminded attitude to such matters it is difficult to imagine what all the fuss was about, times have surely changed, these days contraceptives are on clear view and available in the rest rooms of many hotels all over the country. We ended up that evening having a late meal in a restaurant in Westmoreland Street called "The Paradiso," a popular nightspot of the time, setting off for home sometime after midnight.

We got as far as Bray when the car let us down, in order to get home to Wicklow at that hour of night we had to abandon the car and call a taxi. The taxi driver was not amused when he was informed that as well as Michael and myself we also had a van full of fruit and vegetables to be transported to Wicklow. He decently agreed to take us together with our cargo. I couldn't help but wonder on the journey home; as I sat in the back amongst the crates of oranges and heads of cabbage etc. while Michael sat up front with the driver, if someone from on high was pointing an accusing finger at us for our theatrical undertakings earlier in the evening.

While running the vegetable shop I became friendly with a man who conducted his business just across the street, his name was Tony Burke a most gregarious man who loved playing the piano and the church organ and was also interested in the theatre. He was well known in the district and respected by everyone, rich and poor alike; you could say he was an institution in the town. On quiet days in the shop I would ramble over to Tony's and we would have a cup of coffee. Many an afternoon we would sit in his comfortable bachelor sitting room and chat about matters of all sorts. Tony was the local undertaker, and was always the essence of efficiency while being kind and sympathetic with clients at that difficult time. Occasionally when he was exceptionally busy I would give him a hand preparing the coffins.

Apparently in those days I believe the choice of coffin predicated the entire cost of a funeral, if the coffin chosen was an expensive one then all the trimmings were to the same standard, and of course the same applied if the chosen coffin was of a less expensive category, so the standard of the linings could be from paper to silk and lace, with no mention of money at such a delicate time.

One bright summer morning I was helping Tony prepare a coffin in the workshop, we were having a joke as usual and I noticed that there was a very nice white oak coffin in the racks, if one can describe a coffin in those terms. Tony confirmed that it was indeed the top of the range. Laughingly I said to him,

" Tony I'll bury you in that coffin." About a week after that incident he was at the Post Office posting a letter when he took ill, and was brought home; the doctor diagnosed a severe stroke. Another friend from next-door, Joe Fallon and myself stayed with Tony through the night. He was taken by ambulance to a Dublin hospital next day and died a few days later. We did bury Tony in that white oak coffin with the silk and lace trimmings.

Another frequent visitor to Tony's home back then and a lifelong resident of Wicklow town was a gentleman - name of Jack Barlow. Jack, at that time was well into old age, if I were asked to put a figure on his age I would guess mid eighties. A most interesting man who will be remembered for two very different facets of his long life, both to which he was totally devoted. Firstly his occupation, as long as I can remember and I believe for a great many years before, as the owner of a small ice cream parlour on the seafront situated close to the corner of the Green opposite the Leitrim Lounge. I believe the original location of the "Cosy Corner" as it was known was just close to the west end of the then wooden bridge later replaced by the "Parnell Bridge."

As small children, the rare occasion of a visit to the "Cosy Corner" was always a wonderful experience. My mother would put us sitting at one of the tables by the window overlooking the Vartry River, we would make sure that we were in a position to watch Jack as he slowly went through the ritual of preparing our special treat which included a generous slice of ice cream smothered in thick raspberry cordial. Our mouths would be drooling in anticipation until the single stemmed glass was placed in front of each one of us.

A rotund little man who was always immaculate in starched white coat with matching apron tied high above his generous waistline. His features, particularly when he smiled which was infectious, took on a cherubic appearance. I can clearly see him in my minds eye sitting on a high stool in a small cut-off area just inside the door from where he dispensed the various delights to his many customers; or chatting in his friendly manner, fingers intertwined, thumbs twiddling, hands resting below his chest as he conversed easily with visitor or native alike.

"The Cosy Corner" was an Aladdin's Cave to any child; the walls and coved ceilings were covered with Postcards and Pictures from all over the world. Even at an early age I was fascinated at the wonderful display from so many magical places.

Jack Barlow had another and for many a more interesting facet to his character, he was a local impresario and amateur producer of entertainment over several decades in Wicklow town, particularly in the field of Pantomime. In fact I believe his company,

"The Wicklow Dramatic Society" was the oldest Dramatic Society in Ireland. From the early 1920's to the mid 1960's the productions of the society were passionately looked forward to in the town, raising much-needed funds for a wide variety of charitable causes. In those early days Jack engaged many popular artistes of the time from Dublin to play in his Wicklow concerts, however, it is his pantomimes with full cast of locals for which Jack is still remembered today, almost forty years on since his passing. My mother-in-law Winnie, and many of her friends in their younger days were involved in the pantomimes, while later on May, Peggy and Noeleen continued the tradition, most of the members of my own family also took part through the years. I remember Winnie telling me that Jack had kept a detailed logbook of all his shows - what a record of the social and performing history of Wicklow that would be if it came to light.

Still, if one mentions the name "Jack Barlow" to some of the older Wicklow natives, their eyes will light up and you'd better be prepared to relax awhile and be regaled with cherished memories of days long ago when they "strutted the boards" under the direction of Wicklow's "Panto King."

HOW GREEN WAS MY VALLEY

Business in the shop was not doing very well. I had a young girl Ann Hayden working with me who was very good with the customers and capable of being left on her own, so I decided to look for a job for a while to help subsidise the shop. My friend Joe Murray who was working at that time in the stores in St. Patrick's Copper Mines Avoca told me that there were jobs going there. Copper was an expensive commodity in those days. The very successful operation close to Avoca employed several hundred between miners, administration and ancillary workers and was managed by a Canadian Mining Company. I applied for a job and was called for interview; I was offered a job, as a surveyor's assistant, so I said I would give it a go. The following Monday, leaving Anne in charge of the shop, I headed off to Avoca. The surveyors department was essentially one very large room in the basement of the main administration building consisting of several architects drawing tables and other appropriate furnishing. On a table in the centre of the room stood a large transparent configuration of the different mine shafts in operation. The room had an air of busy morning activity as the surveyors and their assistants prepared for the days work ahead. The Chief Surveyor was Vincent Barry a pleasant man, who directed the operation from a small screened off office to one side of the room. He explained the details of the job to me and advised me to bring a change of clothes suitable for going underground the next morning. I was also issued with overalls, miner's lamp and strong boots.

The following morning I arrived all set and ready to go. I had been assigned to a surveyor who was working in the main tunnel called "The Knight Tunnel," and instructed in the use of the Miners Lamp. It was impressed on me to always check my lamp before going underground. The Knight Tunnel was the main tunnel and was more like a huge rock cave cut into the mountain, not really what I had expected. We got a lift in the back of a pick-up truck on our slow decent down the tunnel, as we continued through the dull light of the occasional lamp hanging from the roof of the tunnel. We passed small groups of miners moving on their way either up or down with the beam of their lamps flashing in different directions as they turned their heads. We also passed what looked like a large store or office cut into the side of the cave. Joe had mentioned to me that he had to go down to the underground store each week to check the supplies, this I thought must be it. We eventually stopped in a huge Cathedral like cavern, big enough for the big Attiewagons to turn when loaded, before making their way back up to ground level. There were several smaller tunnels off this main loading area.

From here on we continued on foot down one of the smaller tunnels, scarcely more than six feet high. Except for the light of our miner's lamps we were now in total darkness. After a few minutes I heard a continuous sound signal. The surveyor chap in front started to quicken his pace to a trot and shouted to me to follow. We came to a deep cutting to one side of the tunnel, which he ran into and unceremoniously pulled me in after him. Within a few seconds there was a loud explosive noise and a fierce rush of air. Almost immediately my companion started off down the tunnel again in a seemingly unconcerned manner. When I caught up with him I said, 'what in Gods name was that'?

'That was just the blasting at the mine face, you'll get used to that after a while' he replied.

I said to myself, 'do I really want to get used to that!'

There were many tunnels in the system at different levels, which were connected by vertical tunnels called Raises. In the course of our work it was often necessary to proceed from one level to a different level above or below you. This was accomplished by climbing or descending one of these vertical tunnels by means of a chain ladder. Some of these raises would necessitate a vertical climb of fifty to seventy feet; more often than not with water running down the rock wall and finding its way to the continuous pumping system in the base of the mines, but also in its descent running up your sleeves as you climbed the ladder, not a pleasant experience.

One morning, about a week after I started, my surveyor said, "we are going down a different tunnel today." He explained that for some months he had been working on two converging tunnels, which he hoped would meet. The object was to join the main Knight tunnel system to another system some distance away. If they didn't meet he joked, - "I think I will be looking for a new job."

We walked to the entrance of the tunnel, which was just off the main road to Avoca. To work in this tunnel you had to climb into an open topped bucket type lift, which rattled its way vertically down in total darkness, I was told to a depth of a thousand feet but I'm not sure if that was correct. As we proceeded away from the lift down below, the roof seemed to be held in place by large timbers supported by pit props. Although I don't mean to say in a reassuring way, this was more like what I had expected and seen in films like John Ford's "How Green was My Valley," except, the miners we met did not have black faces.

One afternoon, a few days later, as we returned to the office from the tunnel having showered and changed we arrived in time to take part in a small celebration and congratulatory party. One of the assistant surveyors named Terry McNamara had passed his examinations and had been promoted to the position of Surveyor. While we were having a drink and talking, the Chief Surveyor said to me "If you are interested in becoming a surveyor you could do the course, it would take about two years, think about it." I thanked him but didn't give him an answer, but thought 'there is no way I want to spend my life in a hole in the ground'; that is, until eventually and in the fullness of time, when I will have no choice in the matter, which hopefully will not be for a great many years to come.

I finally decided that a 'life in mining' was not for me; however, I would not have missed the experience of that short period I had spent working underground in the Avoca Mines. I handed in my notice and my thanks to Vincent the Chief Surveyor who appeared genuinely disappointed that I was leaving. My other surveyor friend connected his two tunnels perfectly that same week, so I suppose his job was secure.

I felt deeply saddened some months after I left, when I was told that the young chap Terry McNamara who had been appointed surveyor while I was there, had fallen down one of the Raises and tragically lost his life.

4

❖

Hayforks, Weddings, And Tropical Islands

NOT THE MOST COURAGEOUS INDIVIDUAL!

Following my sojourn in the bowels of the Avoca countryside and figuring from that level things could only go upwards, I applied for a job in the Circuit Court Office and was lucky to be appointed to the position of Court Messenger. Not the most illustrious title but then I was in no position to choose! The work entailed executing orders made principally in the District Court but also the Circuit Court, and the collecting of overdue payments of Land Annuities. It was serious stuff and the powers were wide-ranging, and not always pleasant to have to execute.

Not long after my appointment I was given a particular Order to execute over in West Wicklow. The sum involved was not large but I suppose possibly considered sizeable for those times. Several approaches for payment were made and formal letters were sent informing the gentleman of the necessary action, if the matter was not settled to the satisfaction of the court. Unfortunately for all concerned there was no response. I had to assume that in the circumstances a seizure of goods might be necessary. I arrived at the small farm place at the appointed time with two local Garda Siochana, which was normal procedure to help keep the peace, in the event of problems with the execution of the order. In this case a seizure of livestock was envisaged, so the necessary means of transport was also part of the entourage, quite an intimidating sight.

I approached the house from the laneway to be met by the owner of the property brandishing a hayfork who told me what he would do with the "F-ing" hayfork if I came another step onto his "so and so" property. I'll leave the expletives to the imagination. Not being the most courageous individual when looking down two sharp prongs of a hayfork, I decided to read the Order from a safe distance and then tried to reason with him. Unfortunately my powers of persuasion on this occasion appeared, from his point of view, to be lacking in conviction. I was getting strong vibes that the wise advice I was dispensing didn't seem to be having the desired effect on the defendant who was still brandishing the hayfork. I was also beginning to wonder if I would have been safer down in my comfortable tunnel with the explosives in Avoca.

By now a small group from the neighbourhood were beginning to gather and it was apparent to me that they did not consider us to be the 'good guys'. I decided to seek the advice of my two 'guardians of the peace' who were standing a goodly distance back from the scene of confrontation. The Garda Siochana in a most erudite, almost conspiratorial manner, advised caution, but did not appear to be making any effort to put themselves between me and the hayfork. Matters were at an impasse and I still had to carry out the order of the court; when a quiet spoken chap sidled over to me from the group of onlookers and said

"You know that man has a brother living up the road a piece". I was delighted with the information and immediately contacted the brother of the defendant, who knew nothing about the proceedings taking place just up the road. He immediately sorted out the problem to the Courts satisfaction and certainly to my relief, although I think the small group of onlookers, as they dispersed somewhat dejectedly having felt cheated out of an afternoon's unusual spectator sport.

Some months later another unusual case was passed on to me for execution, this time I would be working a little nearer home although not in the Wicklow area. The decree in this case was taken against two elderly sisters and involved not a very large sum, for non-payment of goods or services, the actual detail of which is not important. Again all the preliminary work had been carried out in accordance with the order of the court, with no response from the defendants. I had a feeling that this case could be difficult and unpleasant; these poor old ladies were living in a bygone age, a time when their class was almost untouchable by mere mortals. The fact had somehow passed them by, that power today resided with the money makers, the "movers and shakers" to use one of today's fatuous phrases, rather than in the hands of those in the upper echelons of yesterday's class structure. They would not be easy to deal with, and it gave me no satisfaction hassling people, especially vulnerable old ladies.

I arrived at the property and entered through large double gates, the appearance of which would have benefited greatly from a coat of paint. I started walking up the curved tree lined avenue; the time was about mid morning. The house as it came into view from the curve of the avenue was a fine old red brick Georgian style house with imposing granite steps leading to an impressive entrance portico; the house had two storeys over a half basement. It had puzzled me on earlier visits and not having gained admission as to why the occupants of this fine house should have monetary problems and especially with such a small amount involved, it was difficult to understand. As I came closer, as on previous occasions, the telltale signs of neglect could be seen everywhere about the house and garden, the whole property was in fact neglected and had seen better days. I approached and knocked on the hall door as I had before, without success, and again waited for an answer. I knocked several more times getting progressively louder each time, without response.

I would somehow have to get the message over, that this time I could not just go away if the door was not answered; I would have to force an entry. I decided to break the glass in one of the basement windows; I had no idea what I was going to do when I entered the house. However, the sound of the shattering glass echoing through the house appeared to achieve the response that the knocker had not. Immediately one of the upper floor windows opened and an arm stretched out and a hand waving a crucifix, followed by a little old frightened face appealing to me not to do any more damage, that she would open the door. Needless to say, I did not feel it was my finest hour, standing here frightening the life out of an old lady; but at least we were both getting somewhere, the lady was beginning to acknowledge that she had to face up to whatever difficulty was encroaching on her world, and I was getting the chance to talk and possibly reason with her.

I waited for quite some time at the hall door and finally I could hear bolts been drawn back, the door was slowly opened, but little more than a crack. I was aware of another old but maybe a little younger face almost looking over the shoulder of the first lady, their closeness appearing to lend support to each other. When I finally gained their confidence, at least to some extent, the first lady opened the door and let me into the hall. It was like stepping back into another time. The hall way was quite dark and furnished with heavy mahogany furnishings; mounted deer heads adorned the high walls close to the ceiling. There was a musty, almost an unlived in aura of faded grandeur about the place.

Although it was now getting on in the day both ladies were still wearing what appeared to me to be rather old fashioned silk floral dressing gowns of similar style or maybe housecoats. If a somewhat tired Noel Coward had stepped out from one of the adjoining rooms in his smoking jacket with cigarette holder at a jaunty angle he would not have looked out of place. I stayed talking and explaining the situation to them for some time and eventually they appeared to be more relaxed and understanding of the situation; the second lady spoke very little, and both spoke with soft cultured accents. We finally came to an arrangement that I felt would meet with approval all around; which could have been reached without upset had they opened the door on my first call some months earlier.

As I cheerlessly walked down the avenue I looked back once more at that sad old house which had outlived the promise and aspirations of an epoch that was gone forever. During the weeks that followed the memory of those two little old ladies often crossed my mind, and that day when the reality of life today was harshly thrust upon them. I hoped that they could live out the rest of their lives in the peace and tranquillity of their own long forgotten world.

A BEAUTIFUL AUTUMN DAY

One bright sunny early October morning I arose as usual and after breakfast walked down Summer Hill to the courthouse to work, much like any other morning. The neighbours were as usual getting on with their morning chores; as I passed Doyle's shop Angela was there as she usually was, pencil resting on her ear, busily looking after her early morning customers in her normal busy but friendly way. But for me it really wasn't like any other day, after signing in and clearing up a few things in the office I went back home before 10am. In those days annual leave in the Circuit Court Office extended to only ten working days and I needed every day I could save, as well as that I was well due the time in lieu of overtime. No today was for May and I a very special day; it was our Wedding Day - 3rd October '62.

It was a wonderful day filled with very special memories, a day with almost all the family members from both sides present and also with many of our closest friends. Fr. John Hans, our local curate and a family friend officiated assisted by Fr. Tom Power our PP. in St. Patrick's Church Wicklow where in May's case twenty-five years and in my own twenty-seven years earlier we were both christened. Afterwards we paid a visit to the Dominican Convent, more specifically for May to meet with the nuns, which was the norm in those days for all past pupils of St. Anne's College. The wedding reception was in the lovely old "Hunters Hotel." My brother Frank was my best-man and May's sister Eileen was bridesmaid, it was a beautiful warm autumn day and we thoroughly enjoyed the company of all those closest to us.

We spent our honeymoon in England, in Stratford–upon-Avon and then on to Leamington Spa where we stayed with May's uncle Jim and his wife Joan; then on to London where we stayed with my sister Breda and her husband James, both sets of relatives who were unable to attend our Wedding. Breda had booked the show "My Fair Lady" which was playing in Drury Lane; a wonderful show and an opportunity to visit the West End's most famous theatre, the occasion was an evening of sheer glamour. After two unforgettable weeks we returned home to Wicklow and settled into married life.

In the autumn of '62, the year we were married the De La Salle Past Pupils Union came up with a novel fundraising idea a Street Talent Show or series of talent shows involving teams from different parts of the town. You had Ballynerrin, Main street/ Murrough, Church Hill/ Rocky Road, High Street and the group that I was involved with, Summerhill. Each show was to run for precisely one hour, the group loosing points for running overtime or being short of the hour. It was amazing the interest that built up in the town as the heats went on.

The early rounds took place in the Parochial Hall and I remember the place was packed to capacity; of course much of the audience being made up of people from the opposing groups, principally there to see what novel ideas the opposition had dreamed up. Because each group was confined to their own few streets for every aspect of the show, you actually had to go and knock doors to find people to fill parts. It surprised all involved in every group how much latent talent was found in this way. People who in the normal course of events may never have become involved in such activity, found they had a natural ability for the stage. It was all great fun and a wonderful social activity during those winter months, involving people in all forms of stagecraft from imaginative costume and stage props design, to make-up, or to the painting of scenery. The finals took place in the Rialto Cinema to a packed audience and although our group "Summerhill" was in the final, on both occasions the honours went to the Ballynerrin Group. The Street Talent Show competition was repeated the following year and I believe may well have been the forerunner of the immensely successful "John Player Tops" competition, which was so popular on TV for many years.

A MOST STARK AND VISIBLE MANNER

Some months after we were married I was at work in the office when a young American student called, his name was Mike Byrne and he was trying to trace his Irish roots. We talked for a while but it appeared to me that he didn't have much information to go on. I made the point that if he threw a stone at somebody anywhere in the Wicklow area you would most likely hit a Byrne. He was a very pleasant and friendly young man who had just finished college and whose family lived in Chicago. I suggested to Mike that he come home and have lunch with us and May might have some ideas. Mike came home for lunch and stayed with us for a week. We enjoyed his company and had some great parties with our friends during that week.

The following year Mike's brother Stephen came to Ireland and stayed with us followed by his sister Anne, who called to see us on her way to college in Oxford. Each year an invitation to visit Chicago for a holiday came from the Byrne family, but needless to say in the early years of our married life there was little enough cash for putting a home together. A holiday in the United States for us was out of the question. Finally the parents of the Byrne children, Dick and his wife Frances, came to Ireland for a holiday and we met them for dinner and had a lovely evening in the Green Lizard hotel.

Some years after that visit my brother Paddy and his wife Mary asked us if we were interested in going for a holiday with them to the United States. We immediately said 'yes' on the understanding that we spend some time with the Byrne family who had so kindly invited us to Chicago so many times. With all our arrangements made we set off all four of us on our first great trip to the USA. We stayed for the first week visiting with my brother Michael in New York, who, with his wife Marianne spent that week showing us all sights of that wonderful city - The Rockefeller Centre, The Lincoln Centre, The Statue of Liberty and many other well-known locations. The strange phenomenon, on a rainy evening in the viewing room at the top of the Empire State Building, as we looked through the glass in amazement of the rain, which appeared by some elliptical diametric to be falling upwards. I still remember vividly, a bright summer morning, looking down in awe at helicopters flying around well below us, as the five of us stood on the viewing platform of one of the Twin Towers with the whole island of Manhattan spread out like a virtual map below.

On a more recent occasion back in Wicklow, that fateful day in September 2001, which is imprinted on all our minds simply as 9/11, as I stood alone at home, trancelike, watching television, almost in disbelief of what was being played out like a Hollywood Movie, and yet amazingly in total awareness that for every moment I stood watching this double "Towering Inferno" hundreds of people were dying in the most horrific of circumstances three thousand miles away but also right there in front in my eyes. Only an hour or so before those same people had left home at the start of what should have been another routine working day in New York City. This would prove to be no ordinary day; it truly was the day "Hope, for a season, bade the world farewell".

Just a few months before, on a much later visit to the U.S. on a lovely spring afternoon, we stood in Lower Manhattan, May, Michael and myself looking up and as we know now for the last time, marvelling at those two great New York City Icons.

What absolute and utter madness! New York undoubtedly will recover from this outrage but the United States will never be quite the same again. The full realisation has been utterly and absolutely brought home to the American people, that for the first time in its proud history, war in its most horrific form could and had been visited with relative ease, by a terrorist force, right at the very heart of mainland America, and in a the most stark and visible manner on the American people.

As the days passed we watched the unprecedented outpouring of grief on our television screens from all over the world, but especially from here in Ireland. We saw people standing outside the American Embassy in Dublin weeping openly as they waited in line to sign the Book of Condolence. What was it about this awful tragedy that moved us all so profoundly? True there is a strong Irish connection with New York City, and a traditional bond between Ireland and America. As one journalist succinctly put it, which sums up this awful tragedy completely.

"One has to say that most of those who died were unknown to almost all of us living in Ireland. It was more than just grieving for a brotherhood of strangers living so far away. – It was a lament for certainties undone, the loss of a safe world we had taken for granted."

Getting my mind and my memories back to that first trip to the United States so many years ago - we hired a car, Paddy being the principal driver and left New York on our way to Chicago; taking a wrong turn while Michael stood on the corner shaking his head in disbelief, and I'm sure saying to himself, where in God's name will they end up? Having gotten back on the right track we carried on to spend a few days in Washington DC visiting the White House, the Capitol Building The Smithsonian Institute, Arlington cemetery and several other world renowned locations, what memories we have of that most photographed of American cities. We continued our trip through Virginia and West Virginia, the apple capital of America. We stopped to buy some apples at a big roadside farmers store, the lady there told us she had never met another Irish person in those parts before and made us a present of a jar of apple butter. We all had a wonderful time in Chicago renewing acquaintance with Dick and Fran's family, by then the older of them being married with their own children. Dick took Paddy and myself to play golf in the most exclusive course we had ever seen, while Fran took the girls off shopping. Again in Chicago we went to the top of the Sears Tower, the tallest building in the USA at that time.

On that trip May and I fell in love with the United States and have been back many times since, while Dick and Fran have since visited us in Ireland on a couple of occasions.

One particular visit to the United States stands out. About, I would say fifteen years ago, I had some leave to take so we decided on the spur of the moment we would go to see Dick and Fran. It was mid. February and all leave had to be taken before 5th April or forfeited. We called them on the phone and they appeared delighted but Dick said "You couldn't spend two weeks in Chicago in this weather, what we'll do is, you two guys fly to Chicago and then after a day or two when you recover from the flight we'll drive down to Sanibel Island in Florida."

Within a few days we arrived at O'Hare airport, I could see what Dick meant about the weather, although to us as we drove to Woodbine Ave., Dick and Fran's home the world looked like a veritable wonderland.

Next morning Fran fixed us up with warm jackets and boots and we headed off for a walk in the snow. As one would imagine in America, the roads and the footpaths were kept perfectly clear of snow. What amazed us was, now in late February the Christmas holly wreaths were still on many of the doors and as we walked along the path, in many front gardens wickerwork reindeers with their sleighs stood in the deep snow patiently awaiting Santa's return from some nearby chimney. The lovely old clapperboard houses standing bedecked in snow and icicles, some up to 6' long hanging from the roofs and glistening like crystal in the morning sunshine, all adding up to as we gazed, a magnificent living Christmas scene. Later when we returned Dick suggested that he and I go to check on the lake house, their holiday home in Wisconsin about two hours drive away, before we left for Florida next day, while May and Fran visit some of the children. The drive through the countryside was spectacular and completely different from our previous summer visits to the lake. It was really amazing to see Lake Beulah completely frozen over and motionless in thick ice, where we had been swimming in almost lukewarm water on a previous visit. I shouted back up the garden to Dick

"Is it safe to walk on the ice?" He replied

"We could drive the car out across there in safety".

As I walked out across the lake and looked back towards the house, tickled pink at what was for me a totally new experience, but like St. Peter, not altogether confident that I would not sink into the frozen depths.

Next morning we were up at six am. with the summer clothes selected and ready to make an early start on our journey to warmer climes. Dick laid down some sensible ground rules for the journey. We would make an early start each morning; with three drivers Dick, Fran and myself we would take turns of two hours on four hours off (easy to know Dick was a sailing man) with regular comfort breaks, and we would stop driving as near to 6pm.as possible.

Dick took the first spell taking us through Chicago and on down towards Gary, Indiana, where we would pickup the Interstate 65 which we would follow almost to the Florida state line. I took over from Dick; by now we were opening up the great flat planes of Indiana, we had never seen such flat country, as far as the eye could see in every direction. The interstate highway just went on and on completely straight until it disappeared on the horizon. It was a strange driving experience for me, the road was quiet, you simply set the cruise control at 65mph., which is the speed limit, and steered the car on this unending ribbon whose edges appeared to converge somewhere way out there in the distance. I was somewhat relieved when my first two-hour stint was over, this type of driving seemed to have a mesmerising effect on me, being used to the twists and turns of our Irish roads.

By late afternoon we had left the snow and the flat lands of Indiana behind as we approached Louisville and the rolling hills of Kentucky. We made our first overnight at a Fairfield Inn in the small town of Bowling Green having covered over 450 miles. We were off again early on day two with Dick getting us underway while I sat me beside him riding shotgun and May and Fran studied the daily crossword puzzle in the back. This was much more interesting country with more varied scenery, at times reminiscent of Ireland.

Of course Kentucky is horseracing country and the evidence of white fencing was all over as we proceeded south. It wasn't long before we crossed the state line into Tennessee, the home of country and western music, which was evident on all the local radio stations as we drove along. The Interstate sliced through the centre of Nashville, we saw the signs for the "Grand Old Opry" but no evidence of the actual building could be seen on the skyline from the highway. Our comfort stops were generally made at those lovely old western style stores–cum–restaurant places known as "The Cracker Barrel" which appear to be all over the South. The next major city we passed through was Birmingham Alabama, which made news headlines around the world with serious racial unrest back in the days of George Wallace's Governorship. We left Interstate 65 after Birmingham, and turned eastward to pick up the I. 75, the more direct route to our destination. It was interesting to get away from the highway and drive through some of the smaller towns and villages of Alabama, although if at times quite depressing.

One tends to think of the United States as the land of plenty, the land of equal opportunity for all, but on some of those minor roads here in what is known as the Deep South, we saw what could only be described as abject poverty the likes of which I have never seen on our holiday travels back in Europe. We passed through a small town which one could only describe as a shantytown whose population appeared to be totally black, with a number of men and women just standing around aimlessly, their demeanour, appearing to me, sad and dispirited. In a way one felt a little uneasy bordering on shame as we surreptitiously observed the scene from the comfort and luxury of Dicks Cadillac. It looked like a scene from "Porgy and Bess," but it wasn't, it was real, a community forgotten in this great land of opportunity. This was the darker unseen side by most people of the United States of America

We were now well and truly in the "Bible Belt" which was evident from the many churches we were passing along the way. Although we had an interesting day of varied scenery, if at times somewhat doleful, I think we were all pleased to be approaching our next overnight stop, the little town of Tifton in southern Georgia. We got away to a good start on the morning of day three, quite early on we crossed the Florida line leaving the state capitol Tallahassee and the Florida panhandle to our right, we felt we were getting close to our destination but Dick reminded us that we still had almost the complete length of this long state to drive. Like Indiana, Florida is very flat and away from the coast can be quite featureless. In the early afternoon we could almost smell the sea as we approached St. Petersburg and Tampa Bay on the Gulf of Mexico. A couple of hours later we had passed through the city of Fort Myers and were heading out across the causeway approaching the massive toll bridge onto Sanibel Island.

We had arrived - the sun was shining and the temperature was just over 80 degrees.

"Almost Heaven!"

Our apartment complex, "Pointe Santo de Sanibel" was made up of three large blocks, four stories high built in a U shaped configuration; I would say built possibly twenty-five years earlier when land was more plentiful and individual apartment were built to more generous proportions. I believe all the apartments in the complex are privately owned; probably by well-healed northerners, Dick told us that a judge from Chicago owned the one we were occupying. The verandas of all the apartments looked out on to a large central landscaped garden and small ornamental lake with an island in its centre, while beyond on a raised area was the swimming pool and rest room complex. The raised pool area with the lake below was designed in the style of a South Sea Island setting, with many tropical plantings; the scene could have been Bali-ha'i. The whole garden was a riot of colour with many exotic plantings, those known to me included purple and crimson Bougainvillea, the intriguing Passion Flowers in the blue and red varieties, the splendid flowering shrubs of Hibiscus in the most vivid shades of red, pink, salmon, yellow and the purest of white. The simple Geranium we know so well at home was also represented in its many different shades of red, pinks, mauve and white, displaying heads as large as hydrangea blooms in gratitude to the gods of sunshine, and looking anything but simple; all a most colourful celebration of the botanical art at its most luxuriant.

Our apartment, on the fourth floor, looked directly across the garden to the waters of the Gulf beyond. Dick and Fran had insisted, as their guests, that we take the 'Master Suite,' which was luxurious and also opened onto the main insect proofed lanai or veranda as we know it. We could sit out even late in the evening after dark with lights on reading or just enjoying the balmy night air, totally insect free. I arose early our first morning after arrival. Looking down from the veranda I couldn't believe my eyes, right there on the little island in the lake lying sunning itself was an alligator, I guessed it was about six or eight feet long. It had to be artificial I thought. There wasn't the slightest movement, until someone crossed the garden, when it slowly crawled into the water and disappeared. We saw it most mornings afterwards, I was told they appear to be shy of people; anyway nobody seemed to take much notice of it.

In the quiet of the very early morning I would walk through the garden pausing to marvel at the splendour of to-days blooms of hibiscus opening in all the brilliance of absolute perfection, as yesterday's blooms had folded to a sad and faded memory. Beyond the swimming pool, the garden path led onto the most beautiful white sugar sand beach, fringed with coconut palm trees growing at crazy angles bending towards the gently lapping azure waters of the gulf. At the waters' edge many varieties of sandpipers were busily running too and fro obviously finding some kind of feeding in the gently moving water, while in the tall trees just off the beach could be seen large numbers of pelicans perched almost precariously in the high branches. In the peace of this unforgettable early morning scene it would be easy to imagine Mitzi Gaynor there on the beach being "As corny as Kansas in August" in what could have been a truly "South Pacific" moment.

Later on in the morning on that first day as we sat on the beach I was puzzled by the activity of the people, which appeared strange to me. Nobody seemed to be sitting on the beach or sunbathing as they do at home, despite the warmth of the sun, and few people were swimming. Everybody was on the move in quite large numbers going one way or the other all with heads bowed down and sometimes almost bumping into each other as they proceeded in opposite directions, extraordinary! What were they looking for?

Apparently Sanibel Island I discovered is regarded as the shell capital of the world and all those moving people were searching the foreshore for unusual shells, generally having been washed in on the tide during the night; the downward gait of the people is known as "the Sanibel stoop."

Shopping on Sanibel is a different experience than at home, all the shops are set well back from the roadside and really didn't look like shops, as we know them, they all had magnificent flower filled gardens in front, many with water features and fountains. The only concession to shopping that one could see was the unobtrusive carved wooden signs at the edge of the sidewalk, which gave the minimum indication as to the business conducted within.

One particular shop Fran said she wanted us to see. We approached as I remember it along a raised and staggered boardwalk about four or five feet wide the passage way was almost closed over head with palm trees, banana trees and other foliage plants; everywhere was damp as if it had been hosed down, and with the warmth of the sun the atmosphere was almost jungle-like in its humidity. I wouldn't have been surprised if one of those alligators had found it's way here and was dosing under the boardwalk, I looked down at my bare toes, flip-flaps being my only protection; but no here was a different attraction, every few yards as we walked a different cage housed a huge bird of the parrot family, each bedecked in the most colourful of plumage, some showing themselves off in self pretentious movement while others simply turned their backs to us. I'm not sure what the shop was selling or even if we went into it, but the display outside was impressive. I remember another shop with the most unusual tree I had ever seen; I was told it was the Banyan tree. It was seven or eight feet across with a large crown, the overhead branches drop down aerial roots which when they reach the ground root themselves forming pillars about three or so inches across, as each year passes it gets wider and wider and I am told can spread over a large area.

There were two theatres on the Island, one was called the "The Old School House" and that was literally what it was before its use was changed. It had a small stage and a seating capacity of I would say about a hundred people. While we were there that great show "Anything Goes" was playing so we decided to book. It was a most enjoyable evening, with the novel production not only making the best use of the small stage area but much of the time spilling out into the auditorium giving all of us in the audience the feeling of being part of the action of the show.

Sunsets on Sanibel were breathtaking in the sheer magnificence of their effect; we would walk across the garden to the beach each evening at twilight to watch the sunset. From its beginning in the most delicate shades of pink, until the whole sky almost imperceptibly changed to a deep crimson reflected in the shimmering waters of the Gulf, with the now dark shapes of the coconut palms standing out in stark silhouette against the crimson sky. The whole scene was beyond words; one could only gaze in silence - and in grateful thanks for the wonderful friends whose kindness brought us to this beautiful place.

But we were yet to see what promised to be a very special and in many ways unique place in this wonderful part of the United States. Dick and Fran's lifelong and closest friends, Billy Ryan and his wife Charlotte, owned a lovely condominium on Captiva Island, which is approached from the northern tip of Sanibel Island via another causeway bridge which spans what is known as Blind Pass. Billy had kindly made reservations for all six of us for a day trip to what he described as a very special Island on the intercostal waterway. The Island, which is private and can only be approached by special permission, is situated some two hours north of Sanibel/Captiva islands. The special cruise would leave next morning at 10-30am. from 'South Seas Plantation' a resort on the northern tip of Captiva. Dick, Fran, May and myself arrived in good time and were met by Billy and Charlotte. Our cruise boat the double-decked "Lady Chadwick" was tied up at the dock and the tourists were ready to board. The morning was bright and sunny and the water was glasslike. We soon got the call to board and filed up the little gangway, I would say upwards possibly to 150 people had signed up for the cruise and it wasn't long before the Captain gave the order to cast off; we were on our way.

We steamed gently out thorough the channel marks, each one as we passed, its flat top playing host to a nesting pelican or osprey, in some cases the babies peering at us from over the edge the nest. Meanwhile as we gathered speed, progressing out into Pine Island sound, excitement mounted as a group of playful leaping dolphins escorted us part of the way to our destination. The first port of call for our little ship was the island of "Cabbage Key", another small island in the chain; where many of our passengers disembarked. Once the home of novelist and playwright Mary Roberts Reinhart, the Reinhart house was built on the hilltop site in the late 30's and is now the "Hide-Away Inn and Restaurant", I know nothing of its culinary merits but an intriguing feature of the inn is its "wallpaper" worth more than $20,000. At sometime in the past the guests started tacking one-dollar bills to the wall and signing them. Today these dollar bills cover the walls and ceilings. We continued our trip to our destination Useppa Island about a further 30 minutes steaming.

Useppa is considered to be the most beautiful and interesting island in the chain of islands in the Pine Island Sound, in southwest Florida. Its beautifully manicured white sugar sand beach is fringed with a profusion of tropical vegetation including cocoanut palms, royal Poinciana, Banana trees and again that most unusual and which we know now to be Banyan trees - while the indigenous flowers of the region were in evidence everywhere. With no cars allowed on the island peace and tranquillity reigned supreme, we strolled along the pathway known as East Ridge's pink pathway towards the old Collier Inn stooping under massive boughs of hardwood trees whose form and texture was unknown to me but which appear to command priority along the way. The only appreciable sound to break the silence was the ever-present bird song. Following the pathway the trees gave way to the lovely little three-hole golf course and a cluster of tennis courts; some of the special facilities of this island club. Yes, today Useppa is run as a private club, quite obviously for the very wealthy. Publisher Barron Collier bought the island in 1912; many of the rich and famous liked the combination of beauty and privacy, which this tiny half-mile-long island afforded them. Theodore Roosevelt, the Vanderbilts, the Rockefellers, Zane Grey and Mae West have all visited Useppa over the years. Architecture is strictly controlled here; new houses are all white frame with latticework and wide screened porches to match the traditional building style. None of the houses appeared to be occupied as we passed along the pathway.

The air of peace and tranquillity of this beautiful island hides a sinister past, the notorious pirate Jose Gaspar held his favourite female captive here, while the run-of-the-mill ladies were kept on the nearby island named for its unsavoury goings on – Ilse de las Captivas now known as Captiva Island. Joseffa was a headstrong girl who never took to Gaspar; he found this to be so humiliating to his ego that he chopped off her head. As you can imagine this place has its share of ghost stories. Local dialect changed "Joseffa" to Useppa hence the islands name. More recently in 1976, and I suppose because of its inaccessibility, the island served as the training ground for what will always be remembered as the Bay of Pigs disaster.

We made our way back to the boat having dined well in the "Collier Inn" and later as we returned to Sanibel, watching this enchanting and sorcerous island fade away, mythical like into the magical evening sunset. I could not help but think that we had been privileged to visit a place, which I believe, must come as close as it is possible to complete perfection.

Almost thirty-five years had passed since that young student Mike Byrne made his call to the office in Wicklow's courthouse. We had travelled to Chicago several times since, and Mike's parents and other members of the family had on several occasions travelled to Ireland and Wicklow. However, our paths and Mike's had never crossed since his first trip to Wicklow. Three years ago we were back again in Chicago and had driven up with Dick and Fran to their summerhouse at Lake Beulah. Mike over the years had spent most of his time down south and had qualified along the way as a Doctor; he had since our last visit moved back north again and was practicing medicine in Wisconsin. Dick said to me one evening "I've arranged a golf game tomorrow at "Lake Beulah Country Club" and Mike will join us at the clubhouse, is that OK with you?"

"That's great" I said, "I'm really looking forward to meeting Mike again". As we drove into the car park of the golf club Mike had arrived and was waiting outside for us, he looked well and had changed little over the years. As we shook hands, Mike said,

"Hi Jimmy" I said,

"Hello Mike, as we were saying the last time we met!"

Mother - Elizabeth, Father - William, Carmel, Marjorie, Monica (baby).

James Everett, Minister for Post & Telegraphs.

The only photo of all 10 with mother mid-1940's.

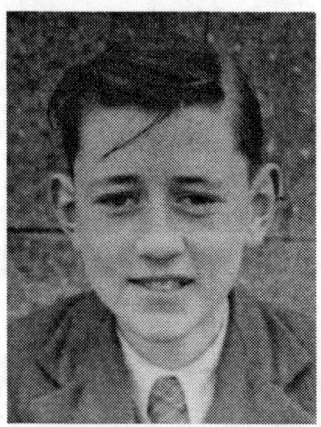

School photo, same period.

May

Hunters Hotel, Ashford, 3rd October 1962.

De La Salle Past Pupil's Dance.
Back left to right: James Devlin, Liam, May, Self, Frank, Noel Furlong.
Front: Left to Right: Breeda, Margaret (Liam's wife), Mai Furlong, Maura (Frank's wife), Lily Murray. Joe (obviously took picture).

Family get-together for Michael and Marianne from New York.
Back left to right Paddy, Carmel, Michael, Liam, James, with daughter Maritta, Noel Boner.
Front left to right: Breeda, Monica(Boner), Self, Marianne, Margaret.

Auntie (Nellie Everett) May's grandmother (Margaret Hughes), my mother Elizabeth.

40th Wedding Anniversary of May's parents Winnie & Jim Lambert with much loved teacher Cecilia Wall.

R.N.L.I. staff Clare Street 1991

GHOSTS IN THE GARDEN

Most of my work as Court Messenger was routine, which entailed in each case receiving the warrant and calling on the defendant. While in most cases quietly collecting the amount involved without serious difficulty; there were however occasions when it was necessary to apply harsher methods. Carrying out evictions or having to make seizures on poor people, who for the most part simply didn't have the where with all to pay, I found these occasions extremely difficult and almost impossible to remain emotionally uninvolved. It was all too much akin to the days of the rack rents and landlordism for my liking.

Fortunately the opportunity presented itself to apply for a transfer to Wicklow County Council to work as a Rent Collector in the Housing Section. I went for interview and was pleased to be offered the job, which I accepted.

The remuneration for the position of Rent Collector in those days was divided between salary and bonus, the bonus being based on your collection. The salary was paid half-yearly; together with the bonus provided you achieved 95% of all collectable rents due over the half yearly period, if you failed to achieve the

95% you lost your bonus. I made the point that we couldn't possibly live on fresh air for six months, so the officials came up with the solution that they would pay a fixed amount monthly on account and then make the necessary settlement at the end of the period, which was reasonably satisfactory.

I would be responsible for collecting the rents on five hundred cottages, my area would cover a section of the county from the sea at Kilcoole to the mountains beyond Roundwood also taking in the villages of Newtownmountkennedy and Newcastle and all the scattered rural cottages within the district. I was much more at home in this job and found the people extremely friendly and most hospitable. I was offered tea in almost every house I called to, which was very kind but not very practical. Of course there was always the few who make life difficult, as much for themselves as for myself or Wicklow Co. Council, then it became necessary to use a heavier hand.

I recall one strange case of an elderly man living alone in a rural cottage. I was finding it difficult when I called to get any answer at the cottage. After calling several times over a period of a couple of months he finally answered the door; he appeared to be in a very agitated state almost hostile. When I suggested that he was in arrears with his rent he shouted at me that he would pay his rent when the Council got rid of the ghosts from his garden. With a strange look in his eyes he said, "all night long and every night they're jumping along the telegraph wires, I can't get a wink of sleep". Well I could do nothing about the ghosts, but the solution for the rent problem came about in a sad and tragic way. Coming along the road on his way home late from the pub one miserable night the poor old man was knocked down by a car. He later died in hospital.

Some months later I encountered a frightening situation, which could also have resulted in a most awful tragedy but thankfully didn't. In this case a young married couple with a little baby had recently been appointed to the tenancy of a new cottage; on one particular morning some time later, by now the couple had well settled in. I called as usual to collect the rent; it was about 11am. when I arrived at the door, having called to quite a number of houses earlier that morning. I was working in a fairly new estate with mainly young people. The lady as usual had paid her rent and kindly asked me if I would like a cup of tea. I gratefully accepted and we chatted amicably as she waited for the kettle to boil. While I was having the tea I noticed a round hole in the centre of the kitchen ceiling, it was about two inches across. I wasn't going to say anything but my curiosity got the better of me and I said in a matter-of –fact way,

"Do you mind me asking, how did the hole happen in the ceiling" with that the young lady burst into floods of tears; needless to say I was sorry I had asked the question. When she eventually composed herself she related what happened. She and her husband had a row a few days earlier, he had been cleaning his rifle and in the heat of the argument his gun went off by mistake, with the bullet or shot going through the kitchen ceiling. The terrifying part about it was, the baby was asleep in its cot in the room above the kitchen, they raced up stairs, and thank God the baby was unhurt, but she could have been killed.

It is amazing how much gossip goes around and how news travels in small communities; or maybe it's not, I suppose all small closely-knit communities are the same the world over. As I did my rounds of the cottages; without soliciting information I would hear all the latest gossip of illness, births, marriages, deaths, courtships innocent or illicit and a lot more that you really didn't want to know, and at all times well ahead of my call on appropriate news-making neighbour. In some cases this information was helpful, you were always well warned of problems you may encounter in advance of arriving at a particular house. I was always grateful when a tenant made me aware of a death or serious illness in the area, as I would then simply call and pay my respects to the family.

THE COTTAGE ON THE ROCKS

Up to this time in our marriage we didn't have a house of our own, unlike today when every young couple would find it almost unthinkable not to have their home completely furnished and ready to move into before they marry. We started married life firstly at home on Summerhill in my mother's house, we then moved on to a little lodge at the other end of town which we rented for £1-10s weekly.

While I was working with the Circuit Court Office the job of Steward at Wicklow Golf Club fell vacant, we decided to apply. We both thought it would be an opportunity to save some money to put aside for a deposit for a house of our own. We were appointed to the position and duly took up residence in Wicklow Golf Club. I would keep on my job and May would look after things in the club during the day, during the evenings I would be home to work in the bar. Things worked out well although free time for both of us was almost nil, either or both of us had to be there all the time, seven days a week. Apart from our two weeks annual holidays the only free days in the year were Christmas day and Good Friday.

We were I would say about eighteen months working in Wicklow Golf Club when an unusual house came on the market, which having viewed we both fell in love with. It was known then as "Riverside", the name, if somewhat lacking in imagination certainly described its position; it was located on South Quay close to the Lifeboat Station and the Sailing Club, built on an outcrop of rock right in the harbour. The Admiralty had built it originally as a boathouse for the Coastguard Station during the British occupation of Ireland. Although it had long since been converted to a dwelling house, it still retained the old slipway, which had been used to launch the longboats into the harbour when the call for rescue came. The original heavy doors stood at the top of the slipway and were still functional, in the reconstruction an inner door and windows had been built so that in summertime the heavy doors could be left open without loss of security. It had for a while in the 40's been the property of my aunt and uncle, Jim Everett and his wife Ellen. They were to feature in the saga of our purchase of "Riverside."

During the early 50's a previous owner had leased the house for a short time to serve as the first home of the newly formed Wicklow Sailing Club. When the property came on the market in the early 60's it was then owned by a Dublin couple, Mr and Mrs Green who had occupied it for some years as their summer residence. On the death of her husband Mrs Green had decided to sell their holiday home in Wicklow; it was being sold fully furnished and the asking price was £2500. Although it seems very little these days, about the price of a continental holiday it might well for us have been two million pounds.

We met with the Bank Managers of the three local banks one after another to ask for a loan, all without success. One must remember that in the 60's money was scarce, loans were very difficult to procure. We had been told that there was no point in approaching the Building Societies because of the unique location of the property this also was the reason given by the bank managers. We decided to call and meet with Mrs Green and see if she would reduce her asking price, we made our way to her home, near Stepaside Co. Dublin. We found Mrs. Green to be an exceptionally warm and friendly lady. Having spent quite some time with her she kindly reduced the price considerably. Again we did the rounds of the Bank Managers and again without success.

We were about to give up and inform Mrs Green of our failure to secure the loan when the manager of the then National Bank, Mr. Dick Seale who was a member of the golf club, and had refused us earlier, knocked on the kitchen door and came in to talk to us. He told us we could have the loan but would have to pay it back in five years. We couldn't understand why he had changed his mind and although we knew we would have our work cut out to clear the loan within the time scale laid down; we were over the moon. Mrs Green was delighted; she told us that she really wanted us to have the house. The day we signed and the keys were handed over to us was one of the happiest days of our lives.

I worked most evenings all that first winter on the house while May took care of things at the club and we moved in the following spring. When we were settled in we felt so much at home and happy that we both knew that we would be here for many years to come. We decided to change the name of the house and choose a name of our own. Taking the fact of it's position with three sides of it literally rising out of the water, together with our good feelings for the place, and our hopes for the years to come, we decided to change the name to "The Anchorage".

Many years later, the loan on our house had long since been paid off, my uncle Jim had by then passed away and my aunt had decided to sell her house and move to somewhere smaller. She asked me about the deeds of her house and would I check in the bank. I was perplexed as to why she would ask me of the whereabouts of these documents,

"But don't you remember" she said;

"Your uncle gave the deeds of this house as security for your loan on The Anchorage."

It was only then that I realised that Jim Everett had given his own house as security with the National Bank and had never told us. We now understood why Dick Seale, the then Manager of the National Bank had changed his position and given us the loan so many years ago in the golf club kitchen.

PASS ME YOUR HEAD LINE

After the long hours and very busy weekends while working in the golf club, we now enjoyed a wonderful sense of freedom. Our long summer evenings and weekends were free again to get on with the work on the house, which I enjoyed, or do whatever we liked, it was like having being released from gaol. With so much free time and the fact of living so close to the water I got involved in water based activities, I joined the Sailing Club, bought a little second-hand dinghy and became very active in all the club activities. I made many new friends amongst the membership of the club, two of whom I was to have an association with for much of the remainder of my working life namely the Desmond brothers Kevin and Dermot.

Although the fleet was mainly made up of dinghies the club was developing a Cruiser section. The big event at that time was the annual Dun Laoghaire/Wicklow Beer Barrel race held each year over the Whitson weekend. It was a very successful fun event, which attracted a huge number of yachts, reminiscent of the old regatta days at Wicklow.

To explain the meaning of the "Beer Barrel" aspect of the

event; the Sailing Club at that time had no liquor licence and naturally when the yachtsmen arrived in the harbour at the end of the race they wanted something a little stronger than tea or soft drinks, so the winner of each class was given a Keg of Beer. Of course it was only natural that a tap was very quickly produced after the presentation was made. In that way no laws were broken and everybody could have a few drinks and enjoy the party that inevitably followed.

During the winter following our move to South Quay the committee decided that the Sailing Club should have it's own licensed bar. Application was made and subject to certain requirements and some alterations within the premises; the licence was granted. A group of us, namely Harry Jordan, Kevin Desmond, and several other willing members, some who are no longer with us including the late Danny Cleary, Capt. Billy Kinsella, Eddie Valentine and Peter Gale all good friends, we spent the winter evenings revamping the inside of the clubhouse and building a secure lockup bar which was a requirement of the court in the granting of the licence. The acquisition of the licence changed totally the atmosphere of the club. It was no longer a simple clubroom where like-minded mainly young sailing types met to chat about their mutual interest in boats and boating matters. The club and the committee had 'come of age', for want of a better expression, and was now taking on the role of running a business with all the responsibility which that entailed.

Wicklow Sailing Club had evolved to a new and different level, with many new members, maybe not all interested in sailing, but the acquisition of the licence would increase the social membership and all the activities of a social nature of the club.

It was at that time, maybe a policy is too strong a word, but as far as possible the practice was adopted for one of the committee to meet visiting yachts, welcome the crews to Wicklow and offer the hospitality of the club, and the very welcome hot shower to the visiting yachtsmen and yachtswomen on their arrival and for the extent of their visit. Since our lounge window faced the mouth of the harbour I had the opportunity when at home to see many of these visitors as their boats entered the harbour. I would hop into the car and travel around to the North Quay where visiting yachts would usually tie up.

One particular visitor arriving for what was his first visit by sea to Wicklow, his little motor launch was named "Coot" and I asked him to throw me his head rope and offered the hospitality of the club to him and his crew. The Skipper's name was Liam King and in turn he welcomed me onboard. I met Liam and his party that evening in the club to discover that he was a magnificent pianist, which needless to say was right up my street. We, all of us present, had a wonderful evening of music and song on Liam King's first of many memorable musical evenings in Wicklow Sailing Club. Listening to such a fine talent, as Liam possesses always brings to mind the one great regret of my own life, that I didn't learn the Piano. We remained friends ever since and on the occasions when Liam would arrive by sea to Wicklow he would give a hoot on the boat's claxon as he passed our slipway; that was the signal to put on the kettle for a cup of tea.

We had many a great musical evening since with Liam on the piano in his home in Dublin or in our own home. Liam and his wife Nonie now live in Wicklow and we still get together for a spot of music from time to time, which I always enjoy.

With my deeper involvement in the Sailing Club and living in such close proximity to the sea I decided to look for a boat somewhat bigger than the little sailing dinghy I had purchased when we first moved to the Anchorage. I couldn't however afford to spend very much. I happened to see a boat for sale on the local paper, which I thought might suit me. She was a double ender with a long bowsprit, gaff rigged with a heavy steel centreboard, and about 22 feet overall; most importantly the price was right. When I called on the owner who lived in Laragh Co. Wicklow, he informed me that the boat was actually housed in a shed in Portumna Co. Galway. With the help of a friend Dr. Austin Kinsella, who holidayed every July in Wicklow and who was always happy to get involved in any boating lark; he kindly offered his jeep and trailer to transport the boat back home to Wicklow. So early one bright and sunny July morning Dr. Kinsella and myself headed off to Portumna; loaded the boat with the help of a number of locals and returned late that evening. We launched the boat next day, and watched as she slowly sank until her deck was at water level.

The boat had been out of the water for a few years and her planking had obviously opened up; we left her submerged for a week to tighten up. When we re-floated her, she was still seriously making water around the base of the centreboard casing, which with some work was easily put right. I sailed her in Wicklow Bay all that summer but found the gaff rig very cumbersome and difficult to manage. At the end of the season I managed to 'squeeze almost' so to speak, the boat into our small garage at the Anchorage and over the next two years I refurbished her totally and completely. The old centreboard and casing was removed and a heavy lead keel fitted. I built a new mast and converted the rig from the original gaff to the more easily handled Bermuda rig. All the decking was removed and a new cabin and coach roof built; complete with two berths and a small but adequate galley. I also fashioned a bracket to take an outboard engine. A self-draining cockpit with under-seat rope lockers more or less completed the refit.

When I decided to do such a major job on the boat I was aware that the garage roof was in a bad state of repair and would need replacing when the work on the boat was completed. You can imagine the remarks and the banter from the locals when I removed the roof and had the boat lifted by crane out through the resultant hole. The boat, which we called "Illyria" sailed remarkably well and much more efficiently with its new rig and gave us a lot of pleasure over the next few years while she remained in our ownership.

DOES THIS LIFEBOAT REALLY GO TO SEA?

Because our home on South Quay was within one hundred yards of the Lifeboat Station, I was always one of the first to arrive when the maroons were fired, indicating that the lifeboat was about to launch on service in response to a call from some person or craft in danger at sea. Not being a trained member of the crew I did not of course go to sea. The then Hon. Secretary Mr. J. T. O' Byrne who was also President of Wicklow Sailing Club mentioned to me that the Royal National Lifeboat Institution was creating a new honorary position at each lifeboat station, that of Deputy Launching Authority (DLA). The Hon. Sec. being the principal launching authority, the DLA would stand in for him in his absence and assist when the lifeboat was on service.

Living conveniently to the station, and obviously being interested he asked me if I would take on the position. I told him I would be delighted to help out in any capacity. Because the Hon. Sec. or the DLA in his absence has the responsibility for actually making the decision to launch or not to launch the lifeboat, the appointment of these two positions are made at a very senior level at head office and ratified by the Committee of Management of the Institution. After a month or so notification of my appointment came through to me both by letter and from the Inspector of Lifeboats in Ireland. This was the beginning of an association with the Royal National Lifeboat Institution, which was to continue for more than thirty years first as a volunteer and later as a fulltime employee.

Within a year of my becoming involved with Wicklow Lifeboat Mr. O' Byrne had retired as Hon. Secretary on age grounds and was elected Chairman of the branch. I was asked by the Inspector and agreed to take over as Honorary Secretary. I approached a close friend Michael Jones to take on the position of DLA. I thoroughly enjoyed working closely with the crew and derived great satisfaction from being involved with the many operational services that the lifeboat was called to. I also approached another close friend Kevin Desmond to take responsibility for fund-raising, which he kindly accepted.

The years that followed were for me very happy years, and fruitful years for the Lifeboat Branch in Wicklow. Kevin, Michael and myself were young and very enthusiastic, we brought new people on to the Committee of the Branch, May was elected Hon. Sec. of a very active Ladies Guild and all was going well. We brought new ideas to the branch, initiated Boathouse Open Days long before it became standard practice throughout the institution. Fundraising by the Ladies Guild and supported by Kevin Desmond soared to the point where Wicklow was the most successful fundraising branch outside the major city branches of Dublin and Cork. The J. W. Archer was the name of the then Wicklow lifeboat; she was by today's standards a very basic craft, capable of a speed of only seven knots and with practically no shelter for the crew in bad weather. Nevertheless she was a beautiful sea-kindly boat, held in the highest regard and confidence by all who went to sea in her. She was at all times maintained to the very highest standard by the mechanic, Jim Bonus, followed on his retirement by Paddy Goodbody. As she stood in the boathouse in pristine condition always at the readiness the whole scene looked more akin to an exhibition than to a working lifeboat station. I remember being asked more than once by visitors to the station "Does this Lifeboat really go to sea?" We were all very enthusiastic and crew and committee alike were proud of our Lifeboat Station at Wicklow.

The Coxswain of the lifeboat for most of the period that I was Honorary Secretary was Charlie Byrne. The Byrne family were part of the lifeboat tradition in Wicklow going right back to its inception in 1852. Thomas Byrne, Charlie's father had served as Coxswain and Second Coxswain and also his brothers as officers of the boat back in the days of the previous lifeboat "Lady Kylsant" and his grandfather Mark Byrne had held the position of Coxswain many years before; while Charlie's brothers Tom and Kevin and his sons were crewmembers continuing the family tradition.

Most of the crewmen of that time were fishermen or worked on the docks so there was never any problem getting a crew together quickly. When the call came they were all close at hand. One of the exceptions to the rule was Harry Jordan, a staff officer with Wicklow County Council and a valued crewmember for many years who later in life held the position of DLA at Bundoran Lifeboat Station. One of the well-known and well-loved coxswains of Wicklow lifeboat was Ned Kavanagh who had retired some years before I became involved. He had been awarded the Institutions Bronze medal for gallantry for his service to the M.V.Cameo many years before. Ned was a very interesting man and most helpful to me in those early years. We spent many a pleasant hour chatting on the seat in front of his little fishing shed overlooking the harbour. One particular occasion which stands out in my memory while we were living in the "Anchorage", tells something of the character of the man.

It was on one bright "St. Stephens Day" morning, Dermot Desmond called me and asked me if I would like to go for a sail, the weather was perfect, I suppose about a force 3 winds and the morning was bright, so I said 'why not'. We rigged Dermot's little Mirror dinghy and took off from the boat slip, the tide was starting to make, so we would head south from the harbour, which would give us a fair tide for our return. As we approached the mouth of the harbour I noticed a familiar figure on the lower level of the East Pier. As we sailed south we were aware of the same figure watching us from over the top of the upper level of the pier. Of course it was Ned. We didn't stay out very long but we did sail well down into the Glen Bay, some distance south of Wicklow harbour before we came about for home; although conditions were perfect it was cold. Ned was still on the pier until we re-entered the harbour when he left for home up across the castle field. That was the kind of man Ned was. I'm sure he said to himself these two are asking for trouble so he couldn't bring himself to leave while we were out of the harbour. I met Ned very soon after but he never mentioned the occasion and needless to say neither did I.

Many of the lifeboat calls were of a fairly routine nature, if you had a change in weather conditions say a sudden strong gale that wasn't well forecast, you could almost guarantee that before long the phone would ring with a request for the lifeboat to put to sea.

One service that certainly was not routine, a film company were shooting in the area the subject of which was the First World War, specifically the war in the air. The film was called "Zeppelin" and stared George Peppard. Most of the filming was done in the Wicklow Mountains although the particular sequence of that days filming was taking place over Wicklow Bay. The subject of the shoot appeared to be a "dog fight" between two First World War bi-planes. I watched the events with great interest through my binoculars from the bathroom window, the two aeroplanes doing their twists and turns and looping the loop while the filming helicopter remained almost static in the air filming the action. Suddenly one of the bi-planes miscalculated a tight turn and dived into the rotating blades of the helicopter, which appeared to cut the plane in two, while at the same time crippling the helicopter; both aircraft plummeted into the sea, as I watched almost dumfounded. It was as if the whole event had happened in slow motion, with the parts of the both craft almost drifting down from the sky, as I watched in heightened awareness at this awful event happening in front of my eyes. I immediately called the Coxswain to be told that he was on his way to the lifeboat and had also seen what had happened, I then called the medical services. I felt sorry for the lifeboat men that evening because of their gruesome task of recovering only body parts from the sea. Four men lost their lives in this freak and tragic accident.

Soon after I was appointed Hon. Sec. an interesting service took place. A number of young people had sailed from Dunlaoghaire to Brittas Bay, a distance of say twenty five miles, the yacht a small twenty-six footer I think I remember it was a "Stella" class yacht owned by the father of one of the young people on board. The day had been a bright pleasant summers day and the trip down I'm sure was enjoyable for those on board, on arrival at Brittas Bay they dropped anchor well off the beach. What they failed to do was listen to the weather reports on radio, which would have warned them of severe easterly gales forecast for the Irish Sea Area later that night. If the forecasts were to prove correct the boat and crew would be in imminent danger, anchored in exposed water and on a lee shore. The first I knew of the situation was when the Inspector of Lifeboats called me from his home in Dunlaoghaire to alert us to the problem, he having been contacted by the owner of the boat, father of one of the young people on board.

Apparently the owner of the yacht must have been aware of the young crews plans to anchor off Brittas Bay. He had heard the weather news and knowing the inspector contacted him at his home. I was instructed by the lifeboat inspector to launch the lifeboat and have the yacht with its crew towed back to the harbour in Wicklow. The evening was still bright and although the sea was fairly calm, the wind was beginning to rise. When the lifeboat arrived on the scene another problem presented itself. The Coxswain radioed back to the boathouse to say there was nobody on board and in the circumstances what were his instructions.

A decision had to be made; lifting the anchor and towing away an unmanned craft without the skipper's permission had implications for the Institution and indeed for me as the launching authority. On the other hand to request the lifeboat to leave the yacht and return to base we would be exposing the young crew if they re-boarded to serious danger when and if the weather deteriorated; and also possible danger to the lifeboat and her crew if they had to launch again later in the night and approach the yacht in the shallow waters of Brittas Bay in stormy conditions to try to effect a rescue. I told the coxswain to lift the anchor and take the yacht in tow to Wicklow, which he did. At least the action of the Lifeboat would ensure that the young people were kept safely ashore. Meanwhile sometime later back in the lifeboat house after my call to the coxswain, a group of young people came into the boathouse, still unaware of the weather warning, demanding why the lifeboat had towed their yacht away from where it was anchored. It seemed that they had gone ashore and were having dinner with friends in their home overlooking the bay when they saw the lifeboat taking their yacht in tow and steaming in a northerly direction. They figured that the obvious destination of the lifeboat was Wicklow. Having explained the circumstances to them they calmed down and were in fact very grateful; they expressed their regret for all the inconvenience caused. The storm did materialise during the night and I'm sure the yacht and its crew were much more comfortable in the shelter of Wicklow harbour than on the exposed shores of Brittas Bay. However, that was not the end of the story.

The Coxswain and Mechanic completed their written 'Returns of Service', which was normal procedure, and I duly sent the reports to head office. Sometime later I received a request from the operations department of head office for a full detailed report of the service by myself, an unusual request, which I completed and forwarded. To complicate the situation further, a new Inspector of Lifeboats had been appointed to Ireland. A few weeks later he called to see me and expressed the Institution's concern, he pointed out that if the skipper of the yacht on the day, although not the owner, had taken a different attitude, the fact that we had taken the yacht from where it was anchored, we could possibly have been accused of 'piracy on the high seas'. An alternative would have been to instruct the coxswain to stand by the yacht until the crew returned, however, we had no knowledge of their whereabouts or if they intended returning to the boat that night. I felt that it would have been unfair to expect the lifeboat to stand by in these circumstances. That was the end of the incident; I still contended however that in the situation as it unfolded that evening the decision to move the boat was the safest one.

Monday 4th of March 1974 marked the 150th Anniversary of the founding of the Royal National Lifeboat Institution; the occasion was celebrated at lifeboat stations and by RNLI branches in general all over England, Ireland, Scotland, and Wales.

Wicklow Lifeboat Station together with Portrush Lifeboat Station were given the signal honour of a launching ceremony symbolic of the thousands of launches on service of present and past lifeboats in this country. These launches had saved 6,000 lives in Irish waters over the past 150 years. The 'Symbolic Launch' of "The J. W. Archer" would take place at noon on 4th of March 1974.

The RNLI's Area Organiser at that time was Capt. Jack Phelan, he gave the committee every support and help with the organisation of the event. It was felt that so many Wicklow people had in fact never actually seen the lifeboat being launched down the slipway, we decided to make the day a very special occasion and issue a general invitation to anybody in Wicklow who wished to attend. For all present we would endeavour to authenticate a launch as closely as possible to a real live service situation. We invited all the many clubs and organisations from around the district; we also invited the pupils and teachers from the five schools in the town and of course the general invitation was issued to all the people of Wicklow.

The day was a great success; the east pier was packed with people almost from end to end. The ceremony commenced with the raising of the RNLI flag by Coxswain Charles Byrne to the music of the Holy Rosary School Band. From the platform on the pier, on the first stroke of noon the order to 'Fire the maroons and launch the Lifeboat' was given by myself as Honorary Secretary of the station. Immediately the maroons were fired the crew who were lined up on the pier raced to the lifeboat. The lifeboat was launched dramatically down the slipway to the enthusiastic applause of the many hundreds present. After completing a slow run around the harbour during which two pupils of the Dominican Convent read "A tribute to the Lifeboat Men" and "A Prayer for those in Peril at Sea," the lifeboat returned and tied up in front of the platform. The Blessing Ceremony took place conducted by Very Rev. A Crinion PP., Rev. Stanley Pettigrew, Church of Ireland and Rev. R.D. Rodgers representing the Methodist Community. Mr. J.T. O' Byrne, Chairman of Wicklow Branch, paid tribute to the Lifeboat Service in Ireland and in particular to the splendid tradition of Wicklow Lifeboat Station dating back to its inception in 1857. The occasion was brought to a close with Kevin Desmond calling for 'Three Cheers' for the lifeboat and her crew.

CAMELOT - A MAGNIFICENT SHOW

In the early 70's a group of people got together to form a Musical Society in Wicklow under the chairmanship of Noel Furlong, with Joe Keegan, a teacher in De La Salle School as the first Musical Director. Having in its first year produced a really excellent concert, the society staged its first full musical production the following year. "The Merry Widow" an operetta in three acts by Franz Lehar opened in the Fatima Hall Wicklow, on Easter Sunday 1973, running for six nights.

I joined the society for that first show but due to illness at the time I had to drop out of rehearsals. However, I did work for the week of the show on the 'front of house' team and continued to do so in subsequent years when the society staged "The Desert Song " and "Oklahoma". Niall Murray, at that time a semi professional singer with a fine baritone voice, played the lead in all three productions. Aideen Lane, an accomplished soprano who lived locally, played the female lead, in each of these shows. The supporting roles were all filled from within the membership of the society and as one would expect in Wicklow, supported by a fine chorus. The first three shows were produced to a very high standard and attracted full houses for the entire week's run in each case.

The society's annual production had by then become firmly established and considered by many as very much part of the Easter season in Wicklow. The show was looked forward too with tremendous enthusiasm; a celebration in music, song, drama and choreography, now that the austerity of the Lenten season was behind us and the brighter days of summer were just around the corner.

I enjoyed the buzz of working 'front of house' with a great team who handled the entrance and seating of the audience with ease, I took particular interest in meeting and welcoming the members of the many visiting societies who attended our productions, making sure that their attendance was acknowledged from the stage, and that they were looked after with a cup of tea and a welcoming chat at the interval, and a 'safe home' at the end of the evening.

After the third production Noel stepped down as Chairman and I was asked to let my name go forward for election, which I was pleased to do. I was elected Chairman and immediately got into the work of our next production, "The Gypsy Baron" by Johann Strauss. For this production we brought two new lead singers to Wicklow in the persons of Philip Byrne, an excellent baritone who had played the lead role in several of the very highly regarded Rathmines & Rathgar Musical Society's shows, and Joan Merrigan who was one of the top professional sopranos on the Irish scene of that time. "The Gypsy Baron" is considered to be one of the best operettas for the amateur stage, with many lovely numbers sung in four-part harmony giving the Wicklow chorus an opportunity to demonstrate its fine choral qualities. Again the society had a great success, and our new leads Joan and Philip proved very popular with the Wicklow audience as they also did with all the members of the society.

The following Christmas the group staged a very successful concert with a cogent seasonal flavour. On this occasion the guest artist was Austin Gaffney with Mirette Dowling as musical director and Sister Rita Mary of the Dominican Community kindly offered her services as our rehearsal pianist. It was a marvellous evening, ending with Austin singing the evocative "O Holy Night" backed by the full chorus of the society, it sounded wonderful, setting the scene for the oncoming season of Christmas and of course also giving a flavour of our forthcoming production, which would be staged at Easter with Austin taking the lead part.

The show, which the society chose for its next production was the lovely Lerner and Lowe musical "Camelot". This was a very different show than anything the society had undertaken here to fore, and had only been produced once before in Ireland. It really could be described as a musical pageant. A new modern show, "Camelot" had a heavier emphasis on high drama than on chorus and had many very good individual parts. Although the chorus had less work to do in the show, the pieces they had were both moving and beautiful.

In order to do full justice to this very ambitious undertaking by the society we agreed that a different approach was necessary. In order to cover adequately the many character parts from our most experienced members we decided to engage three professional leads. We were fortunate to be able to acquire the services of an impressive lineout of top professionals, headed by the internationally known baritone Austin Gaffney, playing the lead role of "King Arthur." Austin was greatly supported by two further top professional singers, our two leads from last year's show; Joan Merrigan playing the leading lady, "Guinevere" and Philip Byrne as "Sir Lancelot". Our Musical Director was the highly qualified musician and teacher Mirette Dowling who at that time was also Musical Director of the acclaimed Wicklow Choral Society. The production was in the hands of the very experienced Abbey and Shakespearian producer Nora Lever who recommended Pat Power as choreographer, the team was certainly impressive and hopes were high for a first class production.

The Fatima hall in Wicklow's Dominican Convent is a magnificent auditorium, richly panelled in oak, and always beautifully maintained, the use of which the society was fortunate to have. However, from a technical point of view, two major difficulties have always existed in the staging of the annual show. The fact that there is no fly space over the stage had created difficulties in setting previous shows. With thirteen full set changes in "Camelot" our set designer Tom Synnott was handed not only a challenge, but also, a real and major problem. Our second difficulty was with the lighting of the show. The lighting bar, which is permanently fixed and suspended from the ceiling, is so close to the front tab curtains, that full lighting penetration of the stage was almost impossible.

I know very little about electricity so the simplest way for me to explain the difficulties of our lighting situation is this. In order to get the best possible lighting effect on stage, we had to work on the maximum wattage output available, if that makes sense, always just on the point of overload during the brighter passages of any show. I remember on one occasion in a previous show; someone brought in extra mirror lighting to one of the dressing rooms; the situation was so critical, not only was the stage, hall and orchestra pit plunged into total darkness but also much of the convent as well. We weren't popular that evening with the Dominican Community in Wicklow.

Tom as always came up trumps with the most imaginative and complimentary set designs, which when built he also painted to great effect. With the assistance and ingenuity of a most efficient set building and back stage crew, most of the set changes could be executed in a matter of seconds. Unfortunately the lighting constraints were something we had to live with.

That is not to say that we weren't extremely grateful to the Dominican Sisters for all their many kindnesses to us over the period as opening night approached, and of course while the show was in progress, we were certainly shown every assistance. I will always remember the support we received from the late Sister Agatha, from feeding us when we were too busy to go home in the run up to the opening night, to supplying anything we requested. I remember Tom saying to me,

"We need a fairly elaborate chair for Arthur's throne scene," I quietly said to him

"I know there is a beautiful seat in the convent chapel, I'll ask Sister Agatha when I get the right opportunity" I diffidently asked for the seat expecting to be pleasantly but firmly refused. Instead Sister Agatha said,

"Certainly, is there anything else you need?"

Visiting societies to our shows were always complimentary and maybe a little envious of the elegance and grandeur of our hall, which in itself added a certain je ne sais quoi to the occasion.

The adjudicator representing the 'Association of Irish Musical Societies' attends all the shows of affiliated societies throughout Ireland, and nominates four awardees in each of the many categories. One of the four nominated in each category is chosen for the award. Our show in Wicklow took place usually in April, which of course was towards the end of the adjudicating year but also a busy performing period with societies, many of whom like ourselves using school halls during the schools Easter holiday period.

Unfortunately the adjudicator's attendance at our show was on the first night of the week's run, which with the difficulties we encountered was really more a final dress rehearsal. We had some lighting problems and one or two first night difficulties; however, the adjudicator was so impressed with almost every aspect of the show she said to me before leaving after the show.

"If I could get back on Friday night, and I can't promise, could you improve on the minor problems of to-nights performance?"

I answered

"Absolutely yes."

I explained to her our limitations with the lighting board, and some of the other problems of the first night, she of course correctly responded,

"The first night should be just as polished as the last night." Her last remarks to me almost as she was leaving were.

"If I can get back and the improvements are made; Wicklow's production of Camelot could win the award for the Best Show of the Year"

As it happened she didn't get back on Friday night and when the awards were announced we didn't win the award of 'Best Show,' we were however delighted to win two National Awards, for 'Best Costumes,' our costume designer was George O'Brien and 'Best Props,' our props designer was Seamus Quinn.

Camelot was a magnificent show, which in my view marked a high point to that date in the annual productions of Wicklow Musical Society and encouraged other societies to stage Camelot in subsequent years.

The following year which was my final year as Chairman of Wicklow Musical Society the show we chose was "Finian's Rainbow." If Camelot was the high point of my period as chairman with the society then "Finian's Rainbow" was the happiest. It was the simplest show to stage having only one set from beginning to end, the lighting plot was also reasonably simple. We again engaged Joan Merrigan for the third year in succession to play our leading lady and playing opposite Joan was a fine tenor named Bryan Hoey. For the first time really, a member of our own society played the pivotal role that of Finian McLonergan and Tom Synnott played the part to perfection.

It is said that in any stage production "There are no small parts, there are only small players," the part of "Susan the Silent" beautifully played by Pauline Carey certainly gives credence to that saying. We also had an excellent production team in Tom Singleton, as producer, Gearoid Grant musical director and Dex

McLoughlin choreographer. They were a wonderful team who through their style of production made this show a very happy experience for the whole society. The show won two nominations for 'Best Programme' and the very coveted nomination of 'Best Chorus', which even though we did not win, placed our chorus within the top four, in musical society terms in the country, high praise indeed.

Over the winter while rehearsals for "Camelot" were ongoing, May and I became very friendly with the Gaffney family, Agnes, Austin and the children Irene, Ann, Una, and the boys Paul and Colm. We spent many happy occasions together at home in Wicklow or with the family in their home in Foxrock. I remember one particularly happy and memorable occasion; we arranged together with Agnes and Austin to spend a week in England to do some shows and play a little golf. What a week it was, we brought the car and Austin and myself took turns at driving. Over the first three days, which were spent in London we attended four West-End shows. The first "Mutiny on the Bounty," a new show with David Essex and Frank Finlay, "Guys and Dolls," in which Lulu played the lead part and "Starlight Express," a spectacular show, but not a favourite with any of us. The final show was "Barnum" with Michael Crawford, a magnificent show with quite spectacular circus effects. After that particular show we went to the stage door and chatted with Michael Crawford. We were the last in the queue to meet him and he stayed chatting with us for several minutes; he appeared to be in no hurry to get away, we all agreed a very friendly and charming man.

For the second part of the break we moved on to the West Country to a Golf Hotel where Austin and I played golf while the ladies relaxed and read and generally enjoyed the comforts of the hotel and indulged in some local shopping. We had a great week with some wonderful memories.

May and Agnes became particularly close as the years passed, Agnes was without exaggeration one of the kindest and most caring persons that either of us had ever met. Her concern for other people and her willingness to really get involved if help was needed; while at all times making light of the problems and concerns of her own busy life. Our family was the recipient of this very caring and selfless side of Agnes's nature on the very sad occasion of the fatal illness of my niece Aoibeann in "St. Vincent's Hospital," which was close by the Gaffney home. Her personal needs or desires she brushed aside as insignificant, with a smile and a shrug, if a friend needed help.

In the early 80's Agnes was hospitalised and had major surgery in the Blackrock Clinic, only the immediate relatives were allowed to see her, it was a worrying time for her family and for those of us who knew Agnes well. After some weeks she rallied and was sent to Dalkey Manor to recuperate. The following Sunday when we called to see her, we found her in the little oratory saying her prayers, she appeared to be in good spirits, and asked me to take her for a little drive. Anne who just arrived as we did, to visit her mother, came with us. We parked on Dalkey Hill overlooking the view of Dublin bay; it was a lovely early June day. Agnes chatted away and appeared if a little frail, to be her usual self, and as always making light of her own condition, while concerning herself more about how matters were with us. She said she was coming to Wicklow to spend a week or two with us when she was discharged from hospital; we were both delighted and pleased that she was making such good progress.

That was the last time we saw Agnes alive. The following week we had arranged to go to Kerry for two weeks holidays. My colleague from the office Dermot Desmond contacted us in Kenmare to let us know that Agnes had taken seriously ill and had been admitted to St. Vincent's Hospital, where she had peacefully passed away. We returned home to a very sad funeral and afterwards spent several hours with Austin and the family. What a great loss she was to her family and what a gap in the lives of the many friends who were privileged to have known her.

Although we remain very friendly with Austin, and the children who of course were forming their own relationships, we didn't see as much of the family after Agnes passed away. These days they occasionally bring their own children to visit us.

Agnes is still and will always be very much in our thoughts and our prayers. Austin's many friends were delighted when several years later he married a lovely lady named Susan who brought the happiness back into his life again.

During all this activity with Wicklow Musical Society I still held the position as honorary secretary of Wicklow Lifeboat Station, which except for certain periods did not take up a great deal of my time. Nevertheless between my work as Rent Collector with Wicklow Co. Council, the Lifeboat Branch, the Musical Society and membership of the committee of the Sailing Club life was fairly hectic. I was also a member of Wicklow Golf Club at that time.

Having served as Chairman of Wicklow Musical Society for three years it was time to make a change, time for somebody new to take over, so with mixed feelings I stepped down.

I can say with total honesty, that no other activity gave me the level of satisfaction I received from seeing our shows finally come alive on the stage of Fatima Hall, on those Easter Sunday nights.

AN UNFORGETTABLE EXPERIENCE

It was pitch dark as I made my way along the road, I was not on my own, the sound of footsteps of many more people were clearly evident as we all moved along in the darkness of the early morning. I, however, was one of a particular group that day who were to meet at Wicklow train station. The morning, although a little blustery, was dry and pleasant answering the prayers I felt sure of the whole country. I met up with the rest of the group, all members of Wicklow Church Choir as we in turn arrived on the platform. During rehearsals our choir had been augmented by the addition of some fine singers from the Church of Ireland Choir. As we all climbed aboard the special train, I looked at my watch, it was a little before 5am.

Our train was taking us on a very special "pilgrimage" to the Phoenix Park the day was Saturday 29th September 1979.

Today as I write, almost twenty-five years on, every detail of that fateful day is crystal clear in my memory. A day that was to fulfil the hopes and fervent wishes of the Irish Nation - that Pope John Paul II, after months of speculation and planning was making his historic visit to Ireland.

The Pope's first Mass on Irish soil would take place at Dublin's Phoenix Park, and promised to be a magnificent occasion. To explain where the members of St. Patrick's Church Choir were involved - the Diocesan Organising Committee decided to put together a mass choir from all the churches of the Dublin Diocese for this very special occasion.

The members of our choir in Wicklow attended many rehearsals for several weeks leading up to the great day, until we were all well up to speed with the music. As the date approached two special rehearsals were called for the Carmelite Church in Whitefriar's Street Dublin. Because of the huge numbers involved we were told that no church in the diocese was capable of accommodating both men and women at one rehearsal so it was decided to hold separate rehearsals. On the evening of the men's, rehearsal, the church was packed to capacity, several hundred men all in full voice, almost as it were - raising the roof. It was truly the most glorious and unforgettable of occasions.

Our final rehearsal was held in the Phoenix Park on a lovely late summers evening a few days before the event, together with the internationally known soloists Bernadette Greevy and the now late Frank Patterson. It was only then, as we saw the scale of the preparations - that the magnitude of the whole event was brought home to us. The choir was sited on a huge raked platform facing the congregation. To our left stood the Great Altar with its massive cross towering above the whole scene, while out in front 160 acres of corrals and aisles, empty now, this evening, except for those putting the final preparations to the site.

As we arrived at Ashtown Station and made our way across the dewy grass of Phoenix Park, dawn was beginning to break. The sight was awesome from our vantage point overlooking the already vast multitude as they streamed through the aisles to take their places in their designated positions. Close to the Altar were the areas assigned to V.I.P's, and also the many hundreds of invalids that were steadily arriving. Off to the right-hand side of the Altar and in front of our position, the Garda Siochanna Band and the Number One Army Band were set up, as were "The Chieftains" – one of Irelands premier traditional groups. During the hours of waiting, we were well entertained by one or another of these groupings.

As 10 o'clock approached a hush seemed to filter through the massive crowd. All heads turned skywards, eyes searching. Then, speck like at first in the Southeast sky, the mighty Boeing 747 slowly achieved its full perspective, as it approached at an altitude of scarcely more then a couple of thousand feet. With its escort from the Irish Army Air Corp, all forming a perfect cross in the morning sky, it passed, slow motion like over the Phoenix Park, as it made its final approach to Dublin Airport. The excitement of the crowd soared. Thousands of flags were raised over the heads of a million people, and the air was filled with cheers of welcome. A day of history was truly in the making.

At 10.30am. Fr. Peter Lemass announced that almost One Million entry stickers had been distributed at the Park gates, and still from all corners of the country and beyond, the people kept coming. By now even from where we were sitting high above the level of the crowd, the view as far as we could see, was just a solid mass of humanity.

Shortly after midday the Pope's red helicopter touched down behind the altar area. Eventually, as he came into full view of the assembled masses, resplendent in gold vestments and mitre, following the procession of Bishops he addressed the multitude in Gaelic, the roar of the crowd was deafening. As our entrance hymn came to a close the Holy Father started the celebration of the Mass again his first words in Gaelic. The homily as I remember it was long but with the Pope's obvious sincerity and confident delivery, the attention of all was only broken by their frequent and enthusiastic applause. While the Pope gave Holy Communion to over two hundred people representing all the Dioceses in Ireland, hundreds of priests delivered Communion to the congregation of the thousands in the park.

When the Holy Father emerged after Mass to take his place in the "Pope Mobile" he was by then over an hour behind schedule. As his car moved up and down the aisles through the crowd the love and emotion of all was almost tangible. As one newspaper put it next morning – "All our excitement, our joy, the deep feeling of honour that the Holy Father had come to visit us was translated into the cheers, waves and smiles of our delighted welcome."

5

Politics - A Lifelong Involvement

THE WIDOWED, THE ORPHANED AND THE AGED

Politics has always been at the top of the Agenda in the Kavanagh family, from as far back as I can remember and for many years before. Jim Everett was first elected to Dail Eireann in 1922 and was returned at every General Election up to his death in December 1967. His entry into public life came about through his work in the Trade Union and Labour movement, which he was responsible for organising in much of County Wicklow. On the death of Jim Everett my brother Liam the then secretary of the Irish Transport and General Workers Union in Wicklow won the nomination as the Labour Party candidate in the ensuing by-election. Although he did not win the seat on that occasion, he more than held the labour vote, ensuring his nomination for the next General Election, which was to follow in 1969. Liam won a seat for the Labour Party in the 1969 General Election, which he held for thirty years.

The special responsibility for the Kavanagh family that Jim Everett and his wife espoused on the death of our father left all of us as we grew up very closely involved on a daily basis with them both, our lives and their world of public life and politics became inextricably linked. All of us from an early age became naturally and as a matter of course involved in political campaigning.

My memories from the time - I was maybe five years old and just about able to fold an Election Address, which was the party literature of the day and distributed by post to all voters in the constituency in the run-up to a general election. Paddy, Liam, Frank and myself were involved while the older members of the family including Michael before he set off to college in the USA were writing the names and addresses of voters on the same literature. As time moved on we also graduated to writing the literature and then when we were old enough to go on the hustings, canvassing for votes in Wicklow Town and throughout the entire County Wicklow. That has been the accepted lot of those of us who continued to live our lives in the Wicklow Constituency or close by up to almost the present time.

Jim Everett was born on St. Patrick's Road in Wicklow town, just opposite the De La Salle National School. After a few short years in school, which was the lot of the working classes in those days, he started work as a junior porter in the Hibernian Bank. From the time he left school, at not much more than a boy; he was possessed of a determination and a tenacity, unusual in one so young, to fight on behalf of the lowly paid, the widowed the orphaned, and the aged.

To quote from "An Appreciation" written after his death by the President of the Irish Transport & General Workers Union - Mr. John Conroy

> *"The late Deputy James Everett TD in his youth was a man– Independent of mind, outstanding in courage, moral and physical, he lived with and was fully aware of the poverty and injustice suffered by working men and women. He saw them in the foulest of winter weather with little protective clothing, tramping a mile sometimes two or three miles, to work at 5/5.30am. in order to*

clock-in at 6am. He knew they worked 60/70 hours a week for wages that little more than paid the rent and provided a poor quality of food and clothing for themselves and their dependents."

In 1917 together with the help of a few friends Jim Everett founded The County Wicklow General Labourers' Association. With his bicycle, and armed with only his dedication, his courage and a gift for oratory; in the market place, at the cross roads and at the church gate he organised thousands of Wicklow men on their first steps to freedom and a modicum of justice.

Strikes and lockouts were many and bitter in those early days. Condemnation from the Council Chamber, the Press, and the Pulpit for daring to organise the working men and to insist that they had rights as human beings, together with continuous harassing, arrest, and personal abuse became part of his daily life. However, the Union he had founded grew in strength, its success spread from town to town and from village to village throughout the county. During 1917 and 1918 he became so well known as a leader of men and accepted as a determined fighter for just causes that he was co-opted on to some public bodies. Later when elections were held he was elected to both the County Council and the Urban District Council at the head of the pole.

During the period of the 1916 Rising, and following the campaign against conscription in 1917 there was a great upsurge amongst citizens everywhere demanding freedom from British rule, Jim Everett, with others was prominent in the leadership of this movement and in the fight for independence.

Early in 1919 agreement was reached with the Wicklow Union and the General Workers Union operating in County Wexford and Jim Everett and Dick King of north Wexford launched the Irish Agricultural and General Workers Union. The new organisation went on to establish a Charter of Wages and Conditions of Employment, not alone for industrial and service workers in County Wicklow and north Wexford but also sought and enforced agreements on wages, and hours of work for agricultural workers throughout the whole area. In 1920 he negotiated a transfer of members of the National Agricultural and General Workers Union to the Irish Transport and General Workers Union, and became that Union's first Branch Secretary in Wicklow.

During the Black and Tan war Jim Everett was appointed Treasurer of Wicklow Co. Council funds, which the Council, in ready response to Dail Eireann had decided to withhold from the British Government. He also acted as Paymaster for County Wicklow for the same period. Following the signing of the Treaty, when the accounts were examined for that period by the auditor, it was found that every penny collected in rates had been accounted for and that the County Council had also received the benefit of interest earned on monies left on deposit.

Following the signing of the Treaty with Great Britain, election to the Third Dail; which was the First Dail of the Irish Free State was called for 16th June 1922. Jim Everett was selected as the first Labour Party candidate for Co. Wicklow. He was duly elected and took his seat at the inaugural meeting of the Irish Free State Government on 9th September 1922; he was the youngest member of the house.

After the signing of the Treaty, Eamon de Valera and the Fianna Fail Party walked out of the Dail refusing to take the Oath of Allegiance to the Crown. For the next five years the small labour party group of members formed the main opposition in Dail Eireann and played a vital role in the establishment of many of the State's institutions still firmly standing today.

Five years later, Jim Everett took a leading part in the efforts to open the way for the Fianna Fail party to take their seats in the Dail (Irish Parliament). On the invitation of Eamon Donnelly, he and Thomas Johnston then leader of the Labour Party held conferences with Mr. de Valera, Mr. McEntee and others. As a result he was one of those who proposed a motion for the abolition of the controversial oath of allegiance to the Crown, so as to reopen the way into the Dail of the Fianna Fail Party. Jim Everett was the first deputy to advocate for the Social Services and to press strongly for independent support for orphans who were living with only the aid of home assistance up to that time.

His special interest in housing for rural and urban workers prompted him to organise a scheme based on direct labour which resulted in more rural cottages being built in his county of Wicklow, in relation to population than in any county in Ireland. He was also instrumental at Council level for the introduction of the Scholarship Scheme which supported numerous children of workers, tradesmen and small farmers to advance to second and third level education.

On the defeat of the Fianna Fail Government and the coming to power of the first Inter-party Government 1948/51, Jim Everett was appointed Minister for Posts and Telegraphs and later served as Minister for Justice in the second Inter-party Government of 1954/57. In his final years as a member of the Dail he recalled with pride the fact that he was the only living member who was present when "The Soldier's Song" was declared the National Anthem in Dail Ereann. A daily reminder even today, can be heard on Radio and Television with the ringing of the "Angelus" bell on RTE each day at noon and evening at 6.pm. which he instituted during his time as Minister for Posts and Telegraphs.

Named "Father of the Dail" as the longest serving Deputy; he contested fifteen general elections and succeeded in all fifteen. On his death on 19th December 1967 he held the unique record of forty-five years service to Dail Eireann and fifty years in public life.

To quote again his friend and colleague Mr. Conroy,

> "Jim Everett is dead, he died as he would have liked, and as he would have wished, serving the working men and women of County Wicklow; may his spirit ever remain to guide the stalwarts of labour in his native town and County"

It would be wrong not to acknowledge the steadfast and unconditional support down through the years that Jim Everett could always count upon from his wife Ellen or Nellie as she was known. I remember my mother telling us about the Black and Tan era when her sister Nellie, as they would have said in those times, was "keeping company" with Jim Everett, on many occasions she delivered documents and dispatches on his behalf when the danger of Jim being apprehended carrying such sensitive material became too great. In the little house where my mother's family lived on Quarantine Hill, Nellie, used to hide the documents wrapped in waterproof material in the gutters over the bedroom window without her parents knowledge; the danger of the house being raided and searched was always present.

Later in more ordered times when he was a member of Dail Eireann, her support was total and unequivocal, their home was always an open house to all who needed his help, to Councillors and key labour men from all parts of County Wicklow who brought him the problems of the people in their particular part of the constituency. All Sunday long these comings and goings continued, well into the evening. These men were Jim Everett's men, fiercely loyal and supportive, in many cases men he worked with and depended on in his Trade Union days, who knew and lived and were of the working class and they were always welcome and well cared for in "St. Patrick's," Jim and Nellie's home on Dunbur Road.

THE UNCERTAINTIES OF PUBLIC LIFE

After leaving school in the local De La Salle College Liam worked in accountancy for two years while taking a Bachelor of Commerce degree in the evenings at UCD. Both Paddy and Liam took a keen interest in Labour Party politics in the County. When the election was called in 1957 they jointly ran the campaign for Jim Everett, who was recovering from illness at the time; writing speeches, organising the canvas throughout the county, looking after the erection of posters and generally managing all aspects of the campaign.

Up to the early 50's, General Election campaigns were for the most part organised through a series of public meetings held each Sunday morning after Mass for several weeks prior to polling day. These meetings were organised outside almost every Parish Church in every constituency in the country; where the Candidates would address the electorate and elaborate on party policy. The "House to House" canvass, now the universal approach by all parties to electioneering was first introduced to Irish political campaigning in County Wicklow by Liam and Paddy back in the early 1950's.

During 1957 Liam was appointed Rate Collector for Wicklow Town, and in addition, took on the part-time position of ITGWU Branch Secretary for Wicklow. He successfully took on the major task of unionising almost every business premises while ensuring rights for employees of new industries such as Veha and Celmac and many more. As he remembers "there was certainly resistance from both sides because some long term workers had a great sense of loyalty to their employers and felt they might be betraying them." However, while membership of the Union increased dramatically, the fact that there was never a strike in his time as Branch Secretary reflects highly on his style of management of union affairs in Wicklow.

On the death of Jim Everett in the 1967, Liam contested the resulting by-election, which it was true to say was frowned upon by party chiefs. The reasons were twofold firstly they felt that the chances of winning would be greatly increased if the party ran a "national figure", and secondly it was not considered party policy that a relative of a deceased member should contest a By-election. The fact that it would have been virtually impossible for the labour party to win that by-election against the combined votes in the case of either of the larger parties, chasing a single seat, seemed to have gone completely over the heads of the moguls of the Labour Party. The figures simply could not add up to a win for labour. Although he was unsuccessful in the by-election, Liam more than succeeded in what he set out to do, which was to hold the labour party vote in the County Wicklow, ensuring his nomination in the following General Election that took place in 1969. He was elected to Dail Eireann in the General Election of '69 on the fifth count with 6444 votes, despite the presence of a strong running mate. His first year in the Dail coincided with stormy times in Irish Politics, the Arms Trial, the Northern Ireland troubles, which were sparked off almost to the day he was elected.

Ireland's entry into the EEC was another landmark, more so in Liam's career than many other deputies and was later to become one of the highlights of his political life. In March '73 he was appointed a member of the European Parliament while at the same time continuing to serve in the Dail, all culminating in an extremely heavy workload and hectic lifestyle. Possibly the most memorable event of his career came in June 1979 when Liam contested the European Elections for the constituency of Leinster and was elected with a massive 40,172 first preference votes, much to the surprise of many people including some members in his own party. He had in the same week headed the pole in both the County and Urban elections in Wicklow.

The main article on the front page of "The Wicklow People", in bold reverse print, the following weekend was headed; "The Magnificent Liam Kavanagh" the article goes on to say,

> *"We may be wrong but we don't think that there is another person in Ireland to Equal Liam's record – Member of the European Parliament, Dail Eireann, Wicklow County Council, Wicklow Urban Council, Wicklow Harbour Commissioners, Wicklow Vocational Educational Committee – just to mention The important ones."*

Two years later party leader Michael O'Leary left Liam in a dilemma by offering him a Ministerial portfolio, which would necessitate his resignation from the European Parliament. Like his predecessor Liam always had the total support of his wife Margaret, who said on that occasion.

"Whatever decision Liam makes is fine with me."

It was a major step to take, but a Ministry would always be an ambition of any politician.

"I couldn't turn it down." Liam said.

Following that June '81 election Liam became The Minister for Labour under Taoiseach Garret Fitzgerald.

In December 1986 the sudden death of my brother Paddy was a devastating blow to his wife Mary and his children Aoibeann, Everett and Michael, and needless to say a great shock to the whole family. From a political standpoint with his deep involvement in politics, Paddy's death was a huge loss to Liam in his political life, as of course it was in his private life. They were both very close and spent a lot of time together apart from their mutual interest in politics. In his own right Paddy's loss to the Labour Party in Co. Wicklow was widely acknowledged, being at that time an elected member of both the Urban and County Councils. Again, the heading of the following weeks "Wicklow People", on this occasion in sadder circumstances read –

"Wicklow has lost an honourable man . . . a man of integrity, a man of courage, and a man who put people first"

Summing up the great many sentiments expressed by members and officials of both councils and other public bodies of which Paddy was a member.

From June 1981 to Nov.1982 there were three General Elections called in quick succession. Fianna Fail won the Feb. '82 Election, under the leadership of Charles J. Haughey which briefly held office until its defeat in Nov.'82 when Garret Fitzgerald again became Taoiseach until 1987.

During the period of Garret Fitzgerald leadership in Government Liam held Ministerial portfolios at the Departments of Labour and The Public Service, Environment, Tourism Forestry and Fisheries where he was instrumental in establishing the independent body "Coillte." If the most memorable moment in Liam's career was his election to the European Economic Community now known as the European Union, the pinnacle of his time in National Politics, with his knowledge and many years experience in local government, has to have been his period as Minister for the Environment. His proud record in providing local authority housing still stands today.

Liam continued to serve as a Member of Dail Eireann until the June 1997 General Election when a cluster of circumstances combined, which resulted in his narrow defeat and the loss of his seat. He continued his involvement in politics as a member of Wicklow Town Council and Wicklow County Council until the June 2004

Local Election when he made the decision to retire. These days Liam has a little more time to spend with Margaret and to indulge their lifelong passion for the game of Golf.

Following Liam's announcement that he would not be seeking re-election in the June 2004 locals, the east area council of the Wicklow Labour Party turned to his son Conal to accept the nomination in his father's place. At the count following polling day Conal headed the pole in the Wicklow Town election and was elected on the first count; while at the count for Wicklow County Council he was elected to the third seat in the Wicklow East Constituency. Conal's election marks the family's involvement in public life stretching back almost ninety years and now entering its third generation. It is not an easy life that he and his wife Kiara are embarking upon, but having grown up in a political household Conal understands that more than most. Wherever it leads them I wish them well on their journey into the uncertainties of public life.

6

A Whole new Life

"CUT YOUR TEETH ON THAT"

One October afternoon in 1980 we had just completed an Inspector's quarterly exercise with the lifeboat and crew, the inspector at that time was Lieutenant Comdr. Tony Course. Tony was a personable chap and he and I had a good friendly relationship on his visits to review the lifeboat station. While he was writing his remarks on the exercise in the station logbook, I invited him home for a cup of tea, as I usually did, before making his journey back to Dublin. Tony thanked me but said he was rushing back to a party for one of the staff, an Area Organiser who was leaving his position with the institution. More in jest, than as a serious remark, I said to Tony,

"I would be interested in that position."

Tony immediately said that I should apply and that he would have a word with Lieut. Col. Brian Clark, the National Organiser for Ireland. I had dealt with Brian Clark on many occasions in our lifeboat fund-raising endeavours; we knew each other well, he being in charge of RNLI fund-raising in Ireland. I did as Tony suggested and forwarded a letter of application. Tony obviously did have a word with Col. Clark, some days later I had a phone call from him inviting me to come and have a chat with him about the vacant position. We arranged to meet the following week and talked for some time about the responsibilities of the position, which he explained was in fact that of Deputy National Organiser. On my return home that evening I was delighted to tell May that I had been offered the job. My particular responsibility would be the building of new branches and the strengthening of the branch network throughout the twenty-six counties of the Rep. of Ireland.

I handed in my letter of resignation to my Staff Officer in Wicklow Co. Council and took up my new position of Deputy National Organiser with "RNLI Ireland" on 1st January 1981; and with it began for me a whole new life, and to a somewhat lesser degree also for May.

With the appointment to the staff of the RNLI, I regretfully had to resign from my position as Honorary Secretary of Wicklow lifeboat station. This was the most painful aspect of my acceptance of the position. For twelve years I'd had a wonderful working relationship with the crew of Wicklow lifeboat. I knew I would miss that contact and also the involvement with the cut and trust of service situations of the RNLB "J. W. Archer".

I was bowled over some weeks later when the committee and crew of the Station invited me to a wonderful party in Wicklow Sailing Club, to mark my departure from the branch at Wicklow. All the lifeboat committee were there and I was particularly delighted to see so many of the crewmembers there also. My old boss Seamus Hayes, Wicklow's Co. Manager, and of course my new boss, Brian Clark, had also come along together with many other good friends. I was overwhelmed when the Chairman, Mr. J.T. O'Byrne on behalf of the Committee, the Crew and the Ladies Guild presented me with a magnificent 'Stanley Pettigrew' painting of Wicklow Lifeboat being launched down the slipway. It is a cherished possession, which hangs proudly in my living room.

The early weeks of 1981 were in some ways pretty uneventful, and yet the learning curve was steep. I would drive to Dublin, arriving at our office in Clare Street at 9.30am. and spend my days studying the branch files. It was not easy, but extremely interesting, trying to get my head around the membership of almost one hundred branches from every part of the twenty-six counties, and all their fundraising activities. The Dublin branch alone led by the very hardworking, if often somewhat intractable, Mrs Penelope Montague Kavanagh, was huge and had its own full-time secretary.

It was fascinating to me as I studied the files, with my background as a volunteer fundraiser in Wicklow, reading about the fundraising activities of all the other branches throughout Ireland. It almost felt in the beginning as if I was spying on their efforts, seeking new possibilities. As the days passed I began to feel more a part of the larger 'national structure' of RNLI fundraising. A gradual change of focus was taking place; from seeing things from a single branch point of view, to looking at the fundraising possibilities from the more managerial and advisory role of a broader countrywide perspective. My knowledge of the operational side of the Institution was of immense help to me, especially during those early years. Working so closely with the operational side of the Institution over so many years, added I believe an important dimension, to the various talks and meetings, through the branch network during those years. I remember at about that time Col. Clark receiving a request for an article on the Lifeboat Institution from one of the monthly yachting magazines. He dropped the letter on my desk and said to me,

"There you are cut your teeth on that"

I chose for the article to write a piece entitled 'A day in the life of a Lifeboat Station Hon. Secretary', which of course was well within the scope my experience. It seemed to work out fine, Col. Clark didn't comment, which as one got to know him better, was acknowledgement of his approval in itself.

The staff members at RNLI Ireland were a very friendly and

helpful bunch of people, it was a pleasure to arrive at Clare Street each morning. Born in London of Northern Ireland parents, Lt. Colonel Brian Clark, National Organiser for the RNLI in Ireland was a larger than life character. If one could imagine the quintessential ex-British Army Officer, every fibre of his being shouted British Army, from his bowler hat, worn on special occasions, to his always immaculately polished shoes, that was Brian Clark. He was immensely proud of his military background having served with distinction in many of the great battles of WW2 with the Royal Irish Fusiliers, including that of "Monte Casino." He also had a genuine respect for the many ex-Irish Army Officers whom he numbered amongst his close friends. I remember on one occasion making reference to the Irish Army; "The Army" he very quickly berated me saying, in the Republic of Ireland there is only one army "The Army". He was not always the easiest person to work with; the more timorous members of the staff could, and were on occasions intimidated by his loud and often tetchy manner. Yet behind the brash exterior I'm sure all of us, more than once experienced the kinder man that was as a rule kept well hidden on the regular day to day activities of office routine.

To recount one incident, which gives some insight into the ostentatious if somewhat quirky character that was Brian Clark. It happened some months after I joined the staff as his deputy; and I'm sure it was a rather painful and worrying experience for him, but it certainly had its farcical side.

Brian, after exhaustive instructions to me had gone on a safari holiday to Africa, meeting up with some old ex-army buddies there. Early one morning just a few days after his departure I was going over some detail or other with John O'Callaghan, a member of staff, when John said to me,

"That's Col. Clark's voice," which appeared to be coming from the general office.

"It couldn't be, he's in darkest Africa," I said.

We both went out to the general office. Sure enough there was

Brian more or less slumped over the counter in what appeared to be some pain and discomfort. With his usual economy of words, when he wanted action, all he said was,

"Take me to a hospital."

I immediately got him into the car without delay and with the minimum of dialogue; I asked him if he had any preferences as to which hospital I should take him.

"Monkstown" was his only reply.

On the way to the hospital I asked him what happened to him. I was aware that Brian had suffered with gall-bladder problems from time to time.

"My gall-bladder started to play up on the aeroplane and by the time we landed in Africa I was in serious pain. My friends collected me and got me into bed, they wanted to get a doctor but I told them,

"I don't want any F...ing witch doctor messing around with me, get me on a flight back home." although I felt sorry to see him in such discomfort I found it difficult to hold back the urge to laugh.

When we arrived at Monkstown hospital he was immediately taken to a private ward. One of the nurses asked me what was wrong with him; I told her what I knew which really wasn't much. After a few minutes I was told I could go up to the ward. Just a moment or two after I entered the ward, a nurse arrived complete with clipboard and pro-forma and started to ask Brian the usual, and somewhat personal questions one is asked on admission to hospital, while I pretended to be totally engrossed in matters that were 'not happening' outside the window. As she proceeded through the questionnaire with Brian supplying as little information as possible, the nurse asked,

"What is your age Col. Clark?" He replied,

"If I live to October (or whatever month he named) which appears to be in some doubt at the moment I will be sixty one" he replied. The questions went on and the answers came back in much the same vein until the unfortunate nurse finally either completed the form or gave up in despair. When she left Brian said to me,

"Are you still here, shouldn't you be getting back to work," I replied,

"I was waiting to see if you wanted anything or if you wished me to take your luggage home this evening on my way through, or in fact if you have made contact yet with Brenda?"

"Oh no! I suppose you better do that."

Now Brenda, Brian's wife, was a lovely lady who was possibly the top fundraiser in Ireland for the Lifeboats and always most welcoming when I or any member of the staff called to their home. Brenda kept a permanent Lifeboat Souvenir shop set up in her garage and never missed an opportunity to sell to anybody who called to the house staff included. When I phoned to tell her about Brian; she of course knew what the problem was.

"That is his confounded gall-bladder," she said,

"It would appear so Brenda" I replied.

"He will just have to go and have something done about it; Jimmy I will not be able to go to the hospital before this evening I have a lot on today" Brenda said.

Brenda of course did go to the hospital that morning. Brian eventually had his gall-bladder problems attended too in Jervis Street hospital later that year; however, believe me that was another story.

The girls were all very pleasant and helpful to me in those early days and couldn't do enough to help me settle into this new situation. Joan was our very hard working office manageress, who rarely left her desk even during lunchtime. Norma held the important position of managing all the branch accounts while Margaret held the often difficult role of fulltime secretary to the Dublin Branch, all friendly helpful people. Then there was Mary, who at that time I was to learn was the receptionist and junior staff member, on first acquaintance a reserved young lady whose place in the scheme of things was difficult to make out. Each morning she would arrive at the office at the regular time, only to take off again, and would reappear approaching 5pm. each evening, extraordinary I thought. Mary was to eventually achieve the most senior RNLI fund-raising staff position in Ireland, that of National Organiser, which after we worked together for fifteen years was no surprise to me. It was only after some several days later I realised that just before I joined the staff, the lifeboat office had been moved from 10 Merrion Sq. to just up the road a piece to a new location at 3 Clare Street. However, the lifeboat's regular telephone numbers had not as yet been transferred. Each morning Mary would proceed to the old office to take the incoming telephones calls returning late in the afternoon. There were two other male members of staff John O'Callaghan a recently appointed area organiser who had just graduated from Trinity College. John and myself became good friends almost immediately. Paul the other male member of the group, a quiet and gentle young lad who looked after the post and all the other necessary jobs that had to be done around the office. Finally there was Alice.

When I joined the staff Alice was at that time an elderly lady, a diminutive Dublin woman with the wit and candour that can only be found in the true "Dubliner." She had been with the RNLI for many years and was loved and appreciated by all the staff from Brian Clark down. She lived for coming to the office very early each day, completing her work and as the girls arrived, having "the chat" with them for a few minutes before leaving for home. Her job was to keep the offices clean and tidy. Alice was a most interesting, and in her younger days a well travelled lady, who had visited many countries around the world. She would often regale us in her amusing way with stories of exotic places she had visited on her travels.

Some years later when Alice was still working with the RNLI, we were having one of our regular visitors from head office, on this occasion it was the Chief of Personnel, David Wilford. We had discussed individually as usual the members of the staff, which was routine and without any problems; that was until he came to Alice. When he asked me her age and I told him she was possibly in her mid to late seventies, he nearly as they say, 'threw a wobbler'.

"Jimmy," he said, "we have a real problem here, do you realise, at that age this lady is not insurable, if she had an accident we would be in serious trouble; I'm afraid you will have to let Alice go," he continued.

I hated having to tell her and I suppose wrongly put off the decision for some weeks. The strangest thing happened; it was as if Alice had sensed the difficulty that had to be faced. One morning she waited for me to come in, having completed her work, she informed me that she wanted to retire. We all gave Alice a great party, which we held in our home in Wicklow, we invited Brian and Brenda Clark; Brian had by then retired. Soon after leaving the RNLI Alice went to live with relatives in the Dalkey area. She didn't enjoy her retirement for very long, and apparently died shortly after the move, we only heard of her death after the funeral was over, which saddened all of us very much, especially the girls.

After her departure from the office we employed contract cleaners who were very efficient, but somehow the place was not quite the same without Alice.

GLADYS WHITE – REMEMBERED.

Gladys Florence White was in the ninety-fifth year of her life when she passed away, and the members of her family and many friends gathered at St. Philip's Church Milltown, Dublin to pay their final respects. Her beloved husband Laurence Arthur, affectionately known as "Nips" had predeceased her some years earlier. Mrs White whose voluntary fundraising service to the Irish Lifeboats spanned over seventy years, which I am certain, must stand as a record throughout these islands – most certainly in Ireland. When as a very young girl her ship was torpedoed during the First World War and she almost lost her life; she made a commitment to the cause of saving life at sea, which lasted to the end of her long and active life.

Prominent in every aspect of fundraising in Dublin City, Gladys White, was a founder voluntary organiser of the hugely successful Dublin Lifeboat Shop in Rathmines. She was to the fore with the monster Spring Sale, and the citywide Annual Lifeboat Flag-Days, also a District Organiser of Dublin House-to-House collection. A very astute lady who would always ask the most discerning questions regarding lifeboat matters and you had better have the right answers or be prepared to say I don't know; she could spot prevarication a mile away.

The first time I met this very remarkable lady was shortly after I joined the RNLI staff as Deputy National Organiser. The occasion was the Annual Presentation of Awards in 1981 at the Tara Towers Hotel, at that time Mrs. White was the holder of the Gold Badge for outstanding service to the Institution. Important as it was to those dedicated volunteers who were receiving awards for their fundraising efforts; my abiding memory of that occasion strangely was not of the formal part of the afternoon but rather of the departure of the many awardees and guests on its conclusion, in particular that of Mr and Mrs White.

Anyone who knows the Tara Towers Hotel will be aware that it faces onto one of the busiest roads in south County Dublin. As I stood at the window I remember Mr and Mrs White in their little Morris Minor drive straight out from the hotel car park, without slowing down, onto Merrion Road; picture the scene, at the height of Dublin rush hour traffic. I closed my eyes and waited for the crash, which thankfully didn't happen. God was certainly looking after them on that occasion.

Mrs White travelled all over the city on her little motorbike; her familiar appearance could be seen everywhere, and is still very vividly imprinted on my memory as she arrived at our office. Always wearing her black crash helmet as she chained the Honda 50 to the railings outside my office window in Clare Street. By then she was in her mid-eighties. She finally gave up her fundraising work when she was in her ninety-first year but never lost her interest in the RNLI; two years later she made a very generous donation towards the new Inshore Lifeboat to be stationed in Dunlaoghaire. Everyone was delighted when she was well enough to attend the Naming Ceremony as a Guest of Honour. The end came on 3rd April 1998.

Mrs White was an extraordinary lady who gave generously over her long life of that which is most precious, her time - a lifetime.

I was deeply honoured and extremely pleased when her son Dick and daughter-in-law Aileen asked me to address the congregation at the Service of Thanksgiving.

While the RNLI continues to attract fundraisers of the calibre of Gladys White the Lifeboat Institution will continue to have good and safe hands at its "fundraising helm".

TWO REMARKABLE LADIES

Going back to those early days with the institution Brian had said to me,

"Don't you think it's time you made yourself known to some of the branches around the country"

"I'm ready to go any time, have you any suggestions where I should make a start," I replied.

"I think you should visit the Co. Cork/Co. Kerry branches, it's quite some time since I visited that neck of the woods."

"That's fine with me," I said.

" Now when you call to Crosshaven I want you to look for a replacement for Marjorie Fitzmaurice, speak to her about it. She was a wonderful fundraiser but she is very old and almost blind," the branch needs a younger and more active Hon. Secretary" he said.

That first trip was the beginning of my visits to every branch in the twenty-six counties, and the making of many new and valued friendships all over Ireland. One of the earliest visits on that trip was to Monkstown Co. Cork to the home of Mrs. Mary Dwyer. Mary was a member of the well known Crosby family of the then "Cork Examiner," now the "Irish Examiner," a wonderful lady, always in good humour, who never appeared to take life, or indeed herself too seriously. A visit with Mary in her home in Monkstown was always as good as a tonic, no matter how difficult the day was proving to be, you could always feel your spirits rise as soon as you crossed Mary's threshold; one of those few special places where you felt immediately welcome and at home when you called. She was in her own very relaxed way one of the most effective fundraisers in Ireland. The events Mary and her committee organised were always quality events and highly successful. She was long widowed when I met her; and was mother to a very close family of boys. I don't believe in my life I have met a parent who had such a close rapport with her children and especially her daughters-in-law. To be in the company of Mary Dwyer, together with the members of her family was to observe a group of people where a generation gap simply did not exist. We were to work very closely on many events, with many happy memories, over the following almost fifteen years.

So on I went to Crosshaven, with Brian Clark's words still ringing in my ears. Crosshaven is a lovely seaside town close to the entrance to the wonderful haven that is Cork harbour, and home of the "Royal Cork Yacht Club" the oldest yacht club in the world. Marjorie Fitzmaurice lived alone in a small corrugated iron cottage on the approaches to the town, originally the family holiday home when she was a girl living with her parents. The family would return to Crosshaven religiously each year for the summer holidays where they would spend the long summer days fishing and sailing in the idyllic waters of Cork harbour.

Marjorie eventually answered my knock on the door, attesting to the poor condition of her sight, she was using a white walking stick. A very tall imperious looking lady, I would say approaching her eightieth year if not more, while still carrying the aristocratic bearing that must have been strikingly apparent in her younger days. Her grey hair was severely swept back into a bun, adding an austerity to her features belied by the flamboyant and gregarious nature of her greeting. As I entered the hall and slowly followed Marjorie as she made her way to the living room, I was immediately conscious of the many now fading photographs and memorabilia of her father's and her late husband's military days both as officers with the British Army; from the photographs, much of her fathers service career was spent overseas. As I entered the sitting room I could see many lifeboat flag-day boxes on the floor on either side of a chair obviously where Marjorie was sitting.

"As you can see, you caught me preparing for my Flag Day!" Marjorie said.

She went on, enthusiastically explaining to me about the flag day arrangements and the number of people she would have collecting and where the best collecting stations in both Crosshaven and Carrigaline were for placing her collectors and so on. While all the time I was thinking about Brian's remarks, and waiting for an opening to broach the difficult matter I had been instructed to address. It was clear from her movement that her sight was very poor; but it was also clear from her whole attitude, her enthusiasm for life, and her love for the RNLI, that this lady was far from ready to relinquish her lifeboat responsibilities in the immediate future. I also thought that it would be churlish and unfair at this point to take away the social contact that her position as Hon. Secretary of the branch afforded her. It was also clear to me that the RNLI would not suffer from Marjorie's continued involvement. I decided not to raise the matter of her retirement.

Marjorie remained on as an efficient and successful Hon. Secretary for another few years, and true to her class and forthright style, made her own decision when to hand over, and indeed who her successor should be; as she herself put it, "to a younger lady who would do the job far better than I could."

In fairness to Brian he did not disagree with the manner in which the situation had been handled. Marjorie was a compelling and fascinating lady; I enjoyed many interesting visits to her little home at the approaches to Crosshaven even after she retired from her voluntary duties with the RNLI.

On one occasion when visiting Marjorie she gave me a cutting of a white Azalea from her garden, which she assured me would grow. It has grown well in our little back garden, during the blooming season in April I often say 'Hallo Marjorie you are looking well today', I know she can't see me, but who knows? Maybe now she can, but I know she would surely get a kick if she can hear me!

THE WEEKLY PRAYER MEETING

As time went on in that first year I travelled all over Ireland visiting every fundraising and station branch. It was particularly interesting for me from the point of view of my previous experience to call to the different lifeboat stations and meet the Hon. Secretaries and some of the crewmembers. I had by now settled in well and was really enjoying the job.

One day I was working in the office, Brian was also working on the copy for 'Irish Lifeboats' a magazine, in which he took great pride and which he edited and published annually. Brian without raising his head from his work suddenly announced! "This is probably the last "Irish Lifeboats" magazine I will edit; I will be retiring soon, well not for about a year or so but I believe whoever takes over should be in place within the next few months so that he or she can get the feel of the job before I finish."

"I have informed Head office that I will be advertising the position in the 'Irish Times' next week, I thought you should know." I didn't know what to say I hadn't thought about Brian retiring although I suppose I should have, everything seemed to be moving along at such a pace. I finally managed to say, if somewhat feebly, although the sentiments were honest.

"I am sorry to hear that Brian, it will be strange to have a new person sitting at your desk."

"You are going to apply for the job I take it," he said in a rather forceful tone.

"I don't think so Brian, after all, I'm only in the job of Deputy National Organiser a few months, and really still only settling in.

"Nonsense, he almost shouted, of course you will apply for the job after all if somebody else gets this job and after six months you are sitting there saying - I could have done this job far better than he or she is doing it, you will be sorry, but it will be too late then," he said.

After some thought I said,

"OK Brian if you think I should, then I will." As with every job I ever applied for I set about preparing myself well for the interview.

Some weeks later the advertisement appeared in the press and my application was duly forwarded to the highly respected firm of management consultants Deloitte, Haskins and Sells who had been appointed to short list the applications. I received a call to attend for interview at "The Royal St. George Yacht Club" Dun Laoghaire of all places, the venue chosen by a Mr. Reeve who would be conducting the interview. I arrived at 5pm. on the appointed day; Mr Reeve was a very friendly gentleman who obviously believed in conducting such matters in a very informal manner, and in congenial surroundings over a drink. Never the less I was aware that this gentleman was a skilled practitioner, and was in his relaxed style, obviously gleaning the information he required. We finally shook hands and Mr. Reeve told me he would be in touch with me. Again some weeks later I received a letter inviting me to attend a second interview, on this occasion at the Dublin offices of Beamish and Crawford the Cork based brewery of which Mr. Clayton Love jnr. was Chairman, and of course he was also a member of the RNLI Committee of Management.

This occasion was a much more formal affair; the board room of Beamish and Crawford offices was a round room with no windows and simply consisted of a very large round table which I would say would normally seat probably fifteen people. Around one segment of the table sat five gentlemen namely, The Lord Killanin, Chairman of the Irish members of the RNLI's Committee of Management, Mr. Clayton Love jnr. also an Irish member of the C of M, Mr. John Leworthy Chairman of the Fundraising Committee of the RNLI, Admiral Wilfred Graham Director of the RNLI and finally Mr. Reeve of DH&S. One lone chair was placed opposite these gentlemen - to which I was directed. My first feeling as I sat down and looked across at the line up of eminent and prestigious people facing me was sheer panic, however, one thought gave me some confidence. I was aware that all these gentlemen except one were Lifeboat people. If the main thrust of the interview remained with matters concerning the RNLI I knew I had a wealth of information and felt I could do reasonably well; which was more or less the way the interview went. Finally at the end of the interview I thanked the Board and left the room. I was pleased with the mode of the interview; I felt I had done well which was very satisfying. Whoever would eventually be appointed to the position, I would be pleased and happy to work with, I had given it my best shot.

On the following Monday Brian summoned the staff to the usual weekly "prayer meeting" as he called it, which was in fact a weekly meeting to review the previous week's work and discuss the week ahead. He opened the meeting by saying "I'm pleased to tell you that Jimmy has been appointed National Organiser Designate RNLI Ireland."

Needless to say I was astounded. The rest of the staff appeared to be delighted and indeed there wasn't much concentration on the agenda for the rest of the meeting. I thanked Brian for his confidence in encouraging me to apply for the position and also the sentiment, which was factual, that he would be a hard act to follow. I thanked the staff for their good wishes and also expressed how important their help and support would be in the years ahead.

There were times particularly in the early weeks following my appointment, which in the peace and quietness of the night hours, the responsibility and the enormity of what I had taken on would suddenly strike me. I sincerely hoped and prayed that I would be up to the challenge.

7

✻

Lifeboat Years

THEY CAME LIKE SWALLOWS

The next several months were at times a little difficult for all the staff, not the least for Brian Clark himself. It appeared to me that the realisation of his impending retirement now fast approaching, was difficult for him to accept. The fact that on my appointment as National Organiser Designate I had already worked closely with Brian as his deputy for almost a year, and was by then pretty well up to speed on the organisation and management of the region. In these circumstances of an internal appointment as opposed to an appointment from outside the institution, the long run-in period with Brian still at the helm seemed somewhat unnecessary and at times proved difficult. While I appreciated his wise counsel and learned from it on the various ongoing events as they occurred, I was always very careful not to impinge on his authority, particularly concerning our relationship with staff. On occasion it became difficult for individual staff members particularly in the latter part of this period, not being quite sure whom to report too.

I accompanied Brian on what he called his valedictory trip around the country to express his thanks and say his farewells to the voluntary workers, while at the same time introducing me to those branch members I hadn't as yet met. Brian drove the car on those long journeys, and I enjoyed, or at times endured some of his heavier classical music tapes played at very high decibels, while Brian at the wheel conducted the London Philharmonic or some such orchestra. I would often mentally switch off and find myself, having studied the branch files in some detail and possibly spoken on the telephone, playing a mind game of trying to envisage in my minds eye the person that we were currently about to meet. Interestingly, sometimes that person was uncannily as I had imagined, while at other times, possibly more frequently, completely different. I remember when Brian introduced me to one rather forthright lady in the south of Ireland her retort was, looking from Brian to me,

"So I can forget your face, and remember yours," which I thought was rather brusque, although Brian didn't seem to mind at all.

On the same mission, on another occasion we were travelling in the northern part of the Republic, we arrived in Dunfanaghy, a particularly beautiful part of County Donegal having beforehand arranged an evening meeting with the members of the branch. We all met up in the local hotel, the branch secretary Mrs Sylvia Robinson a lovely and very friendly lady and her husband Val and one or two other members of the committee, Canon Thomas Doherty the local parish priest was Chairman of the branch. A man of great wit and a very accomplished pianist, in truth one of the funniest men I had ever met, had he not taken Holy Orders I'm sure he could well have made a good living on the stage. After a short and rather informal meeting, he played the piano and told stories late into the evening. An even more memorable occasion in Dunfanaghy took place I suppose about a year later, on what was probably my first visit to that part of Co. Donegal after having taken over as National Organiser.

May decided to accompany me on this particular trip; we arrived in Dunfanaghy late on Saturday afternoon, and checked into the hotel. I called on Sylvia the Hon. Secretary and took care of the branch business before dinner at the hotel. After dinner, we went for a walk and I decided to call and pay my respects to Canon Doherty, by then it was about 8 o'clock. We didn't leave the Parocial House that evening until after midnight, when we quietly made our way back down the now deserted street of Dunfanaghy, not knowing or possibly caring very much if we were locked out of the hotel, we'd had such a hilarious evening. Canon Doherty regaled us with one funny story after another, some told against himself, which didn't seem to bother him at all, until finally neither of us could laugh anymore.

He told us that for many years like myself he had been very interested in cine photography, but he had taken it a step further. As a method of raising funds for the parish when he was a curate in Donegal town he would hire films and hold a monthly film show in the parish hall. As a curtain raiser he would show some footage he had taken himself of local sports and other events that happened in the town, which proved extremely popular with the towns people and always guaranteed a full house. The admission price to the film show was four-pence.

There was one particular man in the town who ran a small garage single-handedly where Canon Doherty had his car serviced and who was a great fan of Barry Fitzgerald. As the Canon related the story -

"Any time I advertised a film with Barry Fitzgerald in the cast this man was the first to arrive making sure he sat in the front row of the hall, and if I played the same show for two nights he would be there both nights. What he wasn't aware of was that Fitzgerald and myself were old friends of long standing and he had indicated that he was coming to stay with me in Donegal for a few days. The morning after his arrival, Barry Fitzgerald and myself drove down to the garage and I parked outside, asking him to remain in the car. I went inside to my friend the garage man on the pretext of having a problem with the car and asked him to take it for a test drive; my friend went out and hopped into the driver's seat, when he turned and saw who was sitting beside him the poor man nearly had a heart attack. Needless to say Barry Fitzgerald played the scene to the full." Canon Doherty went on,

"On that first evening of Barry Fitzgerald's visit, after the long journey, he decided to have an early night. Before going to bed myself I looked in to see if he had everything he needed, he appeared to be asleep, before quietly closing the bedroom door, in a very low voice I sang toora-loora-loora mimicking the scene from the film "Going My Way" as I closed the door I just heard a gentle - Good Night."

Before leaving the house the canon brought us into a room where he kept his projection equipment and films. There were many large reels of 16mm cine taken over a long number of years, he said; rather than seeing them destroyed he had been in touch with RTE to see if they were interested in them.

"The TV station is sending someone to look at all the material," Canon Doherty said.

Some months possibly a year later RTE produced a most interesting hour-long programme taken from Canon Doherty's films, the programme was entitled "Filling the four penny seats."

The last time I called on Canon Doherty, of course by then he was an elderly man, he said to me.

"Have you time to come for a short drive with me" again on this occasion May was with me, I said,

"Yes we would be delighted" he drove along the Ards Forest Park until we came to a large group of ecclesiastical buildings. The Canon went into what appeared to be the main entrance of the building, after a few minutes he returned.

"Come on in and I'll show you the church" we went in to this magnificently peaceful Church and sat there for a few minutes. When we stood up to leave Canon Doherty said,

"This is the place where I will end my days." We returned to

Dunfanaghy without speaking very much; that was the last time I saw Canon Doherty. I often wondered if he did retire to that peaceful retreat, or even if he is still alive, I'm sure after all this time he can't be. I know one thing for certain, wherever he is in Heaven, he is making those around him laugh.

Thinking about Barry Fitzgerald brings to mind the Abbey Theatre. Although I've been to the new Abbey Theatre many times, I regret however that I was never in the original Abbey of Yeats, Synge and Lady Gregory. After the fire, which destroyed the original building in 1951 the Abbey Company took up residence for a short time in the Rupert Guinness Hall and later moved to the Queens Theatre in Pearse Street. My first visit to the Abbey was during the fifteen-year period when the company was in residence in the Queens. The new Abbey Theatre, which was erected on the original site was opened by President Eamon de Valera on 18th July 1966.

I had taken a few days leave, which May and I had arranged to spend in Galway with my sister Marjorie and her husband Henry (Broddie) in their home at Salthill. On this occasion I had a long promised venture in mind, which was not unrelated to the Abbey Theatre. Over the years I had taken particular interest and read a great deal about the birth of the Irish Literary Theatre. I had for a long time intended visiting Coole Park once the home of Lady Gregory and widely acknowledged as the cradle of the Irish Literary Revival. Also in the vicinity of Coole Park was Thoor Ballylee a 16th century de Burgo tower house owned and restored in the early 1920's by W.B. Yeats and used as his summer home.

A tablet in the wall commemorates this as follows-
    I the poet William Yeats
    With old mill boards and sea-green slates
    and smithy work from the Gort forge
    Restored this tower for my wife George;
    And may these characters remain
    When all is ruin once again.

The tower house was further restored in 1965 and is now one of the National Historic Monuments of Ireland and open to the public. So the four of us Marjorie, Broddie, May and myself headed east from Galway on a bright summers morning; at the village of Oranmore we turned south for Limerick, arriving at Thoor Ballylee just in time for lunch. We had a very pleasant lunch in the little cottage attached to the tower house and afterwards attended a short audiovisual film on the history of the tower and the Yeats connection. Not wishing to make the heavy climb to the roof we left Marjorie and Broddie browsing in the souvenir shop. May and I climbed the granite steps of the original spiral staircase linking the various rooms containing an interesting collection of first editions of the poets work. Some of the rooms as I remember had the original barrel vaulted ceilings. The view from the battlements for many miles across the countryside is really spectacular and rewards one for the heavy climb. I remember reading of Yeats relating his experience of hearing the noise of ancient warriors in what sounded like great numbers mounting the stone stairs during the night while he occupied one of the tower bedrooms.

We moved on down the main road towards Gort and within a few minutes arrived at the gateway to Coole Park. Driving up the wide avenue we passed under what can only be described as an imposing and ongoing gothic archway of ilex trees, the avenue then continued through thick woodlands. Having parked the car we continued on foot from the car park, we came to a lectern type stand mounted just off one side of the avenue, displaying a weather protected picture of the once great house. Sadly the view beyond the stand reveals all that is left of Coole Park. Not a stone of the original house remains; only the foundations having been built up somewhat filled and grassed over. In 1927 Lady Gregory in old age negotiated and agreed the sale of the house, the gardens and the 'Seven Woods' to the Ministry of Lands and Agriculture, with a home there for her lifetime; fully believing that the property would be saved and preserved for the benefit of future generations of Irish people.

To the deplorable shame of the Government of the time, on the death of Lady Gregory in 1932 Coole Park was left to lie idle for nine years and allowed to fall into an advanced state of disrepair. In 1941 it was eventually sold to a builder for the value of its stone. Oliver St. Gogarty wrote after the demolition of the house,

> "It makes one wonder what can be worth building in a land where there is no reverence for great times and great men"

Restoration thankfully was later carried out on the woods and the garden through the good offices of the Gort Archaeological Historical and Literary Society and the late Canon G. Quinn.

We walked around what was left of this once great house; which through her support and collaboration, its generous hostess was the inspiration for so many celebrated literary figures, W. B. Yeats, Douglas Hyde, J. M. Synge, G. B. Shaw, Augustus John, George Russell (AE), Sean O'Casey, Sir Hugh Lane, John Masefield, George Moore and a host of other writers and artists, many of whom created literature and works of value while visiting there; as of course did Lady Gregory herself. Four years after her death Yeats wrote of Coole Park,

> "I long for the quiet; long ago I used to find at Coole. It was part of the genius of that house"

We visited the flower garden where the "Autograph Tree" still flourishes, and on which can still be clearly seen the initials of these famous and talented people carved so many years ago at the invitation of Lady Gregory. Again as Yeats wrote of these famous people,

"They came like swallows and like swallows went."

We took one of the laid pathway walks from the remains of the house across Inchy Wood (Island Wood) and were contented to just sit - quietly enjoying the tranquillity and beauty of Coole Lake, and gaze towards the Island of Illaunteige the scene, which inspired Yeats to write,

The trees are in their autumn beauty,	The nineteenth year has come upon me
The woodland paths are dry,	Since I first made my count;
Under the October twilight the water	I saw, before I had well finished,
Mirrors a still sky;	All suddenly mount
Upon the brimming waters among the stones	And scatter wheeling in great broken rings
Are nine-and-fifty swans.	Upon their clamorous wings.

Well the Swans of Coole are still there, upon the brimming waters and among the stones, or maybe these beautiful creatures are the re-incarnation of the famous, like the swallows, who have returned to mourn the loss and destruction of what Coole might have been - A great and lasting Centre of Excellence for Irish Literature and Culture. Lady Gregory wrote constantly in her Journals of her anxiety for the future of Coole -

> "Through the guests who have stayed there it counts for much in the awakening of the spiritual and intellectual side of our country – if there is trouble now, and it is dismantled and left to ruin, that will be the whole country's loss"

It is widely acknowledged that the influence of Yeats, Singe and Lady Gregory and their Abbey Theatre awakened more than a spiritual and intellectual side to our country at that time. Experts would affirm their influence as being very considerable in heightening a desire for Irish freedom.

It was time to leave Coole Park, and the heritage of Lady Gregory; so much of which has been lost to the Irish People by the boorish and tasteless behaviour of those who should have known better.

ABILITY FOR GETTING THINGS DONE

Early in the first year of my appointment the Irish agent for the firm of Sotheby's the Fine Art auctioneers from London, Mr. Bill Montgomery approached us with the offer of holding an Antiques Valuation Day in aid of "Lifeboats Ireland." I knew nothing of such fundraising events but assumed rightly that it would take the form of the "Antiques Road Show" which we are all familiar with on TV. I met with Mr. Montgomery and told him that I would be delighted to accept his kind offer and to please let us know how we could help.

Sotheby's local representative in County Waterford, where it was proposed we hold the event, was Mrs. Julia Keane of Cappoquin. Our fundraising branch Hon. Secretary who would be deeply involved in the organisation of the event was Lady Norah Wingfield who lived in a large country estate named "Salterbridge" located between Cappoquin and Lismore. Through the good offices of Mrs. Keane and her husband David we were able to secure the magnificent Lismore Castle as the location for the event. It was decided that all involved including the agent for the Duke and Duchess of Devonshire owners of Lismore Castle would meet at the castle for a planning meeting.

Seven or eight of Sotheby's experts would travel from London for the valuation day, each having expertise in a different field of the antiques business. We were delighted to be offered the Great Hall of the castle to carry out the valuations; this would add greatly to the prestige of the event and I believe, in itself would guarantee a good attendance. A charge was suggested for each valuation given, which would go towards the Lifeboat Institution. It was also decided that the local lifeboat branch would provide soup and sandwiches on the day the proceeds from which would also go to the Institution. I was concerned that this aspect of the event would be too much for Lady Norah to take on; she was an elderly lady who required the aid of a walking stick to get about.

The day before the event, Mary and John from the office and May and myself drove to Lismore. I called to "Salterbridge" to see Lady Norah and also on Julia Keane to see how things were going. All seemed to be very quiet nothing really seemed to be happening; I was worried! May and I and some of the Sotheby's experts had been asked to stay at "Salterbridge" with Lady Norah while Mary and John stayed with other members of the branch committee.

"Salterbridge" was a large mansion of a house, which must have been beautiful in times gone by, but with no concessions to today's modern lifestyle such as central heating etc. Although it was April time the weather was still remarkably cold with heavy overnight frosts. Our bedroom, which occupied a corner position on the first floor of the house must have been twenty-five feet long by fifteen or more feet wide and had four large windows.

Our bathroom was situated at the end of a very long corridor; unfortunately we were unable to find the light switch in the corridor when it came to bedtime, which left us groping around in the dark. The bed linen was stiffly laundered white linen sheets and pillowcases, and deadly cold. After breakfast next morning we made our way to the castle. As we left the house Lady Norah said she would join us sometime later, I was really worried now about the preparations, particularly from the point of view of the lunches which the local branch of the Lifeboat Institution had taken on the responsibility of preparing. When we arrived at the castle the kitchens were a hive of activity, there must have been at least twelve ladies making sandwiches and preparing all kinds of goodies. The Sotheby's people were working away under the direction of Bill and Julia setting up their tables and signage. There was a lovely fire burning brightly in the massive fireplace in the Great Hall. All the preparations were well under way and all was thankfully going very well. Presently Lady Norah arrived and with a wave of her walking stick gave her seal of approval to all that was happening in the kitchen. With an hour still to go before the great doors of the castle were opened to the public; queues were beginning to form outside.

May and Mary checked the items for valuation and gave the appropriate ticket for the particular expert while John and myself helped out where necessary. The day was a wonderful success with the queue at times over one hundred yards long. A very busy but a most enjoyable day was had by all, and an extremely successful fundraising event; the first of many associations we were to have around the country with Sotheby's, for the lifeboat institution.

That evening we were all invited to Julia's in-laws at Cappoquin House for dinner, the home of Sir Richard and Lady Keane. I remember Lady Norah saying to us when we were driving to the house.

"You will really see a most beautiful home this evening," she was not exaggerating.

Before leaving for Dublin next morning after the other guests from Sotheby's had departed, we had a long talk with Lady Norah, who as the name Wingfield implies had married into the Powerscourt family. She told us of her childhood days in New Zealand, and showed us a most interesting photo album of those early days. Her father was Admiral Jellico of WW1 fame and who was later to become Governor General of New Zealand. She also told us with some sadness how her son had been killed during the last days of WW2.

It was with reluctance that we had to drag ourselves away from "Salterbridge," to collect Mary and John and return to Dublin. Lady Norah was a very interesting lady, softly spoken, but obviously with a quiet authority and ability for getting things done.

Some years later, in fact I was at another Sotheby's Valuation Day, on this occasion in Rochestown Park Hotel in Cork. I was talking to Mrs Mary Dwyer the RNLI's representative in Cork City, when she said to me,

"Did you know, Jimmy, that Lady Norah Wingfield is in hospital here in Cork"? "No" I said,

"I didn't, I'll go now and see her." I collected some flowers and went directly to the hospital. When I arrived at the ward Lady Norah had a visitor, 'a man of the cloth' whom I assumed correctly was her local Clergyman, she appeared pleased to see me and obviously wanted to speak Lifeboats, the poor clergyman was almost shooed, however very politely, out of the ward shortly after I arrived. I am sure had the situation been reversed and I had been in the ward when the Clergyman arrived I would have received the same polite but earnest treatment.

A COSY DOMESTIC SCENE

An amusing incident happened on a visit to the home of a voluntary worker on my travels early in that first year after taking over from Col. Clarke. I was visiting branches down the country and the particular lady I was about to call on I had met several times in the office. She had often called when in Dublin to collect fundraising supplies for her different branch events; her name we will say was Kate. However, this was the first time I called to her home. From enquiries I had made in the district I had been given directions to look out for an imposing entrance to what was in fact one of the few remaining walled estates in that part of Ireland, so it shouldn't be difficult to find. I drove up the almost never-ending long tree-lined avenue, which eventually opened out to reveal a magnificent small Georgian mansion, which overlooked an ornamental lake and a beautiful sweeping view over the rolling countryside beyond.

I was amazed at the style and grandeur of the whole scene. The friendly young lady I had met several times in our office, I had found to be a very down to earth person with few airs and graces what so ever, and although extremely pleasant, displaying little indication of what now appeared to be such a highborn upbringing and lifestyle. I approached the imposing hall door with some reticence, which was opened presently by herself who welcomed me in her usual warm and friendly manner and invited me to come through to the kitchen. We chatted about lifeboat matters and indeed matters in general, Kate told me that she was a keen gardener and grew all her own vegetables and invited me to see the garden. I was amazed, she had every vegetable I was familiar with and many I wasn't all grown as she explained by herself. Needless to say I was full of admiration, this young lady certainly didn't mind getting her hands dirty!

"Let's go in the house and have a cup of coffee, the baby is due a bottle", she said in a casual way, we returned to the kitchen and Kate prepared the bottle; while we were having the coffee,

"O my heavens look at the time? she said, looking at the kitchen clock,

"I'll have to fly to collect my son from play school. Jimmy! Will you give the baby his bottle and I'll be back in a few minutes".

I must have looked alarmed? Kate smiled and said,

"You'll have no problems he is very placid and takes the bottle with no trouble" with that she was gone. I was sitting there in the kitchen, the radio playing, all going well, feeding the baby when after a little while the back door opened and a gentleman came into the kitchen looking quite perplexed at the cosy domestic scene that presented itself, he introduced himself as Kate's husband, more as a question rather than a statement. I very quickly explained who I was and what I was doing sitting in his kitchen feeding his baby. Kate returned almost immediately and I was glad to hand over the quite contented baby to her more capable hands. We all had a good laugh before I left this charming couple, Kate still smiling, with the baby in her arms as I drove away from their lovely home to make my way to my next call.

THE WETTEST DAY

A new breed of self-righting lifeboats capable of over twice the speed of the older more traditional lifeboats, the Arun Class, came into service with the RNLI the year before I joined the institution. Portrush was the first station on the Irish coast to receive this new design in lifeboats. The second of the Arun Class boats to be assigned to an Irish station would replace the 52ft. Barnet Class lifeboat "RNLB Rowland Watts," at Valentia, one of three Barnets on service in Ireland all of which would be replaced within the next few years. The arrival of firstly the Waveney class some years earlier at Dun Laoghaire and Dunmore East and later the Arun class of lifeboats marked the beginning of the end of the older traditional style of lifeboat, so familiar at lifeboat stations around our coasts. It was an interesting period in the history the RNLI; what we were really witnessing was the transition from the traditional displacement hull form to a new and fast hull design. This new design of lifeboat would change utterly the nature of "Search and Rescue" on the coast of the United Kingdom and Ireland, which really had served the Institution since its inception. The Arun was capable of more than double the speed of the traditional boats, with an operating distance of 250 nautical miles at full throttle and without refuelling. With its self-righting capability and the very latest in hi-tech equipment, the Arun would prove to be the ideal lifeboat for Valentia.

The significance for me of the arrival of the new lifeboat at Valentia meant the first Naming Ceremony in Ireland since my appointment. As time moved on with the replacement of lifeboats and the opening of many new lifeboat stations on the Irish coast, naming ceremonies were to become fairly routine events, while still a major occasion in the life of any Lifeboat Station. The Valentia Naming Ceremony of 1983 was also special in so far as it was the first such event to be held in the Republic for several years. From the vibes we were receiving back from around the coast we could expect a very large turnout, it promised to be quite a major occasion.

Having attended an inaugural planning meeting in Valentia as early as April '83 with Tony Course the Inspector of lifeboats, my opposite number in charge of the operational side of the institution in Ireland, we fixed the date of the ceremony for 17th September 1983. The main worry of the local lifeboat committee in Valentia and indeed ourselves was the possibility of an important senior football match involving Kerry happening on that weekend, if the County Football team was to progress well towards the all-Ireland football final. Although that scenario would impinge greatly on the attendance at the ceremony, having consulted with senior staff in the institution, it was decided to take our chances and go for that date.

Regular monthly meetings were held in Valentia; every detail of the occasion was covered and responsibilities undertaken and noted by crew and committee alike. From the exact mooring position of the lifeboat on the day - the positioning of the naming platform - the seating arrangements of upwards to possibly 800 guests - the seeking of appropriate permissions and site cleaning arrangements from Kerry County Council - the finding of a venue to accommodate the full number of invited guests for the tea party after the ceremony - arranging the choir and the Blessing Ceremony with the clergy, all had to be attended to locally. Back in the Dublin office, the preparation and posting of invitations was undertaken with a list of all hotel and bed and breakfast accommodation included for those guests wishing to stay overnight.

The layout and printing of the programme, arrangements for overnight accommodation for VIP's, arrangements for luncheon for the platform party before the ceremony, and as the date approached the writing of speeches were all now attended to.

The day finally arrived, bright and sunny with a blustery breeze blowing, all was well. At the site it was all systems go with some members of the crew putting the final touches to the cleaning of the new lifeboat RNLB "Margaret Frances Love" while a host of other helpers set out the seating, decorated the platform and erected flags and bunting all over the site. The staff from the office and myself named each seat from the list of invited guests, with special seating for crewmembers wives and families, close to the platform. As noontime approached I was talking to some of the local fishermen who were very apprehensive about the weather conditions for the afternoon. Sure enough by 2pm as Lady Killanin who was to name the new lifeboat and the Bishop of Kerry who would jointly conduct the Blessing Ceremony with the Rector of Killarney and the rest of the platform party took their seats the rain had started. By the time Lady Killanin had uttered the time-honoured words

"I name this Lifeboat Margaret Frances Love, God bless her and all who sail in her" and the Lifeboat had slipped her moorings, bringing the ceremonies to a close, the day had seriously deteriorated with heavy rain and strengthening winds.

We all retreated in the now stormy conditions to the warmth of the historic old Cable Station building for the very welcome refreshments. The many hundreds who made the long journey to celebrate this memorable occasion, had a most enjoyable day with the small but very dedicated lifeboat community of Valentia Island.

Greeting the President and her husband at Ballyglass Naming Ceremony 4th May 1991.

Mary Dover, daughter of Wicklow's coxswain making a presentation to Patrick Hillery, President of Ireland in May 1990 with Liam and Self.

"The Anchorage" our first home.

"Illyria I" after total refit.

"Illyria II" with Michael Shortt at Athlone Lock.

Our good friends "Snoopy and Kim" in summer trim.

"The Retreat" our little grey home in the West.

Our 40th Wedding Anniversary – a wonderful gathering of family & friends hosted by Maura & the girls.

My sister Breeda with some of the next generation.

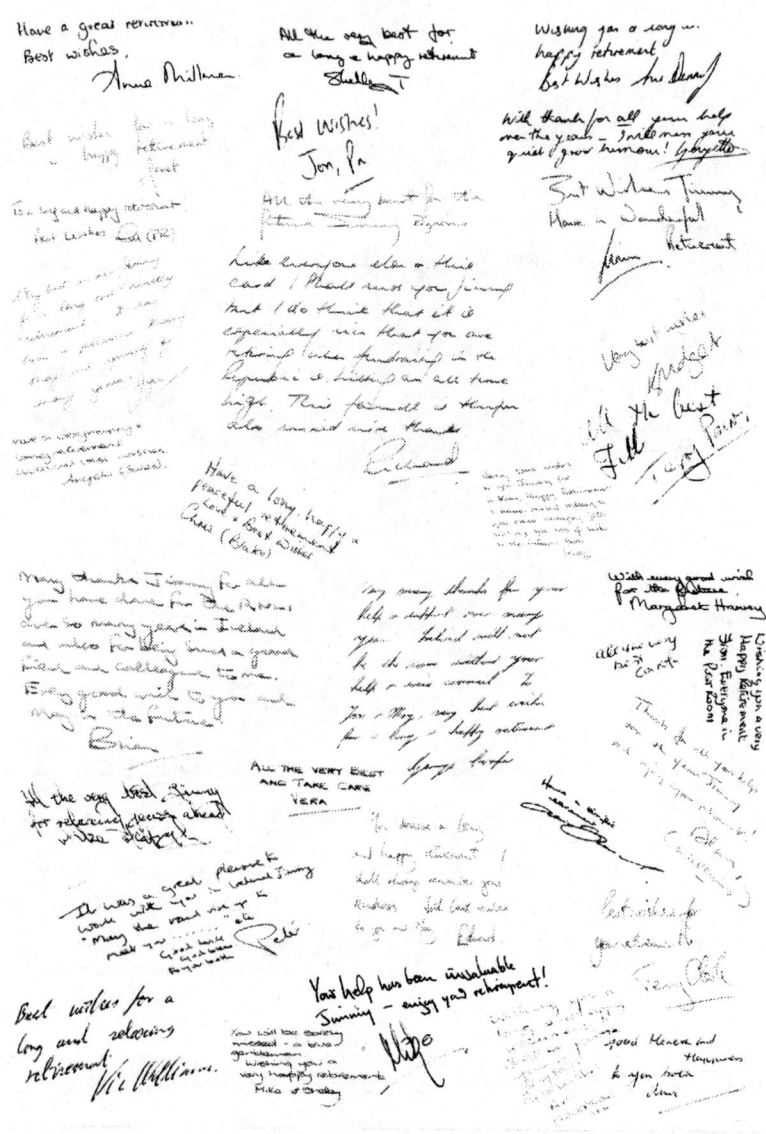

Retirement Good Wishes from R.N.L.I. Dorset.

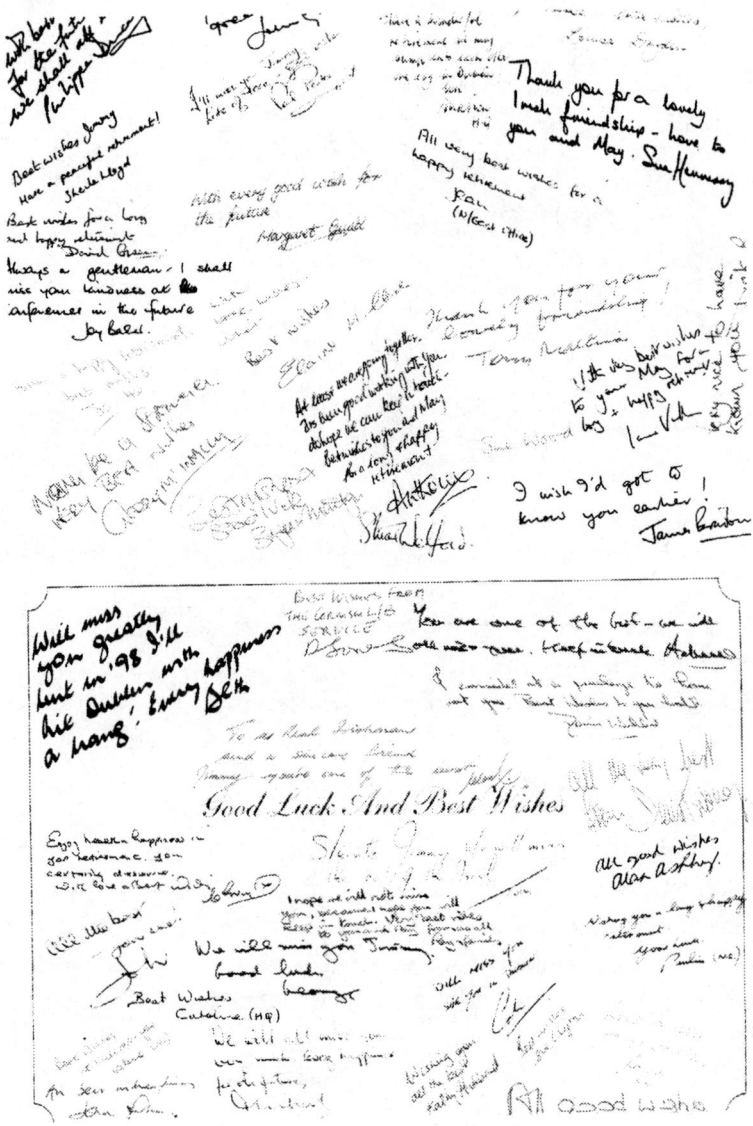

A THRILLING EXPERIENCE

As the years passed I was to take part in organising many Naming Ceremonies all around the Irish coast, all carried out to the same set format, and yet in their own way each one very different. The most rewarding aspect of these events for me was being involved closely again with the lifeboat crews, be it only for the duration of arrangements in the case of each lifeboat station, and working closely with them as we prepared for their special day.

I recall arriving at Ballyglass Lifeboat Station in Co. Mayo with my colleague Mary Newman, currently the National Organiser Rep. of Ireland, for a naming ceremony meeting. We arrived in the early afternoon with the intention of joining the then Inspector of Lifeboats Peter Bradley and the crew for an exercise on the lifeboat, before taking part in the meeting later that evening. The day was fine and sunny with a strong westerly wind blowing. As we arrived at the boathouse, I must admit a little late, the boat was about to slip her moorings and go to sea, the Inspector assuming by now we were not joining them for the exercise.

However, we very quickly donned the oilskins and made our

way to the lifeboat. Having made our apologies for being somewhat late, we were duly strapped into two of the aviation type seats in the after end of the deckhouse. As we steamed from the shelter of Ballyglass Bay we immediately felt the effects of the strong wind on the open waters of the Atlantic Ocean. To someone used to the short choppy and confused seas of the east coast of Ireland the seas off the west coast seemed enormous. The Arun class lifeboat climbed slowly but effortlessly; our seats assuming an angle similar but even much more so, to that experienced in flight as your jet plane climbs from its runway. The powerful twin engines of the lifeboat pushing all thirty two tonnes of her up what seemed to be the side of a mountain, in reality the steep Atlantic rolling seas. The lifeboat appeared to stand for a split second almost motionless on the crest of the wave, while through the side window the sea disappeared momentarily now from our view, and all around us were clear windswept skies; before putting her head down as we charged headlong down the other side of this huge sea with our stomachs suspended somewhere close to our mouths, as the lifeboat crashed to a sickening momentary stop in the trough below with now nothing but sea, spume and spray visible in all directions; only to shake herself and start the steep climb once again. For a few minutes my mind raced to assimilate one of the most thrilling and exhilarating of sensations I believe I had ever felt. However, between the severe motions of the lifeboat coupled with the smell of diesel exhaust fumes being blown back over the stern of the boat and into the deckhouse I soon began to feel quite seasick. I looked over at Mary and could clearly see that she looked no better than I felt.

Having finished the speed drills, the Inspector with a smile on his face, instructed the coxswain to take the lifeboat into the more calm and curative waters of the bay, where our digestive systems recovered much more quickly than our reputations as matelots. As sensational and thrilling memories in lifeboats go this one rated very highly indeed.

I have heard it argued, cynically in my view that the real purpose of Lifeboat Naming Ceremonies is simply to create awareness of the Lifeboat Institution. It is true that awareness of the work of the Institution amongst the general public is vital to its ongoing support. However, it would be very wrong to say that creating a heightened awareness of the institution was the main purpose of these great events. The "Naming Ceremony" is far more than that; it is a celebration and an acknowledgement of the heroic and selfless dedication of crewmen, and in more recent times women, who are prepared to put the lives of others before their own safety. It is a vote of confidence by the Institution in the skill and seamanship of each particular crew, to take on the often difficult and dangerous task of saving of life at sea, and succeeding, even in the worst of weather conditions. Of course it is an opportunity for the fundraisers to take pride in the fulfilment of their ongoing efforts. It is also a time when the local populace, can show solidarity with their own lifeboat crew, both men and women. It is a 'gathering time', a time when crew and committee members from many stations come together in support and comradeship. It is of course also through the Blessing and Dedication ceremony an opportunity to remind ourselves that there is a greater being on whom all of us can call for succour in our own particular hour of need.

Organising "The Naming Ceremony" as part of ones duty, was for me one of the most rewarding aspects of my work during my years with the Royal National Lifeboat Institution. The early meetings, the camaraderie with the crew and committee and getting to know so many people locally from the local clergy, to those responsible for preparing the ceremony site, from meetings with the Choir for the Blessing ceremony to possibly the tutoring of a little girl, most probably a crewman's daughter, who would present the bouquet to the "namer" of the lifeboat. For me it had many of the elements and the excitement of a theatrical production with one essential difference, this was not 'make-believe' this was real life drama. Needless to say, all well organised productions start on time, which we always tried to adhere to.

You had the stage decorated to the last detail, while in front the band and choir ready to do their part in leading the audience with the hymns. You had the "front of house" people showing all the invited audience to their seats, and right on time you had the first set of principles, having been given their "lines," now taking their places on stage for the start of "act one" while the band strikes up our National Anthem.

Of course what could never happen in a theatre, the action switches from the stage (platform) for act two when the "real principles" the Lifeboat Crewmembers take over on the water as the lifeboat is put through her paces for all to see and admire as the chorus concludes with "Home from the Sea;" and a rousing three cheers for the Lifeboat and her Crew. I always felt a wonderful sense of satisfaction when the proceedings went according to plan; I enjoyed every minute of each Ceremony, and like all good theatre when the performance is over it was time to celebrate.

My involvement in the organisation of the Naming Ceremony of the new Tyne class lifeboat RNLB "Annie Blaker" in Wicklow gave me particular pleasure. Coming back into what was "my own" Lifeboat Station and working with friends on the crew and committee was a joyous occasion for me. My brother Liam was at that time Chairman of Wicklow Lifeboat Branch and as such he would be taking a leading part in the ceremony. In Britain if the Guest of Honour at a Naming Ceremony is a member of the Royal family, the ceremony is accorded all the pomp and ceremony of a Royal occasion. The Lord Lieutenant of the particular county where the event is taking place is consulted on protocol and of course the Palace itself is very much involved.

Here in Ireland, when The President of Ireland is participating, the ceremony is given the same status as a Royal event, this was the case with the naming ceremony in Wicklow. His Excellency Patrick J. Hillery President of Ireland was Guest of Honour with

The two Archbishops of Dublin; Most Rev. Dr.Desmond Connell DD and The Right Rev. Dr. Donald Caird DD and Rev. Christopher Walpole officiated at the Blessing Ceremony. The elected representatives of the Irish Parliament for the constituency were also invited. The Chairman of the RNLI Mr Michael Vernon and Mrs Vernon, the Director of the RNLI Lt. Comdr. Brian Miles and Mrs Miles also attended. The Irish members of the Committee of Management were present. Senior members of RNLI staff travelled from head office in Dorset to be present for the occasion together with representatives of the doner, Miss Annie Blaker. Happily the weather was kind, giving us a lovely warm sunny day. The location for the ceremony in Wicklow is particularly good, with the boathouse and slipway adjacent to the East Pier, and all the space in the world to arrange the seating, giving an excellent view of the proceedings to the invited guests. Wicklow lifeboat is a housed slip launching boat as opposed to an afloat lifeboat, which is the case at most lifeboat stations on the Irish coast. The bonus for the huge attendance being, that they had the opportunity at the conclusion of the ceremony to witness the dramatic launch of the lifeboat down the slipway. Michael Jones the station Hon. Secretary and Kevin Desmond who at that time was the Ass. Hon. Secretary, and both close friends of mine, were responsible for taking on much of the local arrangements, unfortunately Kevin found himself in hospital for the event; happily he made a swift and full recovery.

I have seldom in my lifetime seen so many people on the East Pier in Wicklow, all thoroughly enjoying the occasion. As the lifeboat threw off her chains and shackles and ran down the slipway, one was conscious of a real sense of pride uniting all present; in what was more than the launching of another new lifeboat, but an event that was close to the core of every Wicklow person for almost one hundred and fifty years.

The Naming Ceremony of the "RNLB Annie Blaker" was a wonderful event and a memorable occasion not only for the

Lifeboat Crew, the local Committee and Ladies Guild and those of us involved, but also for the wider community who down through the years since 1857 to the present day, have faithfully supported their lifeboat station at Wicklow.

NOW YOU'RE FLYING THE AEROPLANE

We were constantly being approached as I'm sure all charities are with supposedly brilliant ideas for raising funds, and of course many of these ideas were sound and well thought out concepts, however, some could be and were hair-brained, while on one or two occasions we were approached with what I believe were positive scams. The better ones we took on board and gave every help and support to those who wished to run with them. The more hair-brained ideas, although made with good will, we turned down but in a sympathetic and grateful manner.

We were approached with an interesting idea, which one might consider somewhat hair-brained, but which was popular with charities all around the country at that time. The idea was to encourage people to do a Sponsored Parachute Jump. The outfit that approached us operated from a base in County Kildare. They explained the procedure, they would move into a specific district with a caravan and sell the jumps for a fixed amount, in the name of the RNLI, (which started to ring warning bells immediately) a percentage of the return from each jump would go to the RNLI. The figures produced were good and it was pointed out that the sport was very popular; all was without doubt legitimate and above board. Obviously a lack of enthusiasm was coming back from us so it was suggested that we spend a morning in Kildare when we would be shown the whole operation, I hasten to say without doing an actual jump. A few days later Dermot and myself headed off to the Curragh in Co. Kildare. The set up was impressive we were shown how to re-pack your parachute after a jump and all the other techniques which go into the training session of all prospective "skydivers" before they takeoff. The whole business was quite exciting.

"Would you like to go up before you leave, you can see the Blessington lakes from the air?" the pilot said.

"That would be great" I said looking at Dermot, "He agreed." I climbed into the seat beside the pilot while Dermot sat directly behind.

"If we were doing a jump we would remove the rear seats," said the pilot. So off we went into the deep blue yonder.

We circled the lakes turned and skirted the closest of the Wicklow mountains before turning west again.

" Would you like to take the controls?" he said,

"OK, tell me what you want me to do" I said,

"Do you see that mountain peak in the far distance, well steer straight for it - now you're flying the aeroplane" said the pilot. I don't know how Dermot felt, but for me it was the most fantastic sensation. Many many years ago as a teenager I had a great desire to learn to fly, I even went as far as to find out the cost of flight tuition, which of course was prohibitively expensive. I never thought that at this time of my life I would actually take the controls of an aeroplane even if only for a few moments.

We thanked everyone and made our way back to the office, it was time to make our decision. I wasn't entirely happy; there is a risk element in every parachute jump, which I felt did not sit well with a charity whose sole existence was for the saving of life. I decided to talk to Anthony Oliver my direct boss and Head of

Fundraising in Poole. We discussed the inherent danger in such an activity and the implications for the institution if a serious accident occurred. I decided not to go ahead with this particular fundraising idea.

A ROOM WITH A VIEW

In the late 1980's the policy of the RNLI with regard to regional office property appeared to change. Up to this point it was the policy to rent rather than invest the Institution's funds in property such as regional fundraising offices. As one member of senior management put it, "we are not in the property business," although the Belfast office was an exception at that time. Our office situation at 3 Clare Street, Dublin consisted of, four rented rooms, two on the ground floor and two at basement level. The conditions were extremely cramped for the staff, and also the lack of storage space required to service the needs of a nationwide branch network was a serious problem. Although we had two parking spaces at the rear of the office the parking situation for visiting volunteers was next to impossible in such a busy centre city location. On one of the regular visits of the Director Comdr. Miles to our office, I discussed the situation with him and he readily agreed that we needed more space. I was surprised when he suggested that I should look at premises with a view to purchasing rather than renting.

I discussed with the office staff the fact that purchasing would certainly mean moving away from centre city, which would have travel implications not only for the staff but also for the voluntary branch members, many of whom call to pick up fundraising supplies. Together with one or two of the staff I looked at several properties with little success, none of which were entirely suitable. I happened to see a house on Lower Glenageary Road Dunlaoghaire in the property pages of the press, which appeared to have the accommodation we needed. Although four members of staff lived on the north side of the city, with the Dublin Area Rapid Transport System now in place, they all appeared enthusiastic about a Dunlaoghaire location. We made our offer on the property and, despite ours being the highest offer, without coming back to us, the auctioneer sold the property to somebody else, which was difficult to understand.

However, we decided Dunlaoghaire was the correct location for the RNLI's fundraising office in Ireland. We eventually found a fine property, on the sea front overlooking South Dublin Bay, which possessed all the accommodation we needed. The purchase price was IR£195,000, I got the go ahead from Head office and we bought the house. The property needed some major repair work, both externally and internally, which was carried out before we moved at a cost of IR£50,000. We moved into our new offices in 1992, which were officially opened by the then Minister for the Marine, Mr. David Andrews. It was a wonderful environment in which to work. We had all the space we needed to get on with the job.

We developed a new souvenir shop and storage area in the basement. On the ground floor there was a large well appointed reception area with plenty of space to meet with the volunteers when they called. The kitchen with canteen space for staff lunches etc. was to the back of the house. Adjacent to my office on the first floor, which looked over Scotsmans Bay, we had a large meeting room. The property also possessed a large secure yard, which would prove extremely useful as time went on.

In the early period after we moved in, especially during the summer months, the view from my office window could be a distraction. Every time I lifted my head something was happening out on the bay, with yachting or boating of some kind or other. However, as with all things, after a while it became part of the accepted scene. Never the less it always remained a beautiful location, and a privileged location for all of us from which to manage the fundraising endeavours of RNLI Ireland. The new National Office would serve the RNLI long into the foreseeable future.

You can imagine how surprised and a little saddened I felt some years after I retired to hear that the RNLI will soon be selling this beautiful property in Dunlaoghaire to move to a custom built location in Swords, Co. Dublin, which would also house the RNLI's Operational Depot. I believe that a valuation on the Dunlaoghaire property revealed that it should now fetch at auction well over one million euros, quite a handsome return on investment for an organisation which is not in the property business.

"WHITE OF MORN"

Each year I would do a complete tour of all the Branches and Ladies Guilds, throughout the twenty six counties principally to thank the members for all their help and dedication in raising the necessary funds, and of course to encourage them in their future efforts on behalf of the Lifeboat Institution. I would also make occasional trips down the country outside these annual visits, when special fund-raising events were taking place in any specific branch. Through these branch and special visits I made many friends in every county in Ireland. While I had my favourite branches and made special friendships, I thoroughly enjoyed visiting all parts of the country and calling on the branch members in their homes on a one to one basis. If the truth be known, in this area, I was playing to my best strength as National Organiser. Even today having been retired for several years I still miss this aspect of my work with the RNLI. On many occasions as I have recounted, May accompanied me and being hon. secretary of the Ladies Guild in Wicklow she had a lot in common with many of the branch ladies. Over these years I also met many of whom I suppose one would call celebrities, and while I can't say that I was at all times at home in their company, it was needless to say interesting to meet and speak with such famous people.

The governing body of the RNLI since its inception has been The Committee of Management and its various sub-committees. The members of these committees are made up mainly of volunteers and some members of senior management. I believe the name Committee of Management has been changed to "The Council," it fails me to understand why it was felt necessary to change the name of this body which has been to my mind fundamental to the institution's organisation since its inception, it almost smacks to me of "change for change sake" The members of the Council are chosen for their specialist knowledge or experience in a given area relevant to the general operations of the institution. The special knowledge sought to fill such vacancies which may arise on the Council from time to time are in the fields of Business, Finance, Public Relations, Search and Rescue, Maritime, Fundraising, Medicine and Establishment. All of these highly qualified and eminent people give their time purely on a voluntary basis.

Through an agreement with the Irish Government, Lifeboat Search and Rescue in Irish waters is in the hands of the RNLI whose headquarters is in Poole, Dorset. Over the years the RNLI has benefited from having many excellent Irish representatives on its "Committee of Management" and on its various sub-committees, this was particularly so during my years both as volunteer and staff member. The Lord Killanin was the senior Irish member of that body during my early years as National Organiser. I had quite a lot of contact with him in those years, keeping him up to date with all that was happening on the Fundraising and Public Relations side of the Institution throughout the country. I remember he was attending a presentation at one of the branches and I had accompanied him, which was usual for the National Organiser in the case of a fundraising occasion, while it would be the Inspector of Lifeboat's responsibility if the event was operational. We had some time to kill and Lord Killanin started to talk about his involvement with the film industry and specifically with the film "The Quiet Man" and his friendship with John Ford the famous film director.

John Feeney, Ford's father had emigrated from Spiddal Co. Galway in the mid nineteen century and had married Barbara Curran in America, also from Spiddal. They had a son whom they named John after his father. John, junr. later changed his name to John Ford and was destined to become one of the greatest film directors of the twentieth century.

Lord Killanin and John Ford met and became friends in the United States in 1937. Many years later when Ford decided to adapt Maurice Walsh's short story "The Quiet Man" for the screen, he chose the ancestral home of his family, Connemara, as the location in which to set the film. He contacted his friend Lord Killanin, an expert on Connemara to source the main locations for the film. Spiddal, was the original choice for the setting of the village of "Innisfree," Lord Killanin also had historical connections with Spiddal and kept a holiday home there. However, the lack of a hotel large enough to accommodate the main cast members necessitated the move to the village of Cong on the Mayo/Galway border, with its top hotel, Ashford Castle, which would provide the necessary accommodation, located right at the edge of the village. Lord Killanin found the little thatched cottage "White of Morn" in its beautiful setting in the Maam valley which played such a vital part in the story; sadly now little more than an overgrown pile of stones. Those like myself who have been fans of the film will remember the scene with John Wayne carrying the massive mahogany bedstead into the cottage. Lord Killanin told me that when shooting was finished John Ford made him a present of the bed, which he had in his summer home in Spiddal. Lord Killanin was President of the International Olympic Committee from 1972 to 1980 and was at that time arguably worldwide the best-known living Irishman.

Another very well known Irishman, and I am proud to say a fellow Wicklow man, who was a member of the Committee of Management and also a member of its Public Relations sub-committee was Ronald M Delany. Ireland's best-known athlete; Ronnie won Gold at the 1956 Olympic Games in a brilliant and thrilling finish of the fifteen hundred meters. On his return to Ireland at the end of the games he received a heroes welcome all over Ireland. As an Irish member of the Committee of Management he was always very popular at branch events and presentations, and as one would expect, with his background in public relations he was an excellent after dinner speaker. Over the years while I held the position of National Organiser, Ronnie Delany was helpful and constructive, and always supportive of the organising staff in RNLI Ireland, a valued member of the Committee of Management

Vice Admiral Sir Arthur Hezlet was also an Irish member of the C of M of the RNLI and lived in Northern Ireland. In those days in the early eighties the troubles were raging north of the border, and even in southern Ireland we were very conscious of security when we had visitors here from the United Kingdom or Northern Ireland. As well as his membership of the RNLI's group of Irish members Sir Arthur as he was generally known was Chairman of the RNLI's prestigious Search and Rescue Committee. All decisions with regard to new lifeboat placement and the opening of new stations were considered and agreed by this sub-committee before being ratified by the Committee of Management. Sir Arthur was a most friendly and outgoing gentleman and a wonderful conversationalist and storyteller. It was always interesting to listen to the stories of his exploits during the war. He was I believe the most highly decorated sub-mariner of the Second World War, and as such he had many stories to tell. I remember him telling a group of us one evening, that during one particularly difficult tour of duty he and members of his crew did not have time to change or take off their clothes for almost a two week period, snatching the odd hours rest when possible.

Clayton Love jnr., who succeeded Lord Killanin as the senior member of the Irish group achieved the highest-ranking position of any Irishman within the RNLI when he was elected to that of Deputy Chairman. This was an honour, which was very well deserved. Clayton devoted an inordinate amount of time to his voluntary work for the RNLI, both in Ireland and throughout the United Kingdom. In his position as senior member of the Irish group and later holding the prestigious position of Deputy Chairman of the RNLI he was at all times extremely supportive of and helpful to the Irish Region within the structure of the Institution.

The Irish members of the Committee of Management were highly respected and influential within the RNLI, holding responsible positions on key sub-committees. With Ronald M Delany being a member of the Public Relations Committee, Richard Burrows Deputy Chairman of the Establishment Committee, Wallace Clark MBE. DL. member of the Boat and Shoreworks Committee, Sir Arthur Hezlet, Chairman of the Search and Rescue Committee, Terence C Johnson member of the Fundraising Committee, Professor John Harbison member of the Medical and Survival Committee and Wilson Ervin CBE member of the Committee of Management.

HOME FROM THE SEA

One morning in late 1988, Pam, our receptionist who manned the telephones in our office told me that Mr Phil Coulter's secretary wished to speak to me,

"Mr Coulter would like to meet up with you next week when he is in Dublin if that would be convenient," his secretary said.

"I would be delighted to meet Mr. Coulter" I replied. The arrangements were made that I would meet him in "Jury's Hotel" in Ballsbridge. When I met him he recounted how his brother had lost his life in a drowning accident in Lough Swilly and since the accident he had become very aware of the work of the RNLI.

"I would like to help in some way and since I am a song writer I would like to write a song in praise of the work of the lifeboat men," Phil explained. I thanked him and replied,

"That would be great I'll contact our public relations department in Poole, I'm sure they will be delighted."

"Fine, I'll be in touch with you when I have something to show you", he said, I thanked him again and made my departure.

However, when I contacted my superiors in head office I can only say that they were less than enthusiastic about the project.

They made the point that this had been done before and on those occasions it had been largely a waste of time. That did not deter me at all, I made the point that this was Phil Coulter who had written the million seller "Congratulations" and that beloved Derry Anthem "The Town I Loved so Well." I decided I would not mention these sentiments to Mr. Coulter and would press on with the project.

Some weeks later I had a call informing me he had completed the song and would send me a tape to listen to. He explained that it would be his voice on the tape, but the actual recording would feature a professional singer; and would I contact him when I had a chance to listen to the tape. Well, the tape arrived and I listened to it several times "Home from the Sea" was born and it was to become the anthem of all the Lifeboatmen. Phil called to the office shortly afterwards,

"I have an idea for the recording of "Home from the Sea," see what you think. If we put together a choir of lifeboat crew members made up of say two from all the lifeboat stations around the Irish coast who wish to participate to sing the chorus, with Liam Clancy who would sing the verse. The song would be backed with the Phil Coulter orchestra, what do you think," he said,

"I think its a terrific idea, I'll write to each station with the idea and I'll come back to you say within two weeks or so."

The lifeboat men responded with great enthusiasm. On 5th July 1989 we all met up in a Dublin hotel with Phil Coulter and Liam Clancy of the Clancy brothers fame. After a couple hours rehearsal we proceeded to Windmill Lane Recording Studios and recorded "Home from the Sea." Later in July the song with Liam Clancy and the Lifeboat Chorus became the main feature of the Phil Coulter Concerts, which ran for a week in the National Concert Hall, with each night a total sell out. I'll never forget the reception we received each evening from the audience as we marched out on the stage, I couldn't resist joining the lifeboat men many in sea-going oilskins and lifejackets, to be greeted with a standing ovation each evening by a packed concert hall. Soon "Home from the Sea" was No. 4 in the Irish charts, a further series of "sell out" concerts followed in the Cork Opera House and the Belfast Opera House. Guest appearances on the Late Late Show (RTE) and the Gerry Kelly Show (UTV) followed. The RNLI featured the song in a new promotional film entitled

"Home from the Sea, The story of the Irish Lifeboats."

I was delighted when the Public Relations Committee formally acknowledged Phil's valuable contribution in publicising the work of the Lifeboat Institution by awarding him the Special Public Relations Award of the Silver Lifeboatman Statuette.

Home from the Sea
By kind permission of Phil Coulter

I

On a cold winters night with the storm at its height the Lifeboat answered the call
They pitched and they tossed till we thought they were lost as we watched from the harbour wall
Though the night was pitch black there was no turning back for someone was waiting out there
And each volunteer had to live with his fear as they joined in a silent prayer

Chorus of Lifeboatmen.........

Carry us Home Home Home from the sea, angels of mercy answer our plea
And carry us Home Home Home from the sea, carry us safely home from the sea

II

As they battled their way past the mouth of the bay it was

blowing as never before
As they gallantly fought everyone of them thought of loved ones back on the shore
Then a flicker of light and they knew they were right there she was on the crest of a wave
She's an old fishing boat and she's barely afloat please God there are souls we can save

Chorus.......

III

While back in the town on a street that runs down to the quay and the harbour wall
They were gathered in pairs at the foot of the stairs to wait for a radio call
Then just before dawn - when all hope was gone - came a hush and a faraway sound
'T was the coxswain he roared all survivors on board thank God and we're homeward bound

Chorus......

To carry them Home Home Home from the sea, angels of mercy answer our plea
And carry them Home Home Home from the sea
Carry them safely home from the sea.

* * * * *

When Phil wrote the last verse of the song, the words read " 't was the skipper he roared all survivors on board." When we spoke on the phone having received the original tape I apologetically suggested that we don't have skippers by name as such on lifeboats - we have Coxswains. Phil laughed and thanked me for pointing out the inaccuracy. Sometime later at The Annual Presentation of Awards in the Mansion House, Phil Coulter as Guest of Honour, while speaking, thanked me in an amusing way for my input into the writing of the song "Home from the Sea".

A NOBLE VISITOR

During most of the nineteen eighties The Duke of Atholl held the position of Chairman of the RNLI. The Tenth Duke of Atholl lived in a massive Scottish Baronial pile near Pitlochry in Scotland and whose lineage can be traced back to the thirteenth century. During the summer of 1983 the Search and Rescue Committee of the Institution was due to carry out its periodic inspection, in this case of the Lifeboat stations on the east and southeast coasts of Ireland. This would entail meeting with the crews and local committees, reviewing the operational situation, and assessing the future requirements if any of each lifeboat station. The visiting group, as well as members of the S & R committee would also include a number of the Irish members of the Committee of Management. Starting at Dunlaoghaire on Saturday morning and finishing in Dunmore East on Sunday evening. The Duke decided he would fly over to Dublin on Saturday evening and join the rest of the committee on Sunday morning for the second day of the Inspection. I was detailed to collect the Duke at the airport. I asked Comdr. Brian Miles, the Director of the Institution,

"What arrangements should I make for overnight accommodation for the Duke?" He answered,

"Why not bring him to Wicklow and have him to stay in your own home, you have plenty of room and I know the Duke would be delighted"

We were living in "Glebe Cottage" at that time and accommodation was not a problem so I said,

"Fine that's what we'll do."

Saturday was going to be a busy day not only for me but also for May. During the week prior to the visit all the Special Security arrangements necessary at that time not only for the Duke's visit but also for the other visiting members of the S & R people were made. Arrangements were made with Dublin Airport for the use of the VIP lounge for the Duke's arrival. By having these arrangements in place I could park at the VIP exit, and with only hand luggage the Duke could go directly through the lounge to the car.

The Inspection would begin early on Saturday morning when the Search and Rescue committee would visit Dunlaoghaire Lifeboat Station, and the party would be arriving at Wicklow Station at approx.11.30am. May therefore decided that she would prepare lunch at home for the party, in all as I remember being about twelve. The group included Lord Killanin, Clayton Love Junr. Admiral Hezlet, the Director Comdr. Brian Miles, the Chief of Operations Comdr. Cairns, my brother Liam as chairman of Wicklow branch and Michael Jones the Hon. Secretary of the branch. Shortly after lunch when the visiting group had left for Arklow Lifeboat Station we had a knock on the door. It was two members of the Garda Siochana in plain clothes one of whom I knew from the local station, Garda Joe Cumiskey. Joe informed me that because we were having a high profile visitor staying in the house overnight we must have a Garda presence at the house for the period of his stay, he also said,

"We will have to check the house and gardens thoroughly and note any vulnerable points" I showed the two gardai over the house and garden.

"What time do you expect your guest to arrive in Wicklow," I gave them the information, as I knew it, and shortly after left for the Airport. The Duke arrived on time and we left for Wicklow stopping for a meal at the Glenview Hotel on the way home. When we arrived home the squad car with Joe and his other garda friend was parked outside the house. The Duke retired shortly after we arrived home and rather than leave Joe and his friend outside in the car all night we built up the fire and invited them to sit inside in comfort for the night. When I came down next morning two different Garda had taken over from Joe and his friend. After breakfast the Duke and myself left to join the rest of the visiting party in Wexford being followed discreetly by the Garda squad car. When we arrived at the Wexford County border the Wicklow Garda Squad left us to be replaced by a Wexford Squad car.

There was a sequel to my meeting with the Duke of Atholl. Some months later, in December, we were in London for our quarterly fundraising meeting. It had become the practice for the Chairman of the Fundraising Committee, at that time Lord Stanley of Alderley, to invite our group the fundraising organisers to dinner at a special venue on one of the evenings during our pre Christmas meeting. On this occasion the venue chosen was the Dining room of The Houses of Parliament at Westminster and the Duke of Atholl was also invited to attend. After dinner the Duke was expressing the Institutions thanks to our group for an excellent year's fundraising when somebody jokingly suggested having a raffle. The Duke took up the suggestion and said,

"Let us all put our names on a five pound note, with half the pot going to the winner and half to the RNLI." When the draw was made I was surprised to hear my name being called. I came back to the hotel where May, having been to the theatre was waiting, seventy-five pounds better off than when I left.

Before leaving the Houses of Parliament I went to say my goodbyes to the Director Comdr. Miles who was talking with the Duke. While I was speaking to them the Duke gave us both a tip for a horse running at one of the meetings the following Saturday. May and I returned home later in the week, not before having blown the seventy-five pounds on two tickets for the splendid show "Aspects of Love" playing in the "West End". On the following Saturday morning my nephew-in-law Donnacada Murphy called to the house; during conversation he happened to mention that he had been given a tip for a horse running in the afternoon. It immediately came back to me then about the Duke's tip earlier in the week. We checked the races and decided to do a double, putting in ten pounds each on the two horses. To make a long story a little shorter the two horses, the names of which I have long forgotten won their races, giving us a return of six hundred and fifty pounds for our investment of twenty pounds – a good day's work.

The evening we went to see "Aspects of Love" had an interesting twist to the occasion. As we arrived at the theatre in Shaftsbury Avenue it was clear that something more than the normal pre-show activity was taking place. The paparazzi were out in force while many of those attending the performance appeared to be in no hurry to take their seats; remaining outside waiting to see who or what celebrity would arrive. May and I took our seats which were close to the stage, we were aware that several seats in the row directly in front of us were vacant; just as the lights were dimmed at the start of the performance the seats were filled very quickly by a group of people. We discovered that the lady seated immediately in front of us was none other than Lady Sarah Ferguson. At the interval before the houselights came on the party quickly left the auditorium returning only when the lights were dimmed and finally leaving very quickly at the end of the show.

THE GREAT MAUREEN POTTER

Another interesting and as we all know quite amazing character who crossed our path in our fundraising endeavours was Charles J Haughey. Although I had met him earlier at one of our Naming Ceremonies in Howth at which he had officiated when he was Taoiseach this particular meeting was later and shortly after he had retired. We had decided to organise a major fundraising event, the brainchild of that now sadly deceased fundraiser extraordinaire Philip Booth, as part of the appeal for a new Lifeboat for Dunlaoghaire. We managed to secure the support of ACC Bank as the major sponsor for the event, which would entail pushing an Inshore Lifeboat on its trailer from Howth Lifeboat Station all around the edge of Dublin Bay ending at Dunlaoghaire Lifeboat Station. We were kindly offered the use of a very old bus, from the Dublin Transport Museum, which was painted in its traditional livery and would act if necessary as a relief in the event of anybody getting overtired along the way. The actual push would be undertaken by the junior members of Howth Yacht Club who would work in relays with the help of a number of inshore lifeboat crewmembers. Because of the high density of traffic on the chosen route we decided to hold the event on a Sunday. Howth being in his constituency we asked Charles Haughey to start the push from the Lifeboat Station.

The day arrived and what a miserable day it was, with a steady heavy drizzle, which looked like it was going to last through the day. Charles Haughey arrived still with quite an entourage even though now retired as Taoiseach, and although he was now simply a member of the Dail his involvement in any event could still draw all the representative of press and television. Of all the political figures I have met over the years Haughey above all had a special something that was difficult to define. He is quite a small man, and not considered handsome, and yet his presence gave a certain emanation, which was larger than his stature. Before setting us on our way he complimented the great work of the Institution and referred in a comical way to his own rescue off Mizen Head, Co. Cork by the Baltimore Lifeboat. He also commented on the weather saying that had he been Taoiseach he would have made sure that the day was fine for the event. Along the way we had arranged several refreshment stops for the boat pushers and those walking. We had also asked some well-known people to meet up with the walkers along the route and encourage them in their efforts. Being such a bad day most of them were obviously put off by the weather. One lady however who was not put off was the great Maureen Potter who came to one of the refreshment stops and put on a comedy show there and then in the rain. As a result we asked her to present the Annual Lifeboat Awards to voluntary workers in the Mansion House the following year, which she did, and what a night that was. That occasion was not only memorable for the awardees but it was also a hilarious evening for all who attended including Ray Kipling the RNLI's Deputy Director.

Getting back to the Big Boat Push, we arrived in view of Dunlaoghaire Lifeboat station in the afternoon having stopped on the way and very warmly refreshed at Poolbeg Yacht Club. Tired but elated our gallant band completed the walk to be welcomed to the finishing line by the Garda Siochana Band to the strains of "Home from the Sea" which by then, still in heavy rain and soaked through expressed much of how we felt. The event was financially a success although the weather I feel kept many people from joining in along the route. However, on the PR side the event with Mr Haughey's attendance received excellent coverage in the Press, so all was well.

A ROYAL VISIT

The 7th of July 1993 was to be a special day for RNLI Ireland. Earlier that year the President of the RNLI, His Royal Highness The Duke of Kent had intimated his desire to visit a number of Irish lifeboat stations a first in the case of Southern Ireland stations. The Director Comdr. Brian Miles discussed dates with the Irish members of the Committee of Management and in conjunction with the Duke's office the dates were fixed for the 7th/8th July. The east coast was chosen for this first visit of the RNLI's President to Ireland. Starting the visit at Clogher Head and proceeding to Skerries, Howth, and the first day would finish at Dunlaoghaire. Then on the 8th starting at Wicklow and continuing on to Arklow and finishing the visit at Courtown.

It was my responsibility together with the Inspector of Lifeboats, Peter Bradley, to make all the arrangements for the visit. Peter would look after the arrangements at all the lifeboat stations and the movement of the party between stations. The Duke's party would include the Chairman of the RNLI, Mr Michael Vernon, the Deputy Chairman, Mr. Clayton Love jnr., the Director, Comdr. Brian Miles and several of the Irish members of the Committee of Management. It would be my responsibility together with the Garda Siochana as to the security arrangements for the visit, while at all times keeping the British Embassy informed, and also to look after the committees and guilds at each branch and arrange for them to be presented to the Duke. I would also take care of dining arrangements and menus for dinner on 7th and lunch on the 8th of July. In this area Mary Newman, who has a particular interest in culinary matters, was of great help. Needless to say security would be at its tightest and both Peter and myself were told that if it became known that the Duke of Kent was to visit the Republic of Ireland the visit would immediately be cancelled. This meant that all the arrangements were to be made without letting anybody at even station level know who was actually visiting. This situation had its amusing side, on a couple of occasions, as we worked through the arrangements.

The Duke's party, having visited Howth, would be transported by Howth lifeboat over to Dublin Bay, where he and his party would transfer to Dunlaoghaire lifeboat, and land at the East Pier in Dunlaoghaire. With security dictating the need for a location as close as possible to the pier for branch and guild members to be presented we approached the very adjacent National Yacht Club. The Club Manager was most apologetic and explained that the club had a major event, the Dunlaoghaire to Dingle race which would be started by Mr Haughey early on the morning of the 7th of July. He was very sorry that he couldn't accommodate us on that particular day. All the Yacht clubs in Ireland are most supportive of the RNLI and none more so than the National, we thanked him and just before leaving I said – more to get the message over as to the importance of the occasion, than as a criticism.

"Could I say that I truly believe that your committee will be extremely disappointed that you passed up the opportunity of welcoming this person to the National Yacht Club," The Manager realised that this was something very special, the penny had dropped as to the importance of the event, he immediately answered,

"Look, would you give me twenty four hours, we have a committee meeting this evening, if you call tomorrow morning I'll have some word for you," when I called to the club next morning the Manager said,

"We would be delighted to accommodate the RNLI on the 7th of July."

Something similar happened in a hotel near Gorey when we were arranging the lunch for the second day of the visit the 8th July. Again without naming names to the receptionist but making the point that it was a very special occasion I explained what we required. When I mentioned to the receptionist the necessity for security and the possibility of a helicopter landing in the garden she also realised that this was a little bit special and said,

"I think you should talk to the Owner/Manager of the hotel."

It was not my intention in either location to make myself appear important, however, it was necessary to establish the high-ranking level of this visit while not being in a position of disclosing the name. All the arrangements went well and we did take the Hon. Secretary at each station branch into our confidence a few days before the visit. On the night before the visit I was late coming home and May had a phone call from the press asking if it is true that a member of the Royal Family will be visiting Irish lifeboat stations tomorrow, needless to say she answered in the negative - nothing appeared in the morning papers. The visit went extremely well and when the Duke landed at Dunlaoghaire 'remarkably' several hundred people had lined up on the promenade facing the East Pier and clapped as he walked in along the pier. The party entered the National Yacht Club and all RNLI people were given the opportunity to meet and speak to the Duke. An excellent dinner that first evening was provided close by in a private dining room in the Royal Irish Yacht Club; after which I left for Wicklow to ensure that all was ready for the visit next morning. The Duke

To a Garden Party at Buckingham Palace

On Thursday 18th July 1996 from 4 to 6 pm

Needless to say it was quite exciting for both of us, it was certainly something to look forward to, we had seen in the past on television mention of garden parties at Buckingham Palace but never thought we would actually be invited to one. The instructions from the RNLI also arrived; reservation would be made in our name at the Grosvenor Hotel, Grosvenor Square which, we were advised was within walking distance of the Palace. We were to arrive in time for lunch and join Ray Kipling the Deputy Director and meet the other members of the RNLI group. The dress code for the ladies was hat and informal dress, and lounge suits for the men. We arrived in London with the city on a one-day bus strike, and on one of the hottest days I can remember. At the appointed time we all walked, approximately twenty RNLI invitees, to the main gate of the Palace. A long line of people had formed as we slowly made our way across the Palace Yard and through the main entrance, familiar to most people from the many Royal events shown on our television screens.

We passed through the Main Entrance Hall dominated by the Grand Staircase named I believe because of its winding proportions and floral gilt-bronze balustrade. On each side of the main entrance a huge semi-reclining figure in marble or alabaster, which I believe could have been based on the study of Greek or Roman ideals, we proceeded on through a very spacious Salon and following the line of people through French windows to an elevated terrace with steps down to the Palace Garden. The gardens were huge; a small lake could be seen in the far centre. The very tall trees around the perimeter gave the gardens a countrified atmosphere and contributed to the almost total privacy. Ranged down the left hand side was a continuous line of snow-white ornate catering tents where the guests could sit and partake of the finger food wine or soft drinks, and on the day that was in it, most welcome iced coffee, all of which was ongoing for the afternoon. The RNLI party were asked to form a line by the Deputy Director to meet our President The Duke of Kent. May and myself were towards the end of the line, when introduced he kindly said he remembered me from his visits to Ireland and expressed a wish to return to visit the Lifeboat stations on Ireland's West Coast.

It was obvious by now that the Queens entrance was imminent. Under the stewardship of a number of gentlemen in dark suits and bowler hats each carrying a black rolled umbrella, the many hundreds of guests were formed into a wide avenue, from the terrace steps out across the gardens to the left and leading towards a large and apparently more private tent. Presently the Queen, the Duke of Edinburgh and the Duke of Kent and other members of the Royal Family came out on the terrace and after the National Anthem moved slowly down the steps and on down the centre of the avenue of people. Those, who for a particular reason were to be presented, were placed at intervals along the centre of the avenue, after being presented and pleasantries exchanged the person moved to one side and the Royal party moved on to meet the next privileged person. In our position to the side of the avenue we were just about six feet away from the Queen and Prince Philip. Finally the Royal party entered the private tent.

It was now time to mingle with some of the other guests, partake of the refreshments and to find some welcome shade from the very hot sun. As we sat there we recognised several well-known faces from the world of television, and politics. Mr. Edward Heath rather slowly making his way across the gardens, as were several Cabinet Ministers and past members of government whose faces were familiar. We chatted with other members of the RNLI party, as we sat in the shade taking in all the style as the guests moved around the gardens. One lady told us as she and her husband were walking in the trees beyond the lake when they met a gentleman walking two Corgies. The whole afternoon was magical and of course a-never-to-be- repeated experience.

Just before 6p.m., the gentlemen in the bowler hats again became more evident and active as they quietly encouraged our departure. As we made our orderly way out of the Palace the thought amusingly occurred to me, had I arrived in dark suit, which I had, and bowler hat, sporting a black rolled umbrella, which I hadn't, I possibly may have had the freedom of the Palace. Happily we were able to make our way on foot, still through the chaos of the bus strike coupled with the London rush hour traffic, back to the comfort of the Grosvenor Hotel. Later in the evening, which we had pre-booked, we went to a revival of that lovely little musical "Salad Days," which we both really enjoyed, after which we walked slowly and quietly back to the hotel at the end of one of the most extraordinary days.

Over the years while I was Hon. Secretary of Wicklow Lifeboat Station, and also for all of my time as National Organiser, May had held the position of Hon. Secretary of the Ladies Guild at Wicklow. In 1996 she was awarded the Gold Badge of the RNLI for outstanding service in the field of fundraising. Needless to say she was delighted, not only for the recognition of her own service, but also for the recognition of the excellent fundraising efforts of all the members of the Ladies Guild over so many years. Kevin Desmond the same year was also very deservedly awarded the Gold Badge for his many years of dedicated service to fundraising in Wicklow over the same period.

The following April of 1997 all four of us, Kevin and his wife Sandra, and May and myself were invited to the Annual Presentation of Awards at the Barbican in London. It was quite a day for May and Kevin; Prince Michael made the presentations, first the gallantry awards, and then the awards to voluntary workers, which included the Irish awardees. The main hall of the Barbican Centre was packed to capacity with RNLI people from all over the British Isles and Ireland, while The Band of the Royal Marines played as we took our places before the main proceedings began. The whole occasion was quite splendid.

The day had started with all the awardees being invited to lunch, which gave me the opportunity to meet again with past colleagues from the other regions, and also to meet again the other awardees from around Ireland. When we returned to our hotel Kevin and Sandra's daughter Fiona had very thoughtfully organised a champagne reception for our party. Later in the evening, being in London, we decided to go to the theatre; all four of us thoroughly enjoyed the lively show "Grease" with a wonderful young cast. The whole trip was another memorable occasion as Sandra and myself together with our respective and happy awardees returned home to Wicklow the following day.

MY TURN TO SAY GOODBYE

Time was moving on and I found myself in the same position as my predecessor Brian Clark when I was appointed on his retirement fifteen years ago. My successor had been appointed, a bright young lady named Claire Brennan who came to us from the ISPCC. I now could understand to some extent the perplexity that Brian Clark had experienced during his final months. Although I believe, unlike what Brian had felt, I was on the whole looking forward to retirement. Nevertheless there were aspects of the job that I would greatly miss. Some of the staff members namely Joan Gibson, Mary Newman and Norma Sherwood, had been with the Institution prior to my joining, while Anne Sweeney and Pam Semple had been with us for several years, and of course Dermot Desmond whom I had known from childhood, all of whom I would miss. In many ways the Irish Regional staff as we were known within the Institution was like a second family to me, we all worked closely together every day; I was conscious that on the 1st of January '97 that daily contact would abruptly cease forever. I would always be grateful for the loyal and personal support I had received over the years from each and every one of them. I knew also I would miss meeting the many friends I had made all over Ireland during the past fifteen years.

However, as retirement was drawing closer, there were some aspects of the job I would be pleased to leave behind. Although I would miss meeting my colleagues from the other regions I would not miss the constant journeys back and forth to Poole and London and the ever-mounting pressure to raise more and more revenue - the constant fight to keep within Budget while annually trying to attain escalating targets - the ongoing pressure of continuously trying to encourage volunteers to accept these ever-increasing fundraising targets. This treadmill I would be glad to leave behind.

It was now my turn to say goodbye to the Branches and Guild members around the country and on my travels, mostly alone, I thought again about those first trips with Brian Clark, listening to his music; and the lady had she been still there, who would now be forgetting my face and remembering the next face. It all seemed such a short time ago, and yet so much had happened. Brian had passed away just the year before. I had continued to call to see himself and Brenda over the years, Brian had taken seriously ill in 1994 but had made a good recovery, still he wasn't the same, he looked frail and tired. "The old soldier" was beginning to fade away; the end came on 31st of July '95 strangely just three days after his beloved little "King Charles" dog "Verdi" had been found dead by Brenda.

At one time, several years before, the Personnel Department of the Institution had informed me that three of my predecessors, who had held the post of National Organiser were still living namely Colonel Trenham, Col. Rosse and Col. Clark and, of course myself, being the present incumbent. The idea had been mooted of getting us together for a photograph, however, it never happened. Now on the death of Col Clark I was the last.

As my own retirement was drawing closer, looking back over my years with the RNLI, one small aspect of my many duties came to mind. In certain circumstances the responsibility fell to me as National Organiser, to source a suitable name for new lifeboats. In the case where funding resulted from a donation to the RNLI, as happened in many cases, the name of a new boat as a rule came with that of the donor or in some cases a relative of the donor. If, however, the new lifeboat was paid for from the general funds of the institution or some other source, then a name had to be found. This happened on three occasions during my time as National Organiser. While of course I was never the "namer" of a lifeboat it is nice to think that I did actually choose the names for three new Irish lifeboats, "St Brendan" for the then new Rosslare lifeboat, "Hibernia" for a new lifeboat which would relieve station boats for re-fit from time to time around the Irish coast. Finally the "Anna Livia" the present Dun Laoghaire Lifeboat, a name chosen from the writings of James Joyce with his strong connection with Dun Laoghaire. In his writings James Joyce referred to the River Liffey, which flows through Dublin our capital city as "Anna Livia".

I was retiring from a position, which I had thoroughly enjoyed, that in many ways had taken over my life, and which I had given much to, but which had given me more satisfaction and fulfilment than all the other jobs I had held throughout my working life. It was strange the whole gamut of emotions I experienced over those final months and days of 1996 – the joy of great friendships made - the sadness at saying goodbye - the relief of handing over the burden of responsibility - the satisfaction of much achieved over the years - the frustration at not achieving all I had hoped – the bewilderment at the many beautiful presentations - the embarrassment of the many kind words spoken, and above all - the inadequacy at the overwhelming kindness of so many people; so many emotions.

There was of course God willing, the years ahead to look forward to; and the plans that May and I had for our future – Yes despite all the feelings, all the emotions, as I had heard many times from colleagues over the years. There is life after the RNLI! To paraphrase a half remembered line from a Seamus Heaney poem –

Let go, let fly, you have listened long enough, now strike your note.

8

Retirement

A NEW BEGINNING

Christmas '96 was, as usual, most enjoyable. As we had done for so many years we spent Christmas Day in "Mount Carmel" with Liam and Margaret and their family; and yet for me it was different. I was conscious over the holidays of all those conflicting feelings, the joy of freedom, as I looked towards the future, no more facing into another new year of endless fundraising concerns. Yet absurdly, there were also the nagging withdrawal symptoms, I was leaving a period of my life that on the whole had afforded me immense pleasure and satisfaction. Retirement and advancing years held no fears for me, growing older is the normal progression of life, and to my mind really not worth wasting time worrying about. I harbour no envy of the young, I have been there, it is an episode lived and enjoyed, I have no desire to return there. The next phase will be a totally different experience, unlived, new, and I am looking forward to it. I am not a morbid person, however as I entered this new chapter the thought briefly crossed my mind of its inevitable conclusion.

Of one thing I was certain, I would not just sit around and vegetate; we would enjoy our newly found freedom and this new episode in our lives. I had always enjoyed travelling and hoped we would enjoy some respite in warmer climates from Irish winters, in the future. I had all through my life, flirted for want of a better word, with the game of golf never getting very deeply involved, maybe with the time to do so I would take the game a little more seriously. I also for many years had a passion for messing about with boats and the water, which would really appeal to me as time went on. However, I had a project, which would keep mind and body fully occupied in the immediate future.

Christmas was a short break in what promised to be a very busy period over the next several months. Some years before I retired I had drawn fairly detailed plans for a small house to be built in the side garden of our present home. Unlike the other three properties in our cul-de-sac, our garage was a separate structure built in the garden but removed by about twenty-five feet from the side of the house. The plan called for dividing the garden and incorporating the garage into the new structure. When I had originally completed the drawing of the plans some years earlier they simply remained in a cupboard until late 1995 when I again came across them. May said,

"Why don't you look for planning permission and then decide if you wish to go ahead with the building." I had the plans professionally drawn; however before coming back to me the architect submitted them to the Council. The first I knew of the application being lodged with the planning authority was when it appeared in the "Wicklow People", together I might add with all my neighbours, which was extremely embarrassing.

The planning permission was granted and we made the decision to go ahead and build. I decided to get tenders for the building of the structure to completion stage on the exterior. Except for the electrical and plumbing work I would complete the interior myself. This project would be my transition therapy when I started into retirement. David Shannon was the contractor we chose, a very enthusiastic young man just getting started in the building business, and who was delighted to get the job. David completed his contract to our entire satisfaction in April of 1996 leaving the inside of the house as agreed, an empty shell. I had decided to finish all the interior ceilings and also the walls in R&V Pine Sheeting. This I thought with its largely open plan style would give the house a very warm and welcoming ambiance. The timber arrived and when unloaded it almost filled one room of the house. I always thought sheeting, was a strange description, for a product that comes in planks 8ft.long by 4ins in width and in packs of ten.

When I looked at the mountain of timber I thought to myself will it ever be finished. It was now late April of my retirement year and we were extremely busy in work, I also knew that I would be away from home a lot between now and the end of the year. I decided to make a start, but before fixing any sheeting, I had to do a first fix of two by two inch timbers horizontally at sixteen-inch centres on the internal side of all exterior walls of the house and then insulate all the gaps between. I hoped I would get this far before the end of the summer and then be able to make a start on the actual sheeting. Each morning before driving to work I would spend a couple of hours working in the house, I also spent every weekend working away on the timber. It was of course very convenient, living just next door to the site. I started work in the bedroom and the upstairs bathroom and worked my way then out to the gallery over what was to be the lounge. By November, I was only a little behind schedule but, of course, because with all the flurry of activity as retirement approached, I didn't get much work done on the building. There was no hurry we were still in the house next door with no finishing deadlines to meet.

With Christmas over and all my farewells expressed to lifeboat friends and supporters, I was free to devote my time totally to the building. Work went on a pace with electrical and plumbing where necessary being carried out as we went along. We had promised ourselves a good holiday to celebrate our retirement, so in February we packed up the work, locked up both houses, and took ourselves off to Florida. This time we went to Anna-Maria Island in the Gulf of Mexico and relaxed and enjoyed the wonderful climate and considered our retirement plans for two glorious weeks. When we returned from holidays I really got into the work and by early April the mountain of sheeting was reduced to no more than ten packs. At this point we had no stairs to the upper floor with access still by ladder. My friend Sean Behan who had dropped in to see how the work was coming along said to me,

"I have a large quantity of well seasoned oak planks left over from building the house, you are welcome to them if you wish to use them for your staircase". Needless to say I was delighted. Now I needed to find a special kind of carpenter/cabinet maker to make this rather complicated staircase. I was extremely lucky; I approached a chap I knew from schooldays who had retired back to Wicklow, having spent most of his working life in a very specialised area of the trade in London. Sonny O' Toole agreed to do the job. Sonny whose Christian name was Bartholomew, called after his father, hence the pet name is much more than a carpenter; he is truly an artist with wood. Having taken very exacting measurements he arrived some two weeks later with the completed staircase in several parts. For me, who enjoys working with wood, it was fascinating watching a true craftsman assemble this complicated staircase which he had machined in his workshop and which fitted to absolute precision. I still admire Sonny's wonderful skill and artistry almost every time I climb the stairs.

We had made the decision to sell the existing house where we were living, so in late March we put the house on the market, expecting the sale process to take at least a couple of months. The fact that the house sold within three weeks put me under some pressure to finish the work and vacate the house. So with the help of my nephew Stephen we completed the new house by the end May and moved in. Eight years later we are still very happily living in "Friary Lodge" as we called it, with its view of the old

Franciscan Friary in the Abbey Grounds. There is no doubt, the house is very comfortable and has a lovely atmosphere, and is also extremely economical to run.

Would we move again? We have lived in eight different houses in Wicklow since we married; some of our friends say we are inveterate movers. If the right property came along, in the right location and had a project for me to get involved in, of course we would, but it would have to be a bit special for us to leave "Friary Lodge."

A VISIT TO THE ARAS

A few months before I retired we made an application for permission to bring a group of volunteers to meet the President of Ireland, Her Excellency Mary Robinson, at Aras an Uachtarain (Home of the President). The request in time was kindly acceded to; the President would receive a representative group of twenty-five RNLI volunteers and staff. By then I had retired and indeed was glad that I did not have to choose from the many hundreds of dedicated volunteers from all over Ireland. This unenviable task would fall to my successor Claire Brennan, and I was grateful to her for kindly including May as an RNLI Gold Badge holder and myself amongst the group. The 20th of May '97 was the day the visit would take place. We gathered close to the visitors' gates of Aras an Uachtarain; it was a beautiful sunny afternoon, it promised to be the perfect day for this splendid occasion to meet the President and visit this historic house. The group was made up of Station and Fundraising volunteers, four Gold Badge holders and representatives of the Committee of Management and Staff. At the appointed time we were escorted to the car park close to the main entrance of the Aras.

Aras an Uachtarain, formerly the Viceregal Lodge, was the official residence of the British Viceroys in Ireland. Built in 1751 by Nathanial Clements the house was bought by the British Government in 1782 as the residence for the British Crown's representative in Ireland. After Ireland achieved its Independence in 1921,when its status became that of a Dominion, the house became the residence of the first Governor General Timothy Healy and for a time his successors the representatives of the British Monarch in the Irish Free State. Following the passing of the 1937 Irish Constitution and the creation of the new office of President of Ireland the former Vice Regal Lodge, after some debate became Aras an Uachtarain - the home of the President. The first President, unanimously selected by all parties of Dail Eireann, was Dr. Douglas Hyde a former president of the Gaelic League.

Interestingly the choice of this house with its past steeped in colonial tradition as the official home of the President of Ireland was extremely unpopular with certain members of the Irish Government of the day, and was in fact in danger of being demolished. Several other properties were considered, one being "St. Anne's" Clontarf the former home of Lord and Lady Ardilaun. Each property in turn was found to be unsuitable for one reason or another. Eventually this former historic home of many British Viceroys became and remains today Aras an Uachtarain na hEireann, the home of the President of Ireland.

From the Entrance Hall with its magnificent ornate barrel-vaulted ceiling we entered The State Corridor also known as The Franchini Corridor, which is lined on one side by busts of each of the seven former Presidents to date, mounted on marble columns. The other side of this grand corridor as we proceeded along features stucco panels, the work of the Lafranchini brothers who during the 18th century worked in many of the great houses of Ireland, Carton and Castletown to name but two, and of course nearer to home, Avondale House, the home of Charles Stewart Parnell. We were escorted into The State Reception Room, formerly the Ballroom, now used for the reception of visiting Heads of State, and the many formal Presidential occasions. The ceiling centrepiece, again by Lafranchini, we were later told depicted - Time Rescuing Truth from Discord and Envy. The particularly striking hand-woven Donegal carpet designed for the house, depicted on its four corners the Riverine heads from the Custom House, representing the principal rivers of Ireland, and in its centre the Phoenix rising from the flames. The beautiful fireplace is by Bossi, whose family was reputed to know the secret of how to colour marble. The very large sash and French windows open onto terracing and steps which in turn leads to the manicured lawns and formal gardens of the Aras, where over the years many visiting heads of state have ceremonially planted trees. The President's Aide-de-Camp instructed the group in the manner in which we were to be presented to the President, Her Excellency Mary Robinson.

When all was ready the President entered the room and welcomed the group expressing her admiration for the work of the RNLI and for the dedication of those volunteers to the saving of life at sea; also the many who give so much of their time in the fundraising support of this great voluntary institution. Mr. Richard Burrows a member of the Committee of Management replied thanking the President for her kind welcome. She then moved along the line and spoke to each person individually. I had met Mary Robinson some years before at the Naming Ceremony of the new Ballyglass lifeboat in Co. Mayo, her native county. On that occasion I was seated beside her father Dr. Bourke a most friendly and affable man who practiced medicine in Ballina. I mentioned the Ballyglass ceremony to the President, an event that took place in the early months of her presidency, she said she remembered the occasion with great pleasure. I also took the liberty of asking her how her father was keeping; she thanked me for asking and told me he was keeping very well.

After the formal introductions were over the afternoon took

on a much more informal air, we were invited to have tea while the President mingled with the group. She then brought the group through The State Dining Room, where portraits of past Presidents line the walls and interestingly explained that the huge table seating upwards of twenty was used for Cabinet meetings in Leinster House up to 1960; and is still used for the first meeting of the new Cabinet after its ministers receive their seals of office from the President. In the State Drawing Room the President kindly offered to have an informal photograph with anyone who wished, and later we gathered on the terrace for a formal group photograph. The visit concluded with a tour of the recently completed interpretive centre; formerly the old basement kitchens.

It was a delightful and memorable occasion, which we all thoroughly enjoyed, our visit to the home of our President and first Citizen of Ireland. It was also nice to meet and chat again with the lifeboat branch members from all over Ireland.

THE LAKE OF KINGS

During the summer months of '97 I explored the possibility of acquiring a mooring in Wicklow harbour. With the sale of the house completed I said to May that I might get back into sailing again and look around for a small keelboat. I discussed the matter of the mooring with the Harbour Master. I had no interest in keeping a boat in the outer harbour with all the attendant problems of having to move it, possibly during the night in the event of easterly gales. I had hoped if possible to keep the boat in the inner harbour, however, I was assured that the particular part of the river in which I wished to lay the mooring would not have the required depth of water at all states of the tide to facilitate a fixed keel yacht. Although the harbour Master was extremely helpful I decided I would re-think my ideas on the type of boat I would look for. Strangely at the time I never thought of checking out the mooring position in our neighbouring town of Arklow which I am sure had excellent facilities.

I had followed all the "Waterways" series with Dick Warner on television with great interest and admiration. The different series illustrated several trips in various craft on Irelands Inland

Waterways, covering in the main the River Shannon and the Grand Canal. We had in fact been involved in a small way with Series 3 before I retired when the subject matter on that occasion, was an old converted lifeboat. The internationally acclaimed series, mainly through the professionalism of Dick Warner and the excellence of the photography, clearly demonstrated the peaceful tranquillity of the majestic River Shannon, its history and folklore all portrayed in a most appealing manner. May and I had spent a very enjoyable week boating on the upper Shannon a few years earlier with two other couples; so with the mooring problems in Wicklow I decided to investigate the Shannon as an alternative. I had a chat with a friend Michael Shortt who had done his share of boating over the years and had been a prominent member of Clontarf Yacht and Boat Club prior to he and his wife Eileen coming to live in Wicklow. So Michael and myself decided to check out the boating scene and the boats for sale on the Shannon and also on the Grand Canal.

We made several trips to many different locations along the river and checked the boats for sale in various boatyards along the waterway. Although we didn't find the boat that I could say, 'that's the right boat for me' the trips were very enlightening and enjoyable. In truth we did find a very nice boat, but the sale fell through, however more about that later! Eileen and May would pack a picnic lunch and Michael and I would head off at about 8am. I remember one particularly lovely summers day, sitting at a picnic table enjoying our lunch at the little harbour at Terryglass the sun glistening from the rippling water as the boats arrived and tied up or departed for another destination on the river, whichever the case; the whole scene was idyllic. There were several days much like that as each week we took off for a day to check out different locations along the river Shannon.

The lovely harbour at Dromineer with the remains of the old ivy covered castle, standing sentinel over all the activity of the river, a wonderful place to linger for an hour or two or maybe a little longer. Another special memory was the day we spent checking out the boats for sale at the marina at Ballina. We again relaxed having our lunch at the beautifully maintained waterfront park beside the ancient narrow bridge connecting comparatively modern Ballina with the old and historic Killaloe. These twin towns live in peaceful harmony and co-existence through the year except when the two great rival counties of Munster hurling, Clare and Tipperary clash in their efforts to progress to the All Ireland Hurling Final. Ballina, not to be confused with a town of the same name in Co Mayo, is situated on the east side of the bridge in Co. Tipperary, while Killaloe, at the other end on the west side of the bridge being in Co. Clare.

The connecting bridge across the Shannon, which saw many skirmishes over the centuries, I am told then becomes a veritable 'no mans land.' The young boys and girls from each side, dressed in their county colours display a little more than passive support for their respective counties. It may be difficult to believe as one explores this small but most historic of towns, that Killaloe, now a centre of tourism, was once the Capital of Ireland, the seat of the great warrior Brian Boru, High King of Ireland. In many ways the history of Killaloe mirrors the history of Ireland in microcosm; the Vikings came to plunder, the Normans to conquer, they came and left. King Magnus of Norway, King John of England, the armies of Cromwell, King William and King James all passed through Killaloe. If you wish to be transported back in history, in fact, to the 13th century pay a visit to St. Flannan's Cathedral; it's style is mainly Gothic though there are traces of earlier Romanesque influences such as the rounded central arch of the east window. Digging a little deeper into the history of this district, you begin to get the feeling of the early civilisation of this very special place dating back to prehistoric times and nestling here at a strategic position on the lower shores of Lough Derg.

On the day Michael and I spent in this particular district of Shannon side, we discovered a wonderful Old Dutch barge a beautifully maintained craft of great charm and character. I would say approximately 70 feet in length. She was tied up on the Ballina side of the river. While we were enviously admiring the barge an elderly and very friendly lady, obviously one of the owners we thought, came struggling along, carrying two five litre bottles of water. She could see that we were taking an inordinate interest in the barge and kindly asked us if we would like to see around her, needless to say we jumped at the opportunity. It transpired that the lady was the sole owner of the boat and lived quiet alone on board. She had led a most interesting life in the art world working for many years in various Art Galleries around the world, and quite obviously was delighted with having company to chat to for an hour or so. "But how do you move such a big boat from one place to another on the river?" I asked her

"I get a few friends to come and help when I have to move." She said. We were given the grand tour of the boat, which was extremely interesting.

The boat was well fitted out below with an excellent galley, which opened onto the main saloon, and must have been 25ft long by 12ft across its beam and easily accommodated the large three-piece suite and ancillary pieces of furniture. A large oil-burning heater kept the whole boat warm and snug. Forehead of the galley and saloon were two good-sized and well-appointed cabins. The lady said,

"Come and see the after cabin which in the old days before the boat was converted for pleasure use was the Skippers cabin; it has never been altered since the boat was plying its cargo through the Dutch canals." It was interesting to compare this traditional old cabin, with its miniscule gravity fed hand basin and double sleeping nook, to the more modern cabins forehead of the saloon. We were told the barge was for sale, which was also very interesting. If one were looking for a very comfortable home afloat, with the option of a change of scene at the press of a button to bring the massive engine to life, then this would be the ideal boat.

However, it was not what I was looking for even if I had been able to afford it, which I was not. I was to meet this interesting lady again many months later on the Shannon.

By the end of August we had made several enjoyable trips to the Shannon and gained a lot of information regarding marinas and harbours. We had spoken to many people all along the waterway without success with regard to finding the right boat. I happened to be talking to a close friend who was also May's boss, Leslie Bradshaw, telling him of our trips to the Shannon, Leslie said.

"I'll get in touch with my brother-in-law Bob Marktelow in Portsmouth, he is very interested in boats we'll see if he can dig up something interesting over there, it can't do any harm."

Within a week I had a call from Leslie,

"Can you come to the office today? I have a facsimile message several pages long coming through from a yacht broker in Southampton, just glancing at it stretched across the room, its content appears very interesting" he said.

Needless to say I went immediately. The facsimile concerned just one boat which was described as a steel barge type motor yacht 40'x12'and of very high specification, she was only five years old. The reason for selling was, that the owner, Mrs. Constable whose husband had commissioned the building of the boat for cruising on Southampton waters had since died; his wife had reluctantly decided to sell. The text message described every detail of the boat complete with line drawings and plans of the layout. There was no doubt this was a quality boat with the interior completely finished out in oak. I phoned the brokers direct, Brinton Marine and spoke to Mr. Bob Brinton whom I found to be extremely helpful with no high-pressure sales talk whatsoever. The price however was more than we had hoped to pay, Mr Brinton suggested it was well worth making the journey and having a look for myself, if she suited me then make an offer; he went on to say,

"The boat has been for sale for a while now, although designed for the inland waterways, with her beam of 12' she is not really suitable for use on the British canals, which are narrower than the Irish canals, he said, the interest in the boat over on his side would be limited."

From the details on the text this appeared to be the right boat, at least it was worth a trip to Southampton to have a look at her. The following week Michael Shortt, Leslie Bradshaw and myself took an early flight and met up with Leslie's brother-in-Law who took us to meet Mr. Brinton and see the boat. She was moored on the Itchen River literally at the bottom of the garden beside a little timber jetty. It was a beautiful hot September day and as we descended the garden steps down to the level of the river, the boat looked very impressive indeed. We spent a couple of hours checking her over, Michael took particular interest in the engine which was in pristine condition, we were all very impressed, there was no doubt she was a magnificent craft.

Before we left I chatted with Mr. Brinton, he kindly gave me a copy of a recent survey which had been carried out on the boat. He said if I went ahead with the purchase he would make the arrangements for lifting out, if we could co-ordinate the loading to coincide with the transport to Ireland. I said we would make the decision and get in touch within a few days.

We decided to buy, we made our offer, which was accepted and I sent on our deposit. We made the arrangements for transport to Ireland and again Michael Shortt and another friend Willie Brown and myself crossed by ferry and drove on to Southampton, I paid over the balance of the purchase money and made the final arrangements for transporting to Ireland. Two weeks later the boat arrived in Lowtown on the Grand Canal. May who had not seen the boat yet and a few other friends arrived. They were as amazed as I was to see the size of her on the trailer. On the journey from Southampton to Fishguard the police had to be notified in each Shire all along the way by the transporters. On her arrival at Lowtown on the Grand Canal we had a crane in place and had her lifted in; after a short run on the canal with all hands on board, we tied her to her mooring, where she would remain for the winter.

Over the winter months Michael and myself went over to Lowtown for a day each week and worked on the boat. Because she had not been used I suppose or properly maintained, beyond having the engine run regularly, for a two-year period she really needed some tender loving care. There were lots of jobs to be taken care of over the next several months. Each week we would run the engine while over the period Michael did a complete overhaul of all the electrics including the navigation and cabin lighting. The boat was equipped with both 12 and 220-volt circuits, so with the use of a small generator I was able to get on with some changes in the layout of the galley area.

As Spring approached and the weather improved we gave the whole boat a fresh coat of paint from the water line up, and prepared for the move down through the Grand Canal to the Shannon. We christened her "Illyria ll"; again over a two-day period, Michael and a friend of ours Pat Hickey, now sadly departed this life, brought her across to Shannon Harbour. Making our first 'land fall' in Tullamore, it was a most enjoyable and happy trip with many laughs and some anxious moments as we manoeuvred our beamy craft through many locks and under narrow bridges dating back well over a century. As we steamed slowly across the midlands of Ireland, we all acknowledged there is no doubt boating on the inland waterways is a slower and very relaxing way of life.

I had arranged to have her dry docked in Shannon Harbour and have her bottom professionally brought back to the new metal, primed and painted. Looking like new and in first class condition, we were now ready to take her up the Shannon to her permanent home. We had tried several different marinas for a berth with not much luck, when by chance, we were told of a new marina on Lough Ree near the River Inny. May made the phone call and we went to see the marina and meet the owner a Mr. Dermot O'Leary. The Marina was first class and we were given a berth. We only discovered sometime later that Dermot O' Leary was the principal singer of "The Bards" a very popular country band on the music circuit. The marina was new and apart from a hire fleet of five other boats owned by Mr O'Leary we were the first to be given a berth. Michael Shortt, Dermot Desmond and myself at 6pm. on Saturday evening steamed from Shannon Harbour through the last two locks of the Grand Canal and started our journey north through the wider waters of the River Shannon towards our home berth in Lough Ree.

We tied up for the night at Shannon Bridge with its massive power station the chimneys of which can be seen for miles across the flat lands of the Shannon region. After having a meal on board we repaired to Michael Killeen's Pub, a famous watering hole on the river where one is assured of great music each evening, a house well known to all who ply the river for pleasure. We made an early start next morning and it wasn't long before we were abreast of the ancient monastic centre of Clonmacnoise (The Meadow of the sons Nos); founded by St. Ciaran in 548 A.D. Clonmacnoise from its modest beginning became a great monastic city and Medieval University renowned throughout Western Europe, for its cultural reputation that was to endure for almost 700 years. I had visited this fascinating settlement with some friends just a few weeks earlier when the boat was in dry-dock. Pat Lalor, Willie Brown and myself spent a memorable day at Clonmacnoise exploring the many antiquities of this ancient monastic site and its excellent Interpretive Centre. Just to see the 1000-year-old Cross of the Scriptures, depicting episodes from the life of Christ, which now stands within the Centre is in itself worth making the visit to Clonmacnoise. With so much to take in I would suggest taking one of the regular guided tours to make the best of your visit to this serene and beautiful place.

After a little more than an hour's steaming we were approaching Athlone, with the unmistakable twin spires of the Church of St. Peter and St. Paul in distant view across the landscape. The capital of the Irish midlands, Athlone (An Sean Ath Mor) meaning, the Great Ford of Antiquity. The modern name, Athlone, comes from two Irish words: Ath meaning ford or crossing, and Luan a man's name meaning the Ford of Luan. The most intensive artillery bombardment in Irish history took place here in 1691 during the historic siege of Athlone. On more than once this historic crossing of the River Shannon was to be the scene of fierce and bloody battle. In more modern and peaceful times Athlone is celebrated as the birthplace of Irelands most famous singer Count John McCormack.

We tied up at the quays beside the huge Athlone lock and being Sunday we made a quick dash for Mass. Except in certain locations and situations, there is no speed limit in open water on the Shannon so after leaving Athlone and passing under the new bridge constructed as part of the Athlone By-Pass we were able to increase the revolutions and get the boat really moving. We soon entered the southern reaches of Lough Ree (The Lake of Kings). I was amazed how broad the lake really is as we steamed along, it was like being on the open sea, suddenly our boat seemed very small indeed. We followed the navigation marks and after an hour or so rounded Hare Island, which was our landmark for what would be our homeport. We slowly entered the channel leading to the marina and tied up in our new berth to be welcomed by Dermot O'Leary and his son Shane who manages the marina.

" THE DECENT CHURCH "

Over the next three years we spent a lot of time in the Shannon region, we would go down for weekends or for periods in between. After all the work and help that Michael put in over the previous year, he was only out in the boat once after that first trip on the Shannon, which was a pity. Michael and Eileen sold their home in Wicklow and moved to the pretty little village of Clogheen in Co Tipperary, where they still happily reside.

Many of our friends and family spent relaxing days and star-filled nights with us on the boat, as we gently moved around the historic Lough Ree. It should also be recorded that we got our share of rainy days, but thankfully one doesn't seem to easily recall them. Being the main arterial route to Ireland's interior from earliest times, the whole length of the Shannon, its islands and shores abounds with historical sites many of which date from the very dawn of civilisation. Be it the Vikings, the Normans, the English they all left their mark. Although Clonmacnoise may be the most notable and extensive of the ecclesiastical sites it is just one of many along the length of the Shannon. We became very familiar with the Lough Ree area and quite often we would run down to Hodson Bay and tie up at the lovely little harbour there and maybe have a meal or a drink at the friendly Athlone Golf Club, the Clubhouse of which stands just over the harbour, or the imposing Hodson Bay Hotel almost next door.

Looking at the map of Ireland it is clear that Lough Ree is close to the centre of the country, as one approaches the entrance to the little harbour from Hodson Bay one is aware of what is known as the Hodson Pillar, which is reputed to be the exact centre of Ireland. Much of the time when May and I went down to the boat by ourselves, we would tour around the area by car and simply use the boat as a base. The mooring was close to one of the loveliest villages in the midlands, namely Glasson, known as the 'Village of the Roses.' Glasson is at its best in summer when climbing roses embellish almost every house in the village, it is also home to one of the most charming little pubs in the Athlone district, 'Grogans,' which, more in our line than its beverages, serves very good food at reasonable prices. My brother Liam and his wife Margaret spent a few very pleasant days on the boat with us, on the first day of their visit they played a round of golf at the lovely Glasson Golf Club with its renowned views of different aspects of the Shannon. A few miles to the north is 'Goldsmith Country;' the following day we did a tour of the Goldsmith haunts.

Born in Pallas Co. Longford the son of Rev. Charles Goldsmith, the family moved to the village of Auburn when Oliver was still a child, and settled at Lissoy Parsonage where Charles Goldsmith ministered at Kilkenny-West Church for the rest of his life. Little remains of Lissoy Parsonage and nothing remains of Auburn village.

'Sweet Auburn, loveliest village of the plain' was how Goldsmith began his much-loved epic poem 'The Deserted Village.' Although much of his life was spent in London, it was this area of Longford and Westmeath that inspired the "Deserted Village" and where so many of the landmarks were located. Kilkenny-West Church, site of, "The decent Church that topped the neighbouring hill", much of the church still remains in tact today, or "The Busy Mill", which survived in use until 1860. The old millstone is set into the entrance of the local pub, 'The Three Jolly Pigeons.' Nothing remains, except the site of the School House where Thomas Byrne taught Goldsmith; the poet portrayed Byrne in the 'Village Schoolmaster' sequence of his great poem with the lines

'A man severe he was and stern to view; I knew him well, and every truant knew;' and ended with the famous lines '

'And still they gazed and still the wonder grew that one small head could carry all he knew.'

Much of the evidence of Goldsmith's life in this area is no more, and yet his association with the district still attracts many thousands of visitors to seek out the locations of his early life in what was once 'Sweet Auburn.'

After three years cruising around the upper Shannon I changed "Illyria " for a smaller craft named "Carolan". When Michael and myself were doing our trips around the marinas of the Shannon some years earlier I almost bought a boat, which was moored at Shamrock Marina near the Town of Banagher. "Carolan" was the only boat we had seen on the Shannon at that time that I liked. Although built in the style of a classic narrow boat she had a beam of 10ft. and was 30ft. in length and built in steel, she was almost 12ft. shorter than "Illyria", but a very nice little boat. However, the sale at that time fell through. The owner was a chap named Martin Guinan, a retired merchant navy captain whom I again met when in dry dock following our trip down the Grand canal. Martin was very taken at that time with "Illyria" and mentioned that if I decided to sell to let him know. When I decided to look for something smaller; the reason being that we were spending a lot of time by ourselves on the boat and I found her very big and heavy to manage, mainly on my own.

I contacted Martin and we did an exchange deal between "Illyria" and "Carolan," I also secured a mooring at Shamrock

Marina which was quite a busy marina with lots of family activity. I got to know many of the boat owners who were all very friendly and helpful and of course Martin continued to keep "Illyria" there. It was a real treat to see how Martin could handle her, docking single-handedly in difficult tidal conditions at the marina. If I felt any sadness at letting her go I took great pleasure in Martin's pride in "Illyria" and his seamanship ability, he was also a great help to me in getting to know "Carolan".

Banagher is an interesting little town with many very pretty Georgian houses along its main street, which runs down to an imposing fortified bridge linking Co. Offaly with Co. Galway. On the west side of the bridge stands a Martello Tower, a small circular fort built to guard against possible invasion by the French during the Napoleonic Wars. At the lower end of the town to the right of the bridge is the very busy harbour and beyond, two thriving Cruiser Hire companies. We would often drive into Banagher in the evenings have a meal in Flynn's Commercial Hotel and then ramble around the harbour looking at the boats coming in to tie up for the night.

Banagher can truly boast it's own literary tradition; Sir William Wilde, Charlotte Bronte, Anthony Trollope and Sir Matthew de Renzi all have connections with Banagher. On one of our trips to Banagher we were encouraged to visit Cloghan Castle, we had on occasions walked by the castle which looked very interesting. It is described as the only ancient castle in Ireland still lived in by a family. St Cronan built a monastery here 1400 years ago and the castle was built on the site some 600 years later. The castle was absolutely fascinating and lived up to all expectations. A rather tall imposing gentleman did the tour and in one particular room showed us a photograph taken of one corner of that room the furnishings in the photograph were just as they were in the room on the day of our tour, however when the film was processed the photo showed a clear outline of a monk kneeling at prayer. Another interesting visit we made by road while staying on the boat at Banagher was to Clonfert Abbey just a few miles on when you cross the bridge into Co. Galway. Clonfert, which is well worth taking the time to visit, dates back to the fifth century. The sandstone doorway of the Abbey is particularly interesting with its elaborate stone carvings. The Abbey has a special significance or import for all who sail or cruise the river; St.Brendan the Navigator founded the monastery.

Of the historic and religious sites visited along the river the one that stands out in my mind above all others is the simple little Church at Meelick. We left our mooring on a pleasant afternoon and gently steamed down river with some friends who had called to the marina to visit us. Some forty minutes later we approached the boardwalk where boats tie up to await the opening of the lock at Meelick. We tied up and secured the boat I was told that the Church was about 15 minutes walk away. The little stone building was approached through a very old Graveyard and when we arrived a lady was preparing to lock up the church for the day, but she was delighted to let us enter and pause for a while. The church which was comparatively narrow for its length of I suppose 100ft. and was built of rough cast stonework as were most church buildings of the period. The building had been re-roofed and serves as a living place of worship with Mass each Sunday catering for the small local community. I can truly say that I have never before or since experienced such a feeling of calm and serenity as I did on that occasion in that simple little 15th century Franciscan church. I was told that it is the oldest Catholic Church in continuous use in Ireland.

We kept our mooring at Shamrock Marina and "Carolan" for two years although we were not using the boat as much as we had been earlier; much of the time I appeared to be driving down by myself, so we reluctantly made the decision to sell. So we were back to square one, however I suppose I did get the boating bug out of my system.

OLD KYLEMORE

One of our favourite parts of Ireland when I was working was Connemara Co. Galway and each time we visited that part of Ireland we would look in the auctioneer's windows at the properties for sale. Needless to say the prices being asked put the possibility of buying out of the question. Over the years while working with the RNLI we had made friends with some of the crewmembers in Clifden. We were particularly friendly with the Honorary Secretary of the station and his wife Jackie and Marion O'Grady with whom we always stayed in their excellent guesthouse on my RNLI visits to Clifden. One evening some months after we sold the boat I was surfing the Internet at home when I clicked on "Properties for sale in Connemara" and went on to check Matt O'Sullivans, the Clifden based auctioneer's website. Listed was a property in the Inagh Valley described as a small dwelling; the price appeared to be very reasonable. I said to May, I think I've found you a house in Connemara? She looked at the listing with a degree of scepticism, I said, it wouldn't be any harm to phone and check it out, which she did. We decided we would go to Connemara for a few days, visit Jackie and Marion and check out the property at the same time. A few days later, in appalling weather conditions, we arrived in the Inagh Valley.

Although we had arranged with the auctioneer to see the cottage the following morning, I thought that in these conditions it would be a good idea to have a look. The lane off the Inagh Valley road was in bad condition and very narrow, I parked the car at a slightly wider part of the lane and put on my Wellington boots, suggesting to May that she should stay in the car, I made my way in driving rain under a golf umbrella up the lane. I arrived at the cottage, which I recognised from a photograph and went in through the gate. The auctioneer had told us that the owners had gone to live in Spain several months before; and on the day that was in it here in Connemara, one felt that they possibly had the right idea.

When I looked around May was just behind me, I climbed up and looked in through the window of what I could see was the living room and I said to May, this isn't half bad! Next morning we met Adrian from the auctioneer's in Clifden and again made our way out to the Inagh Valley, the weather had changed completely, the day was bright and sunny and from the cottage we now had a glorious view of the majestic Maamturk mountain range from the living room window, what a location! The cottage certainly needed some renovation and upgrading, however, the potential was clearly there and I felt that most of the work was not beyond my own ability to undertake. I told Adrian we would have a talk between us and I would call to his office in Clifden that afternoon. We decided on an offering price based on the work that needed to be done and made our decision not to go beyond that price. We happened to meet Adrian on the main street in Clifden and made our offer there and then, which was accepted within a few days.

Over the next year we put in a considerable amount of work on the cottage. We applied for mains electricity, unfortunately the installation of which was held up on account of the Foot and Mouth problem in Northern Ireland. All entry by the ESB onto farmland was suspended for the duration. This held us up, not having the advantage of using power tools, and having to stop work in mid afternoon with the short winter days. Because our water supply was a direct feed from a mountain spring the pressure was not strong enough to operate the showers, necessitating the installation of a large storage tank and electric water pump. We were very lucky to make friends with Michael Fitzpatrick a builder from Renvyle who was a great help to us in getting the work finished which would have been a long drawn out operation, we being so far away in Wicklow. Within a year the work was more or less completed and the cottage was very comfortably finished and furnished; we called it "The Retreat." We have made many friends and acquaintances in the area and without exception they are all extremely helpful and friendly people. We tend to spend some time in Connemara most months of the year, and on many occasions some of our friends have come and spent some time with us.

With the work completed we have more time now to enjoy the wonderful Connemara countryside. Just five minutes drive away from the cottage is the world famous Kylemore Abbey, sheltered by the Twelve Bens and the Maamturk mountains this beautifully proportioned fantasy castle in glistening white granite and grey limestone was built by Mitchell Henry, a Manchester business man in1826 as a gift for his wife. The romantic battlemented castle sited in a magnificent setting beside a lake, is built in the Gothic Revival style. After the sudden death of his wife and daughter Mitchell Henry left Kylemore, but not before he built the exquisite Neo-gothic chapel in the grounds of the castle as a memorial to his wife, the chapel with beautiful stained glass is a miniature copy of Norwich Cathedral. Kylemore Castle was bought together with the lands and Victorian Gardens, by the Benedictine nuns, fleeing from Ypres in Belgium during World War 1, and became an Abbey. It is now run as a boarding school for young ladies. The public rooms, the grounds and the Victorian gardens of Kylemore

Abbey are open to the public. The extensive shop and restaurant is one of the most popular stopping off point for the many thousands of visitors to Connemara each year.

Another interesting place where we tend to end up when we have visitors is the very peaceful and historic Renvyle House Hotel originally the holiday home of the writer and indeed the many-faceted Oliver St. John Gogarty; he was also a surgeon, a senator, a poet, a pilot, and a playwright. During the War of Independence and the Civil War, Michael Collins frequently sought and was afforded sympathetic shelter in the Gogarty home in Ely Place in Dublin; the writer had a great admiration for Collins.

'Napoleonic! But a bigger and more comely specimen of manhood than Napoleon,' was how he once described him.

Gogarty suffered for his involvement during these troubled times; he was taken prisoner but luckily escaped, thereby possibly saving his life, however, Renvyle House was burned down with the loss of a magnificent library and many other valuables including letters from James Joyce. Gogarty rebuilt Renvyle House as an hotel and although no longer in the ownership of the family, it is still a very popular hotel today with its own challenging 9 hole golf course and fishing lake and many other facilities including an outdoor swimming pool. It is the idyllic place in which to relax over afternoon tea in the conservatory, try your hand at clay pigeon shooting, take a stroll in the extensive grounds or if you are feeling energetic, play a few holes of golf. But beware! The pace of life is so relaxed in Renvyle that you may not be able to raise yourself to such energetic pursuits.

THE DOG SIMPLY DISAPPEARED

We have all heard the old saying, 'a dog is man's best friend', and certainly it was our experience that it would be difficult to find a more faithful, undemanding and less questioning companion. Over our married life we had two dogs, very different in breed and temperament, but in their time both were devoted companions. Our first dog was a lovely 'Old English' sheepdog which we called Kim, while the second a 'Jack Russell' terrier, an independent little character who thought he was capable of taking on the world. Our friends Mary and Dermot Desmond gave us "Snoopy", as May's young nieces Tracy and Lynn insisted he be called, to mark my fiftieth birthday. Mary's dad had been breeding a very good strain of Jack Russell terriers in Kilkenny for years; the stock had originally come from "Mount Juliet"

The Old English was a very highly bred animal, which we had bought from a breeder in Co. Sligo. She had proved as she matured to be of very nervous disposition. Around the house she had to be close to one of us, if May or I were sitting down she had to have her head resting on your foot or her paw on your knee. She loved to sit in the car and as long as the engine wasn't running she would stay there for hours. Once the engine was started and the car moving she would go frantic and froth at the mouth. We tried every suggestion to calm her down, to no avail. We were both working at that time and the dog appeared to be fretting when left on its own during the day. When May came home for lunch, Kim would stretch out against the kitchen door and refuse to move, May would have to physically drag her away from the door in order for her to go back to work. We both agreed that it was unfair to be leaving the dog on its own for such long periods. We decided to give Kim to my niece Breda in Clondalkin Co. Dublin, whose own dog had recently died. Kim would have company all the time and be part of a family situation.

Everything went very well for a year or two until one day the dog went missing, the whole family was devastated. My niece who was quite young at the time did everything humanly possible, she pestered the duty officers in the local Garda station, and couldn't understand why a 'special detail' hadn't been assigned to the case. She put photographs of Kim in every shop in the Clondalkin district; she even followed some travelling fairground people down the country, who were believed to be in Clondalkin when the dog went missing. Breda's parents my sister Monica and her husband Noel were getting quite worried about her spending all hours of the day and night out and about around the whole area looking for the dog; all to no avail, the dog had simply disappeared.

Some eight months later Breda's mother and father were in the kitchen in Clondalkin when, low and behold, as they were looking through the window they saw Kim jump in over the back wall into the garden, needless to say they couldn't believe their eyes. The dog was in a bad way, from the deep weal around her neck she had obviously been kept tied up but somehow had broken free, her condition and poor state of health required professional attention. Nevertheless Kim was back and the family were thrilled to have her home again. Breda with the help and support of their local veterinary surgeon nursed the dog back to her former self.

Around 1985 "Snoopy" arrived on the scene, he was only eight or nine weeks old and the cutest little pup you have ever seen. He very quickly made himself at home and within a matter of a few months, regarded himself as the VIP in the pecking order of the household. In my travels around the country, if May decided to come along, Snoopy would also accompany us. We were never refused accommodation at any hotel or B&B, when we presented ourselves together with the dog. On one occasion I got delayed on a call with the result it was nearly 9p.m. when we called to a house seeking accommodation for the night. May explained that we had our dog with us and that we usually brought the 'bean bed' to the room and early in the morning we would take him out to the car. The lady explained that her children were very frightened of dogs, however, she went on to say that they were in bed now and with the lateness of the hour she would let us have the room. Next morning May was up early and as she descended the stairs with Snoopy on the lead she met the children in the hallway. When I came down some time later the children were rolling around the lounge floor, with Snoopy all over them, all enjoying themselves immensely. The kid's mother said to me that she couldn't believe it and was delighted, she told us we would be welcome with Snoopy anytime.

There was one occasion when he let himself down badly. We were living in "Glebe Cottage" at the time and May, as secretary of the branch, was holding a Ladies Lifeboat Guild meeting in the sitting room with more than a dozen ladies present. When right there in the middle of the proceedings Snoopy decided to have his evil way with one of the cushions, to the general hilarity of all present.

On another occasion we were on holidays in Donegal with my sister Monica and her husband Noel whose father hailed from Kincasslagh, the village where we were staying at the time. The four of us and of course Snoopy went for a drive to a small village named Churchill, best known as the birthplace of St. Columba, (Colmcille in Gaelic). However, we were not, on this occasion, on a religious pilgrimage, no! we were on our way to visit the well known Glebe House and Gallery the home of the late Derek Hill a painter who was also a keen art collector, whose collection included such varied works as Picasso, Renoir, Jack B. Yeats, and Sean Keating and also works by a number of Tory Island artists. The house was not far from the village of Churchill and after a very interesting visit to the gallery we drove on to the village for some food and refreshments.

Monica and Noel went into the local hostelry while we took Snoopy for a short walk for a few minutes to do his business and stretch his legs, after which we decided to join Monica and Noel in the pub. As we entered I spoke to a lady working behind the counter, instead of going to the table where Monica and Noel were sitting Snoopy decided to go and meet the nice lady. As soon as he ventured behind the bar counter the lady screamed that she was terrified of dogs and ran through the back door, through the house and into the yard, never to be seen again, while Snoopy happily enjoying the game went after her in hot pursuit. I ran in behind the counter and followed them making my way eventually out into the yard to try to retrieve the dog, however, matters were to deteriorate even further. Meanwhile Snoopy had discovered a goose in the yard, lost interest in the lady and decided he was going to have a go at it. With the commotion that the goose was making, a man who apparently appeared from one of the outhouses, whipped up the goose. When I came on the scene, having exited from the bar through the house and found my way to the yard the man was running out through the yard gate onto the street with the goose under his arm and with Snoopy making valiant efforts to relieve the goose of some of its tail feathers. When I finally got my hands on Snoopy; I hastily put him into the car, and without further refection on Monica and Noel's part, and indeed none on ours we made a speedy retreat from Churchill also never to return.

I don't have a lot of experience with other breeds of dogs, but I have always heard that Jack Russell terriers were extremely intelligent animals; certainly with Snoopy he almost seemed to know what you were thinking. When we went away on holiday my sister Breda and her husband James or our neighbours Pat and Phil Lalor kindly looked after Snoopy who was always very happy and contented in their company. Strangely maybe once over the period of our holidays, when Pat would let him out for a run he would for some reason make his way to Margaret and Liam's at "Mount Carmel", this happened religiously on every occasion we were away. Phil often remarked that it was uncanny, how the dog would be quite happy all the time we were away but on the day of our return he would hardly leave her lounge window all day long. May of course talked to him all the time and he would turn his head from side to side as though he was taking in and understood every word. Mrs Lambert, her mother, would often say to her.

"One of these days that dog will answer you back."

Snoopy lived to be almost fifteen years old, and was a well-loved companion and a wonderful little character. He would refuse to go near his food until I returned home in the evening from work, and then conversely, showing me little more than the slightest sign of recognition, would go straight to his food.

When eventually we knew that the kindest thing we could do for Snoopy was to put him to sleep it was one of the most difficult tasks I ever had to face. I decided that day, maybe selfishly, never to put myself in the position of having to make that decision again.

A HOME FOR THE ARTS

Over the last year or so a group of us have been involving ourselves in various artistic endeavour here in the Wicklow area. A committee was formed, which we called "Wicklow East Arts", with the objective of making the case for the provision of a Community Arts Centre and Theatre for Wicklow. The centre would cater for the growing population of East Wicklow District, which in the latest census exceeded 15,000 residents. As a means of highlighting the arts activity in the district we put together a special 'Arts Awareness Day' in the Grand Hotel in December 02; showcasing every aspect of arts activity form Music to Drama to Dance, from Writing to Painting to Mime and so on. Performances commenced at 2pm. in the Abbey Room involving all the performing groups and continued with a change of group every 15 minutes until 7pm. Meanwhile at the same time in the Friars Suite of the hotel an exhibition of 25 stands was mounted, each stand offering to those interested, information on its own particular arts discipline, again every aspect of the arts was represented. The day was a great success with large numbers attending and visiting the various stands, and as intended –

highlighted the necessity for such a centre in Wicklow.

In the New Year of 03 the Hon. Secretary, Pam Beacom and myself made an appointment to meet with the Department of the Arts to discuss the possibility of funding for the venture. We were received very well and informed that we should prepare our case by having a formal feasibility study carried out together with a Business Plan which should be lodged with the Department early in 04 for consideration later in the year. Unfortunately after a number of poorly attended meetings of Wicklow East Arts no further meetings were called and the plan was shelved for the moment.

In the late spring of 2004 I approached a number of people with the object of holding an Arts Festival in Wicklow in September. Many of those approached I had worked with back in the musical society days many years earlier. We also asked some of the more interested and enthusiastic members of the Wicklow East Arts committee to join us. I was certain from previous involvement with most of the members of the group that their individual commitment to the success of the festival would be total. We all worked extremely well throughout the summer putting the programme together, publicising the event and working through the myriad of tasks that such an involved programme necessitated. The dates were set for 19th, 20th and 21 of September with Saturday being the main day for the outdoor and street events. After many months of brilliant weather, that particular Saturday was the wettest it seemed for years. Some of the outdoor events were held in the Holy Rosary School while others unfortunately had to be abandoned. However, the evening concerts held in the Church of Ireland, The Holy Rosary Hall and The Grand Hotel were very well attended and judging by the warmth of the applause throughout, enjoyed by all. The messages of congratulations from many, including a formal letter from the Wicklow Town Council, also the verbal reports expressed at the following meeting of the committee were very encouraging with a massive affirmation in the district for the first Wicklow Arts Festival.

One particularly gratifying facet of the festival which was received with total accord by all in Wicklow was the decision to honour a great Wicklow lady, Miss Mirette Dowling for a lifetime dedicated to the teaching of choral performance and music skills of the highest quality.

Where we will go from here is very much a decision for the committee. Will there be another Arts Festival in Wicklow in 2004? When I approached people to join the committee it was on the basis of a once off commitment only, and after to review the success of the event and decide if as a committee it wished to organise future festivals. There is no doubt; the support of the community was clearly demonstrated.

As so many lesser towns throughout Ireland have, will Wicklow have its Art Centre? It's hard to know. I don't really see it happen without a much greater level of support and involvement on the part of the members of the myriad of arts disciplines that have always been part of the fabric of Wicklow life; equally necessary is the desire and enthusiasm of the local community as a whole, backed with the support of both local authorities.

Without a suitable modern and well-equipped venue where the broad spectrum of arts activity in east Wicklow can be supported and nurtured, of equal importance, where those attending can be assured of a reasonable degree of comfort, it is difficult to see how the Arts in Wicklow can thrive and flourish to the point where it can achieve its full potential.

THE FULLER VIEW OF RETROSPECTION

What continues to amaze me as I reflect on these pages of past memories is the enormity of the changes that have taken place in such a short period of time, in our country, our town and indeed in all our lives. Changes so subtle, so imperceptible as to go almost unnoticed in the daily march of time, and yet so enormous when looked at in the fuller view of retrospection.

We live today in a throwaway world, so foreign to those of my generation whose ingrained philosophy and indoctrination was to mend, to repair, rather then to replace. This applies not only to consumer goods, but also to almost every aspect of Irish life today. The work ethic today is approached in almost the same throwaway manner. No longer is a job for life, longevity in a single place of employment, so highly prized down through the years, is now seen by many employers as showing a lack of drive, a lack of ambition.

Even religion appears today to be accepted as an "a la carte" activity in the lives of many of us, how confusing it must be for a generation reared and educated on the strict observance of certain precepts and principles. I see no problem with the acceptance of change, if those changes become the legitimate and stated truths and teachings of the Church. Neither do I have the right to be judgemental or critical of people trying to make a life for themselves in problematical circumstances; what I do find difficult to understand, is the tacit acceptance by some Churchmen, without comment or explanation of what appears to me to be this new latter day status quo.

The entertainment ethic has also changed drastically; for many, relaxation and entertainment has to be drink orientated and to a lesser extent, unfortunately for some, punctuated with the use of drugs. Aggression in young people is rife everywhere. Yet where the opportunity is available and the help and support is there for them we see a desire for involvement in more wholesome activities, such as our national or international sports games. The immense pleasure gained by the members of one little group in our town, MYTh. (Musical Youth Theatre) a Musical Society for young people, who in turn give so much pleasure to those who attend their performances. Again the need for suitable facilities is vital to encourage the wider involvement of our youth in all such healthy and desirable activities.

The real scandal of the so called enlightened Western World in the late twentieth and as we enter the twenty first century I believe is, the way we have squandered the worlds non-replaceable resources of fossil fuels with utter disregard for the needs of future generations. History will I believe point an accusing finger at this generation with all its knowledge as having done little to conserve and much to deplete these vital resources. The ever-increasing demand by the major powers and the emerging nations such as China, on the earth's diminishing supply of such resources, while it seems to me paying little attention to conserving or finding alternative sources of energy, is in my view, a very serious and worrying situation for future generations.

The threat by extreme fundamentalist terrorists, to maim and murder anybody who disagrees with their so-called religious beliefs and philosophies, is the reality of life today all over the western world. The Middle Eastern States hold the key to 63% of the world's oil resources. Terrorist activity is well capable of knocking out much of that production almost over night on which our whole way of life depends; thus throwing the world economy into the total chaos approaching that of another dark age. The dreadful tragedy of what will always be known as 9/11 and the killing and maiming of over 1200 innocent people in Madrid, these and the ongoing daily threats are creating a sense of fear throughout the free world. Which of us board an aircraft anymore without looking at our fellow travellers with some niggling shred of concern. It is true that life was hard as we look back to our youth. Our parents' generation lived a life of frugality and comparative hardship, but even in those times the future was surer, more dependable, the evildoers were more visible, more identifiable.

These of course are problems on a world scale, the responsibility of the Bush's and the Blair's and others in high places, on which to bring their skills of statesmanship and diplomacy to bear. We in our little community of Wicklow can only observe and pray. In the meantime being ever the optimist, 'hope springs eternal', comes to mind.

The hope for the future is that a younger generation of leaders will emerge, more enlightened, with a greater understanding of people's real needs and with a much keener awareness and sympathy towards the environment; and of course above all a greater respect for the sanctity of human life.

As for those of our generation, well we always have our memories of less frenetic, more placid times.

AMONGST THE MEMORIES

Some months ago I was out for a walk and happened to be coming home via Dunbur Road, I noticed a "For Sale" sign on our old family home at No. 2. Although the family had moved to "Springmount" on Summer Hill when I was in my teens, the house on Dunbur Road was the home of my formative years, the treasure house of all of my childhood memories. I thought to myself I would love to see around it once more. Had it changed? Would seeing over the house again awaken some long forgotten memory or would the updating over the years to today's reality shatter those vivid childhood memories, so important to all of us? Would it be just another old house from a time long passed? Whatever, I was determined to visit 2 Dunbur Road once more.

A week or so later, not having made any arrangements concerning the house on Dunbur Road, I happened to be talking to my neighbour Tony who is retired but takes on the occasional little job. For some reason, in the course of conversation, I happened to ask him was he working these days. Tony providentially told me he was doing a little job in a house on Dunbur Road. A friend of his had bought it and he was helping him out, getting it ready for letting. Tony confirmed that the house where he was helping and my old home were one and the same. I arranged to call the next afternoon while Tony was there.

It was a strange feeling as I knocked on the door the following afternoon. No longer the grained solid wooden door of my childhood, with the heavy brass knocker and letterbox that my mother polished to perfection every week, today's modern UPVC had replaced all that. As I waited for the door to be opened I could see that the front garden bore no resemblance to that of our day, my fathers Rockery and Sun-house were understandably no longer there. I wondered if I really should have come here, should I have been content to live with my cherished and long-held memories of this old place. Maybe I could still slip out through the gate and forget about this visit. I was quickly brought back to reality as the door swung open and my friend Tony invited me in.

Most people recount re-visits to places they had known intimately in their childhood days as being much smaller than they had remembered. This certainly was the case with me; every room appeared smaller, although the house apart from the kitchen was little changed. As one would expect the kitchen had been enlarged and modernised and a bathroom had been added off the back hall. The addition of a modern fireplace replacing the lovely old cast-iron surround was the only change in the sitting room or parlour as we called it, and of course the ugly gas metre, which in our day stood in an alcove to the left of the fireplace, measuring the amount of gas that flowed through it, was I'm sure long gone. One of the abiding memories of my father was during that final illness, I remember him trying to come down the stairs, and my mother insisting he go back to bed. This was the memory that assailed my consciousness like a faded vignette as I began to climb the stairs - the most unchanged area of the house - I could almost see the scene as I climbed.

The bedrooms were essentially the same apart from decoration; my mother's bedroom was in the back of the house and had a good view of the sea. I stood there for a few moments looking over, what was back then, our little bungalow and once again remembered the wartime shipping of my childhood. In those days my mother's large old iron and brass bedstead had stood with its head slightly 'alcoved' where the well of the stairs encroached on the bedroom, and my youngest sister Therese's cot stood along the foot of the bed, where so many years ago Santa Claus left her Christmas morning gifts.

I crossed the old yard to the little bungalow, where a young man was fitting new bunk beds. There was nothing left of my old memories here, all had changed totally. I carried on out around the back entrance, looking up the now almost over grown lane, remembering our old neighbours the Mitchell family, at no.3 and the two Brennan brothers Paddy and Jimmy at no.1 all long gone. Further up the lane, Mr. Keogh's workshop of long ago, now I am told a luxury apartment. Two new houses stood where my father's prized garden once was.

It was time to return to today's world and let the ghosts of the past rest in peace. I expressed my goodbyes to Tony and the workmen in 2 Dunbur Road together with my thanks; and with my memories and emotions continued my walk back down Summer Hill and home.

THE END OF THE JOURNEY

Well that brings us up to the present; we have more or less come to the end of the journey!

These days as I go on my daily walk I occasionally smile and say hello to a pretty girl, I am always reassured when she ignores me and looks away - I know the sad day is fast approaching when she will smile and say hello back. I will have then achieved the final stage when I am simply considered to be just another harmless friendly old guy!!

What I have tried to do in committing these memories to paper is to write about my own relatively simple and uncomplicated life, and the many good friends I have made over the years, the many interesting people I was fortunate to become acquainted with along the way. How the twists and quirks of fate have carried me along that journey up to today's actuality. Being one of a large and very close-knit family naturally the recounting of my memories over the years is inextricably linked with each of my nine siblings. However, in committing to ink what has been an interesting experience, in many ways an awakening of long forgotten memories; it was at all times my aim not to encroach on their individual privacy more than that which I considered essential to the progression of my own journey down through the years.

Over those years contact between my brother Michael in New York and the family on this side of the Atlantic was mainly confined to exchanging Christmas Cards and of course making contact at times of a more serious nature concerning the family. One of the great advantages of modern technology and specifically the advent of E-Mail communication is the ease and simplicity of maintaining contact. I now converse with Michael at least a couple of times each week. The younger members of the family, the next generation are also in regular contact, all bringing him up to date and forming closer relationships into the future generation of family members, which I believe is important and worthwhile.

As we inexorably advance through the early years of the twenty first century our family's number has been sadly depleted by half to five, I suppose we must accept this loss as the natural cycle of life.

My sister Monica who very early in her young life assumed the role of my mother's confidant and assistant with the younger members of the family after our father's death. Year after year up to the very year of her demise Monica never missed phoning me on my birthday, which I very much appreciated. I remember one particular birthday just before I retired, it was the practice in the office that if the birthday of one of the staff members was known the other members would buy a cake and candles and at the 11am. tea break all would proceed to surprise the unsuspecting birthday person at his or her desk. On this particular occasion the girls were just coming through my office door with the cake bedecked with many lighted candles when the phone rang, Monica to wish me a happy birthday. I suppose still conscious of some reflective responsibility from those early years. My sister Marjorie with whom I had many a laugh when I called anytime my work brought me to Galway and who loved to hear all the news from Wicklow.

My brother Paddy with whom I played golf every Saturday, I never really played regularly since his death. Frank, almost two years my junior, and maybe for that reason we were possibly closest of all. I was delighted when he and his wife Maura had decided to settle back in Wicklow, but again sadly for too short a time. Finally, the oldest of the family Carmel, whose life in many ways was the saddest of all. They are all deeply missed by those closest to them and needless to say by their siblings who remain.

Where do we go from here? Only a Greater Being than us can answer that question. While we both thank God for the blessings of so many healthy and happy years together, one thing is certain that while we continue to remain healthy we will continue to live life to the full - then, just a little time to smell the "Roses" as we all approach our "Decembers"!

Epilogue

FEBRUARY 2004

The time was 7.45am, the sun was warm the temperature I would say - in the low seventies and rising, the sea was calm just a gentle lapping of the water on the white sand of the foreshore. Groups of busy little sandpipers were skittering around at the waters edge. Meanwhile further out to sea the pelicans, kamikaze like, were diving from great heights fishing for breakfast. The early morning shelling enthusiasts were on the move heads bowed down intent on their business. Yes you've guessed? We're back on Sanibel Island after a gap of eight years. As I walked along the beach earlier on I stood watching the pelicans, not by any stretch of the imagination a pretty bird, unlike the beautiful white Ibis or snowy Egret or the many other attractive birds, native to these latitudes. However, in flight the Pelican is king, a sight to behold, magnificent, they appear to have mastered and brought the science of aerodynamics to the point of perfection. Almost without any movement of their wings, they glide effortlessly, slow motion like, sometimes only feet above the waters edge. I was absolutely fascinated as I watched them land high in the huge pine trees along the perimeter of the beach, as they glide in over the treetops they appear to hover just for a moment and very softly land on the slenderest branches at the very top of the trees; amazing control for a bird that is as big as a small turkey.

It was great to meet up again with Dick and Fran when we arrived at Fort Myers airport. At first meeting, Dick looked thinner than we remembered, but was making a good recovery from major surgery; Fran had not changed at all, she looked just as we remembered. It was all of three years since our last meeting in Chicago and again we had a lot of catching up to do.

As I walked back across the beach and over the boardwalk to the main condominium precinct, careful to avoid the occasional falling cocoanut from high above my head, the early swimmers were making their way to the pool. I picked up the usual copy of "USA Today" from the nearby newspaper dispenser and took the lift to our apartment. As I approached I could hear May and Fran happily chatting away in the kitchen.

"Well what's new out there this morning" Fran cried as I opened the door.

"O- nothing new really, the sun is warm, the sand is cool, the sea turquoise and very inviting; just another normal day on the island".

"Breakfast is ready" May said, as Dick made his appearance from the bedroom and we expressed the pleasantries of the morning.

"Anybody pick up the paper," Dick said,

"Yes Dick, its on the coffee table" I replied, as we all sat down to breakfast - How really good it is to be back in Sanibel, I silently thought.

* * * * * *

Life

Life is a book of which we can have but one edition. Let each day, as it adds its page to the indestructible volume, be such as we shall be willing to let an assembled world read.

ACKNOWLEDGMENTS

It is an honour to have a man of the stature of Ronnie Delany to read the manuscript and write the Foreword and I owe him my sincerest thanks and appreciation.

I am deeply indebted to Mr. Tim Pat Coogan who made important suggestions which helped me greatly in the chronological presentation of the book.

I am most grateful to my good friends firstly, Joe Murray for allowing me to use his photograph for the front cover illustration, Mary Murray for kindly assisting with proofreading and Rose Butler who first suggested and urged me to begin.

I particularly wish to mention my brother Michael, domiciled in the USA for more than half a century, whose enthusiasm for the content of the work encouraged me to publish.

Finally to all those whose paths crossed with mine and helped to build the story -

Thanks for the memories.

ISBN 1412068925-4